GW01375131

SIGNS SYMBOLS PICTO GRAMS

Cube Collection: Signs, Symbols and Pictograms
Copyright © 2010 FEIERABEND UNIQUE BOOKS / info@feierabend-unique-books.de

Published in Asia in 2010 by
Page One Publishing Pte Ltd
20 Kaki Bukit View
Kaki Bukit Techpark II
Singapore 415956
Tel: (65) 6742-2088
Fax: (65) 6744-2088
enquiries@pageonegroup.com
www.pageonegroup.com

First published 2010 by FEIERABEND UNIQUE BOOKS / www.feierabend-unique-books.de
Authored by www.zeixs.com

ISBN 978-981-245-948-0

All rights reserved. No part of this publication may be reproduced, stored in any retrieval system or transmitted, in any form or by any means, electronic, mechanical, photocopying, recording or otherwise, without prior permission in writing from the publisher. For information, contact Page One Publishing Pte Ltd.

Printed and bound in China

zeixs

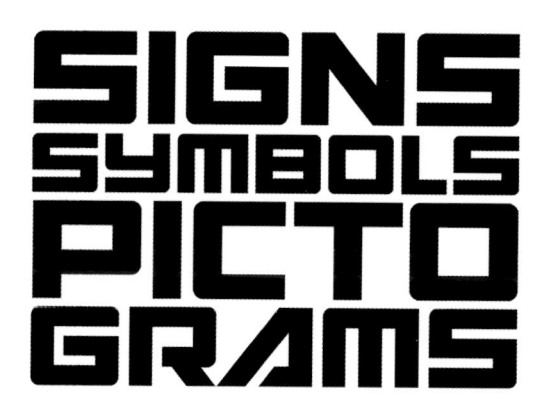

SIGNS SYMBOLS PICTO GRAMS

PAGE ONE

Sings, Symbols, Pictograms

The world is full of signs, symbols and pictograms. And every single one of them is adapted to a specific function. The message they convey has to be comprehensible, regardless of region of origin, language or culture. Their language, as a result, needs to be universal: easily understood, unambiguous and intelligible - not least because they serve to substitute actual, written language. Still, in spite of these requirements, there is enough room for variation and innovation. And the quest for such new forms, which are still able to convey meaning in a universal way, is an intriguing undertaking.

This should be reason enough to devote a whole book to new approaches to the task of designing signs, symbols and pictograms. And this is the result - a book presenting new designs for a great variety of purposes, an overview of: "Signs, Symbols, Pictograms".

Signs, Symbols, Pictograms

Die Welt ist voller Zeichen, Symbole und Piktogramme. Alle haben gemeinsam, dass sie eine Aussage universell transportieren und einem bestimmten Zweck dienen sollen. Wie unterschiedlich die Aussagen der jeweiligen Zeichen auch sein mögen, sie müssen doch allgemein verständlich sein. In anderen Worten, ihre Zeichen- oder Bildsprache muss universell und eindeutig sein. So muss ihre Botschaft kultur- und länderübergreifend verständlich sein, dienen sie in manchen Fällen doch gerade dazu, Schrift und gesprochenes Wort zu ersetzen und Übersetzungen überflüssig zu machen. Diese Anforderungen engen den Raum für künstlerische Variationen natürlich erheblich ein.

Aber dennoch gibt es Raum für Variation und Innovation. Denn gerade die Gestaltung von Zeichen, die neu und innovativ sind, und dennoch dem Anspruch gerecht werden können, universell verständlich zu sein, ist ein spannendes Feld. Deshalb haben wir neue, erfrischende Varianten gesammelt, die originell und dennoch funktional sind: „Signs, Symbols, Pictograms".

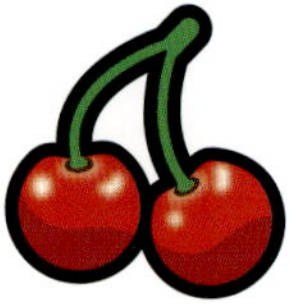
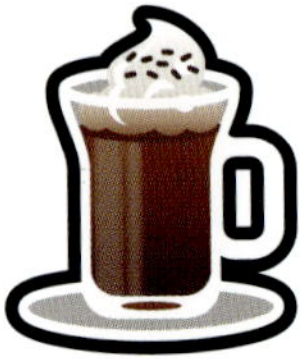
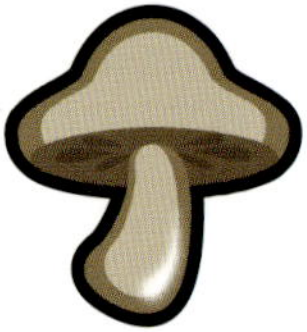
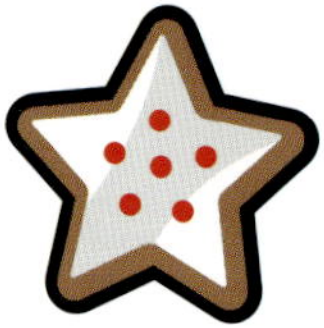
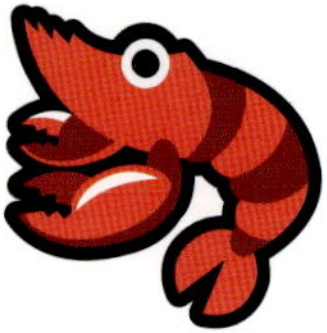
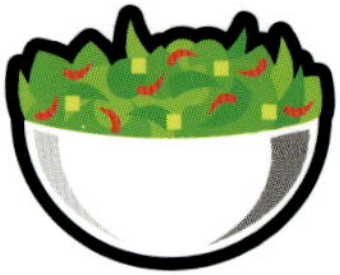

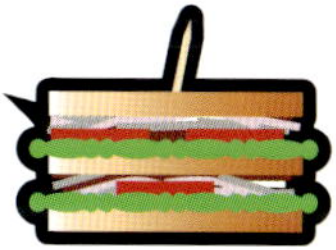

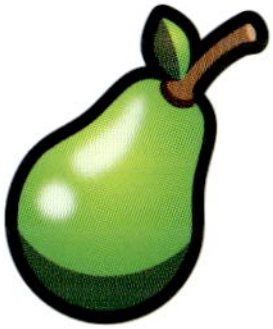

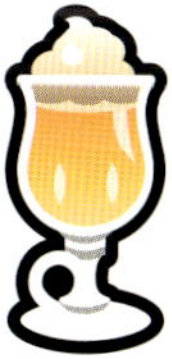

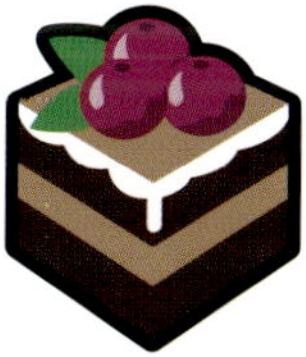

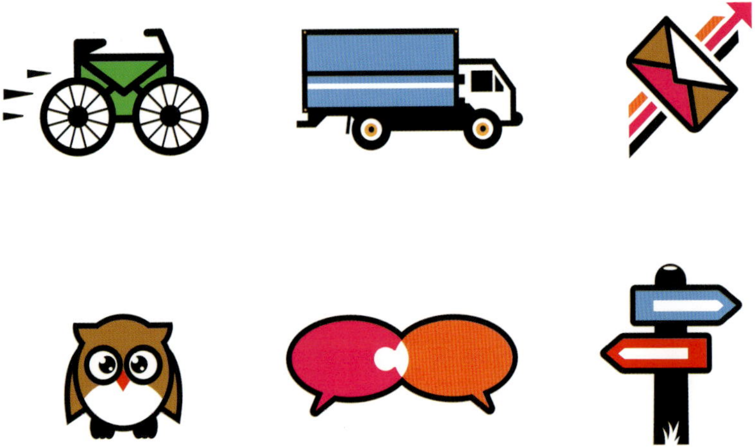

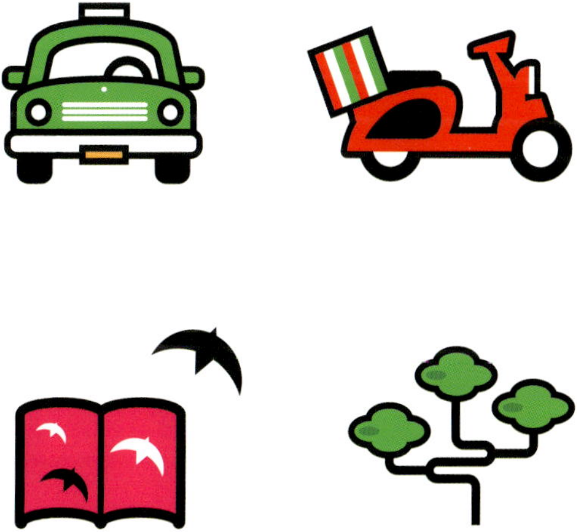

Puk Fenneman (NED) www.coolpuk.com

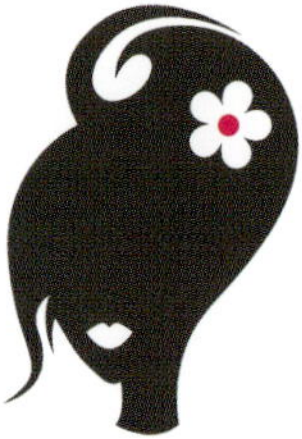

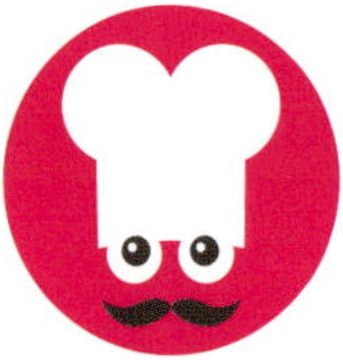
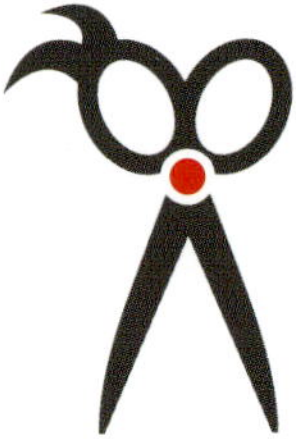
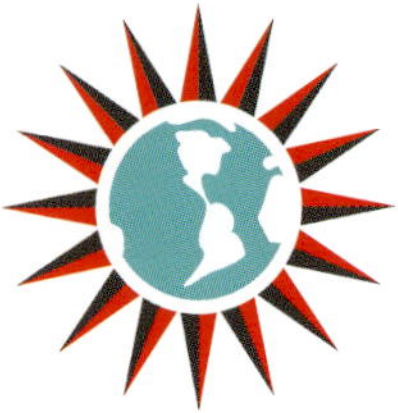

Puk Fenneman (NED) www.coolpuk.com

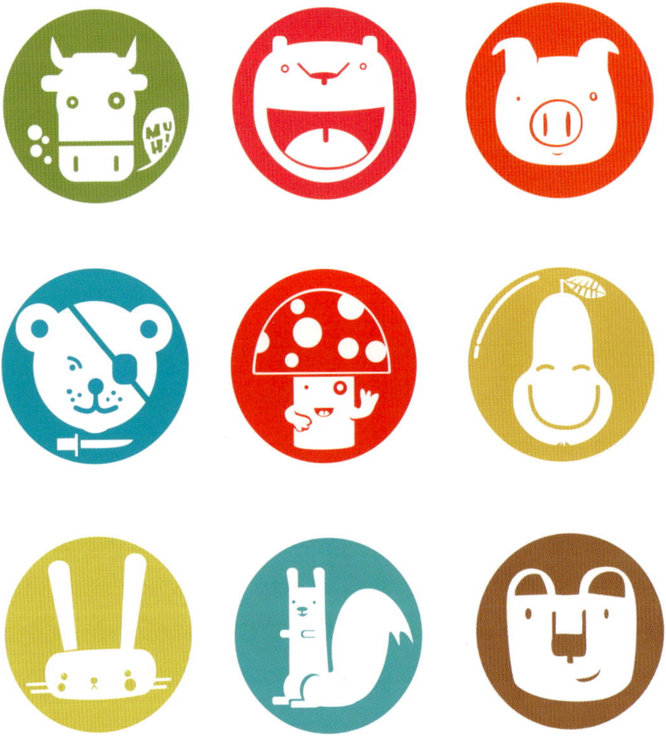
MUH!

Jamie Oliver Aspinall (SUI) www.schnuppe.ch

Jamie Oliver Aspinall (SUI) www.schnuppe.ch

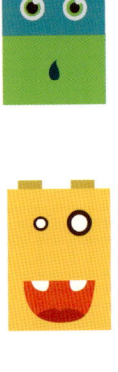

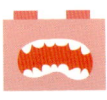

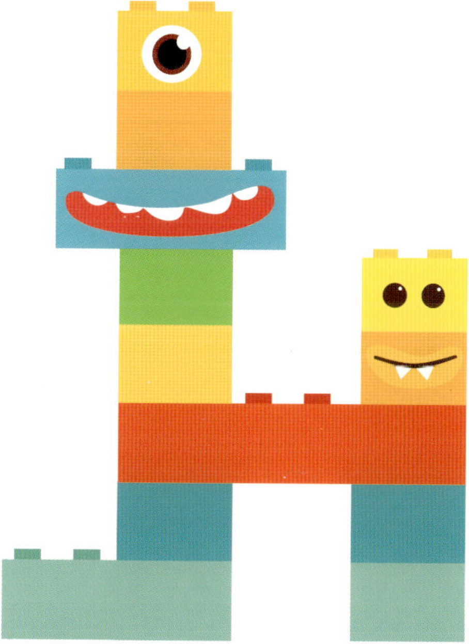

Jamie Oliver Aspinall [SUI] www.schnuppe.ch

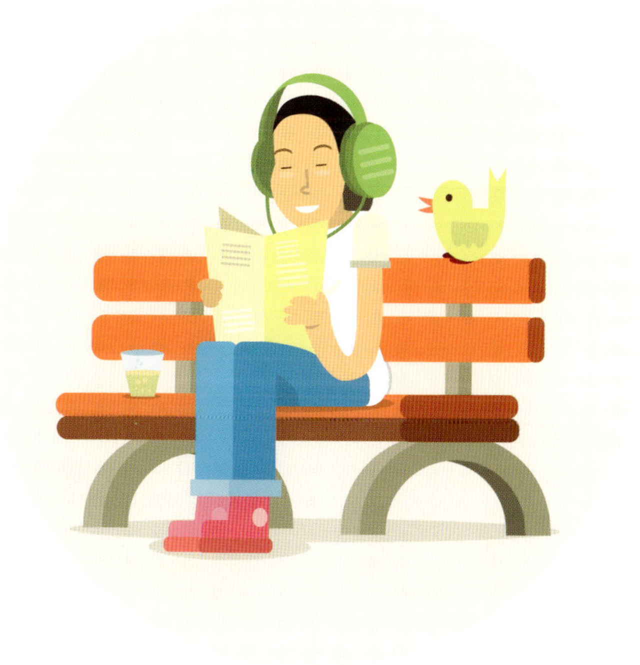

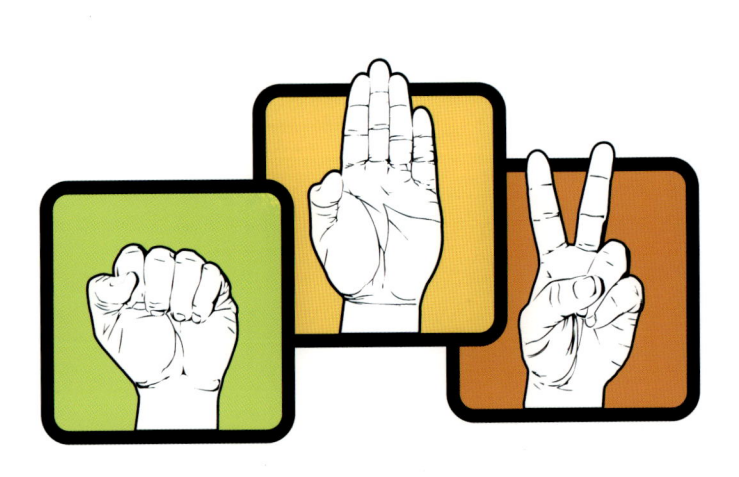

Marco Antonio Castillo [MEX] www.behance.net/el_mrk

Kama [INA] www.oxidizzy.com

Benjamin Koh [SIN] pepper-cinnamon.net

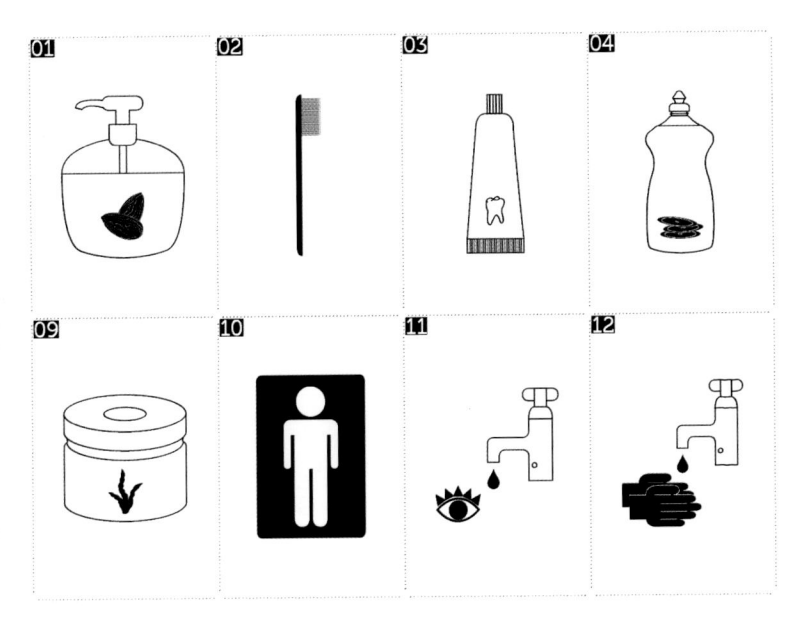

22

05

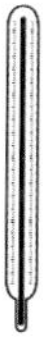

06

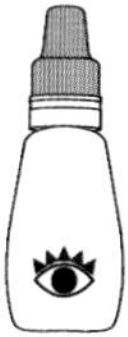

07

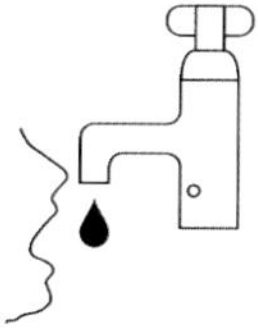

08

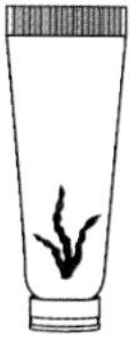

13

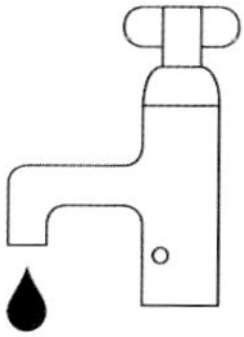

14

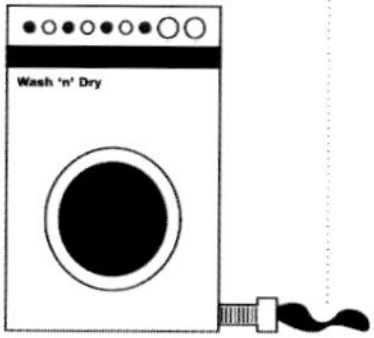

15

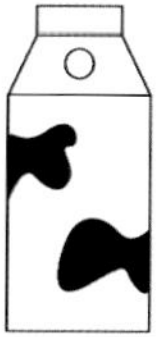

16

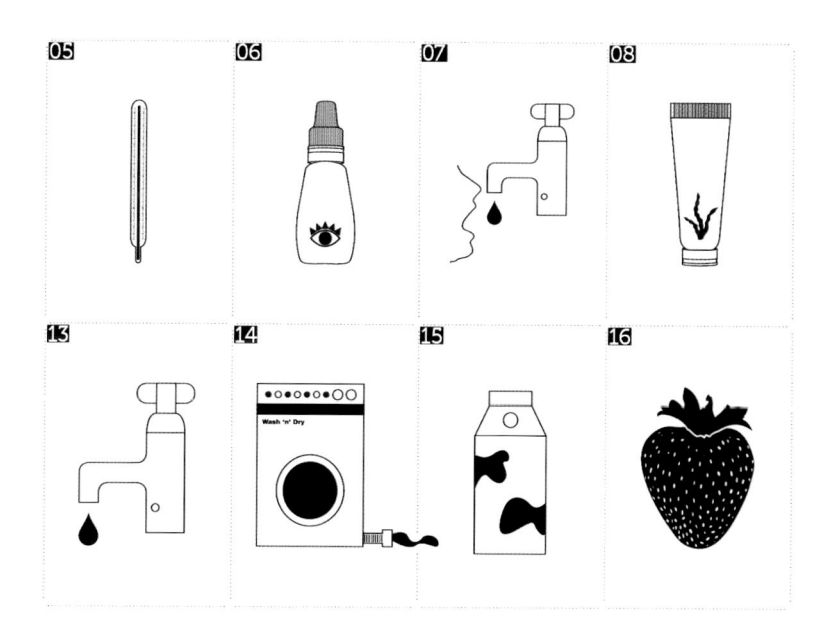

17	18	19

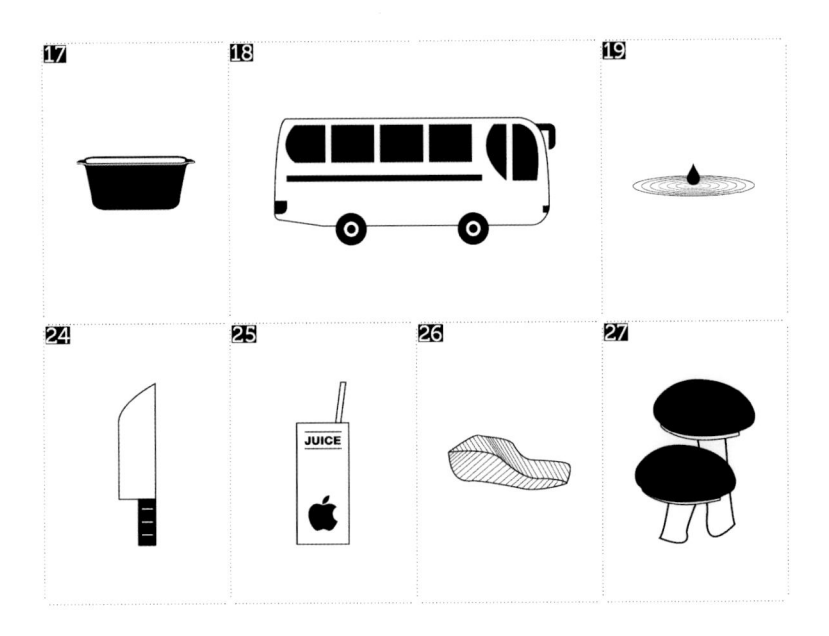

24	25	26	27

20	21	22	23
28	29	30	31

32	33	34	35
UNSALTED BUTTER		Camera	

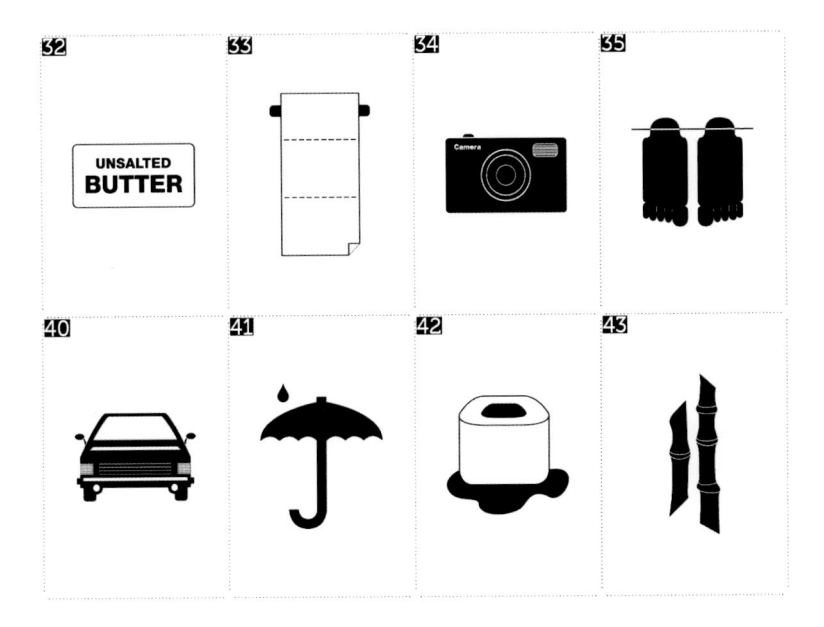

40	41	42	43

36	37	38	39
		COCOA DRINK	

44	45	46	47
		ASIENCE	SOAP

| 48 | 49 | 50 | 51 |
| 56 | 57 | 58 | 59 |

Benjamin Koh [SIN] pepper-cinnamon.net

28

52	53	54	55 Cape No. 7
60	61	62	63

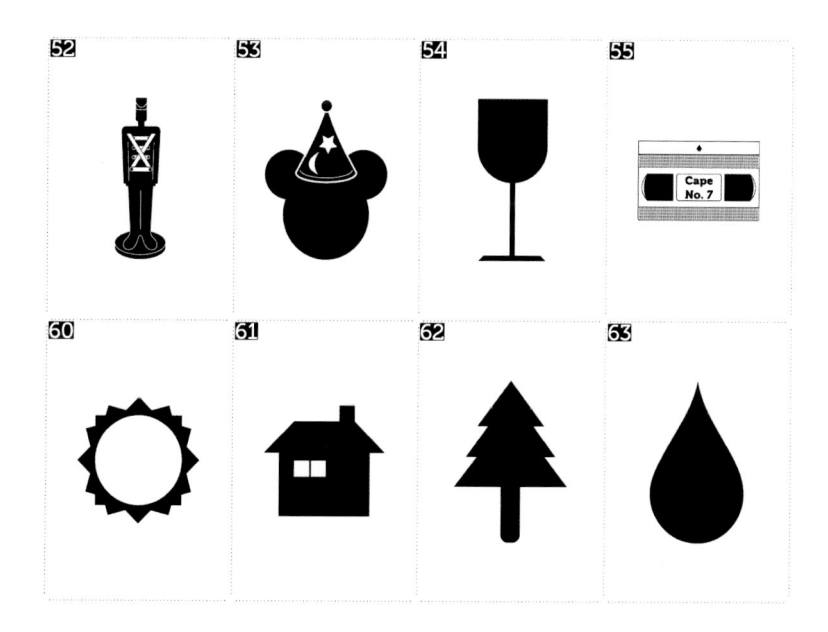

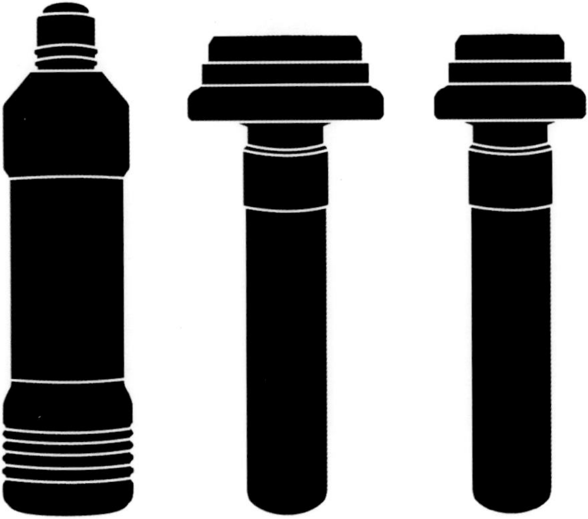

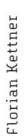

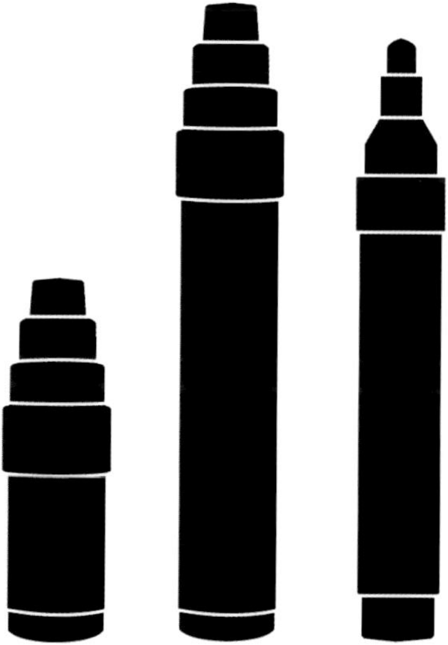

Florian Kettner [GER] www.rv20.com

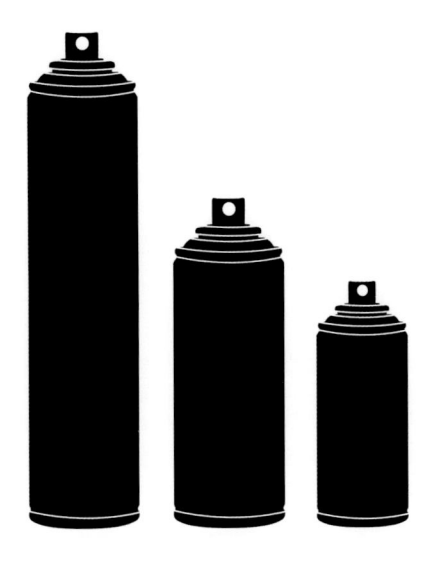

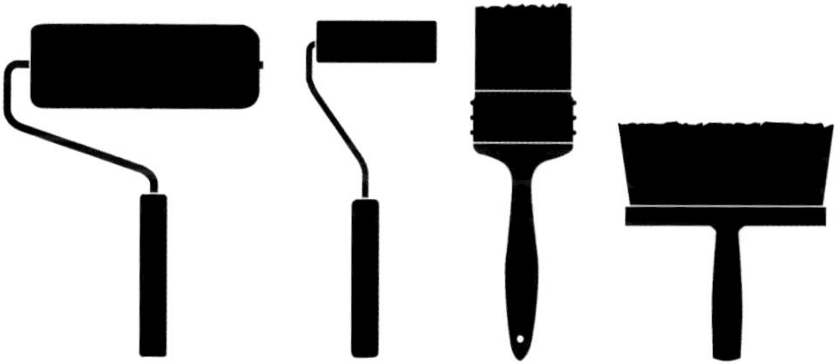

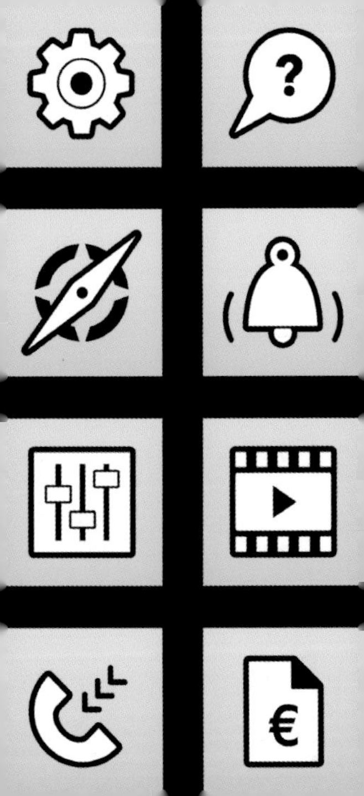

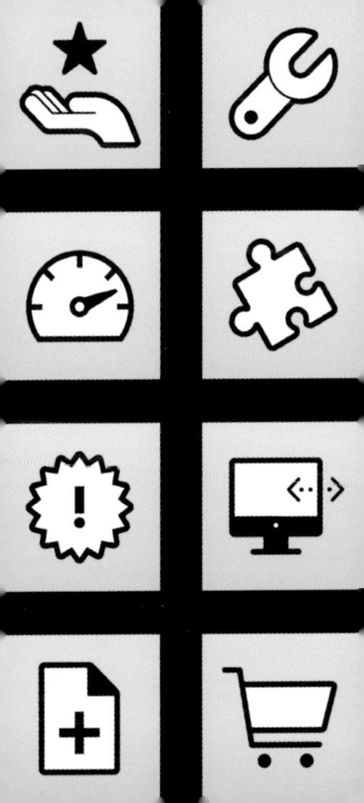

Michael Hartmann [GER] www.finalart.de

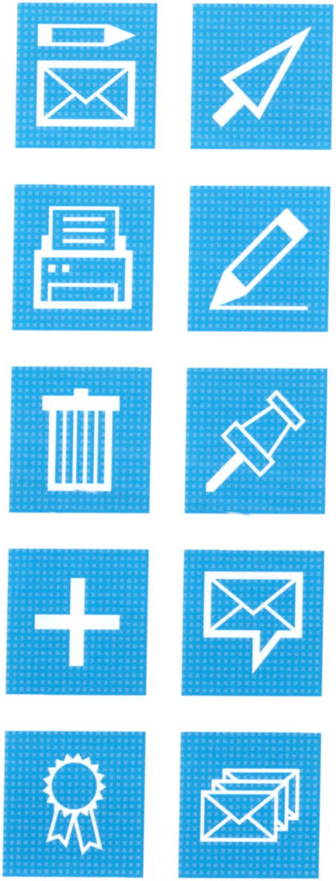

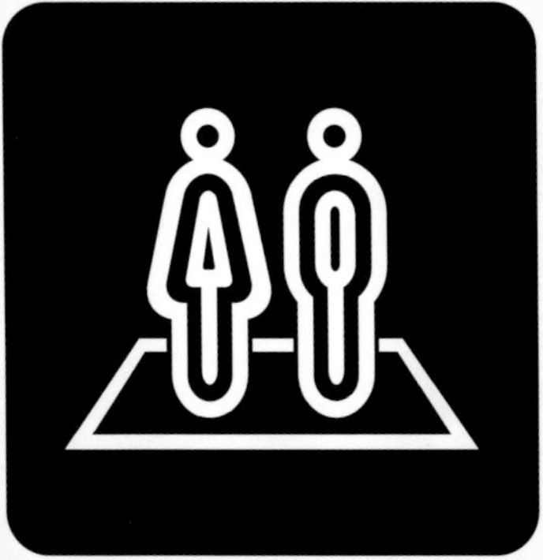

Masood Bukhari   [USA]   www.masoodbukhari.com

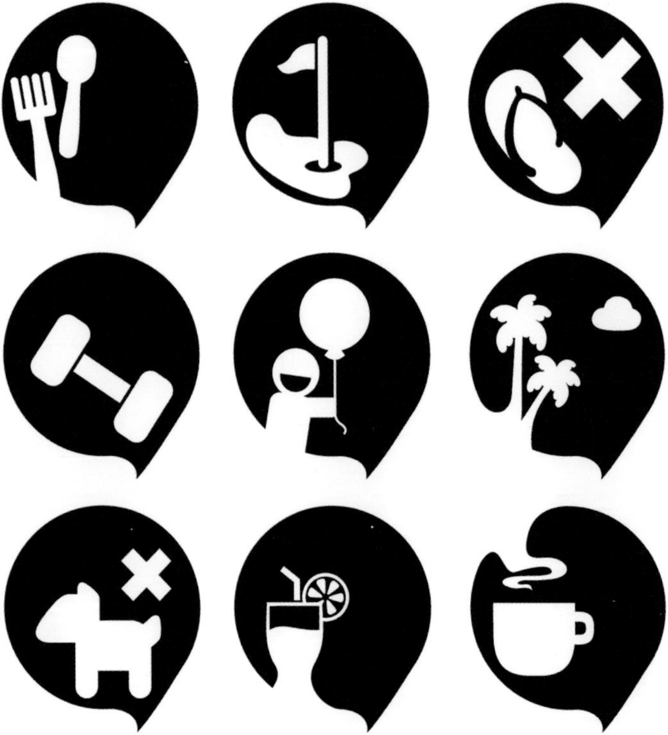

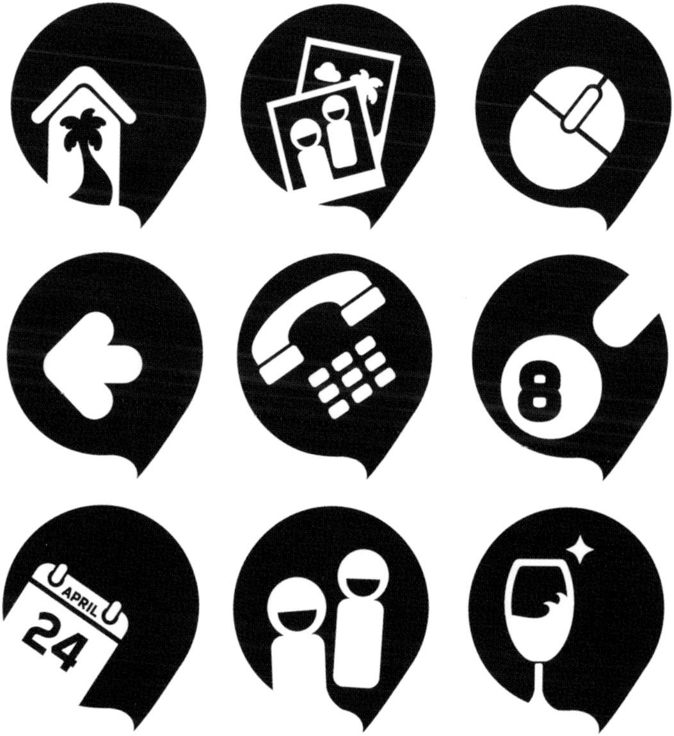
8
APRIL
24

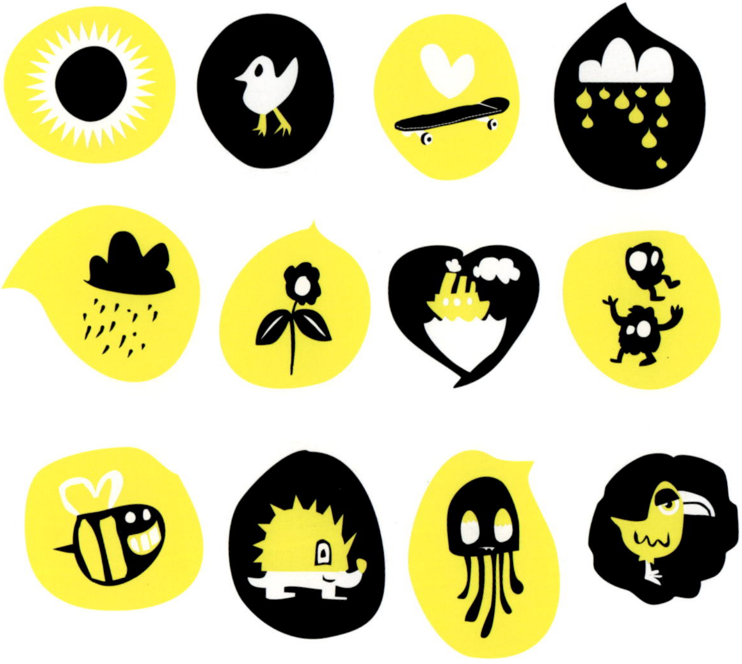

Jamie Oliver Aspinall [SUI] www.schnuppe.ch

Andreas Dümmel [GER] www.pyruswerbeagentur.de

Andreas Dümmel (GER) www.pyruswerbeagentur.de

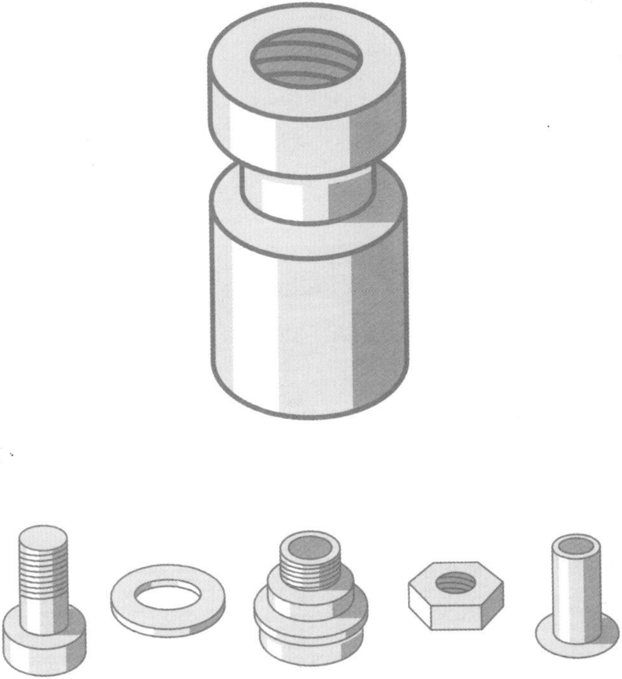

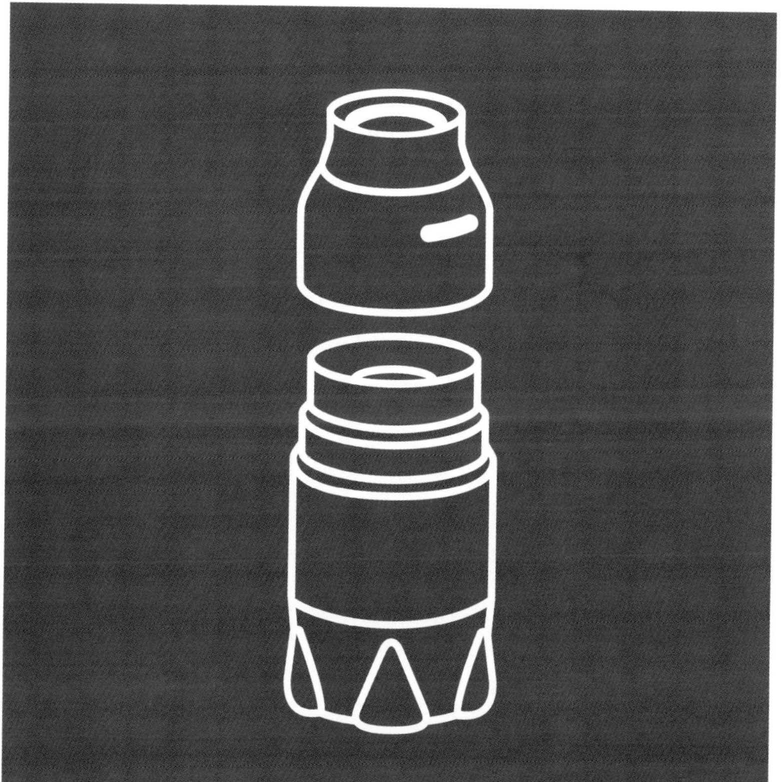

Marco Antonio Castillo   [MEX]   www.behance.net/el_mrk

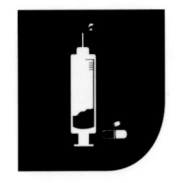

Diego Velásquez L.   [COL]   www.flickr.com/photos/diegovelin/

50

Bo Virkelyst Jensen   (DEN)   www.addsoul.com

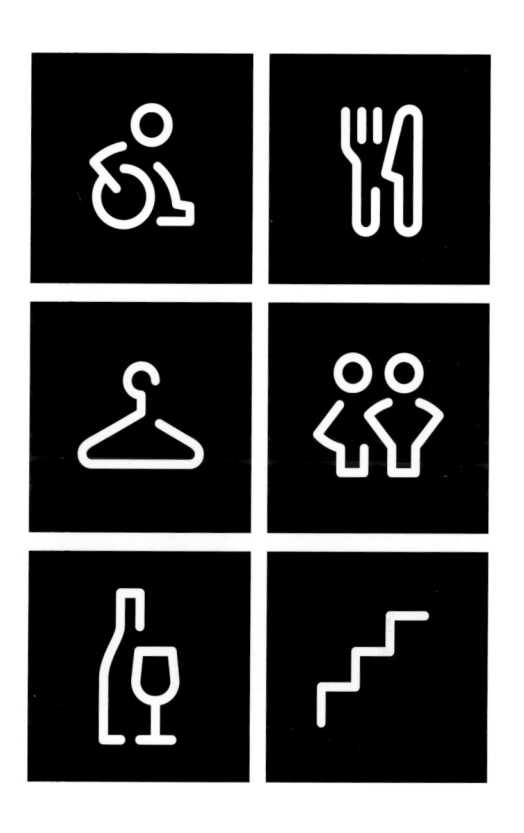

www.masoodbukhari.com

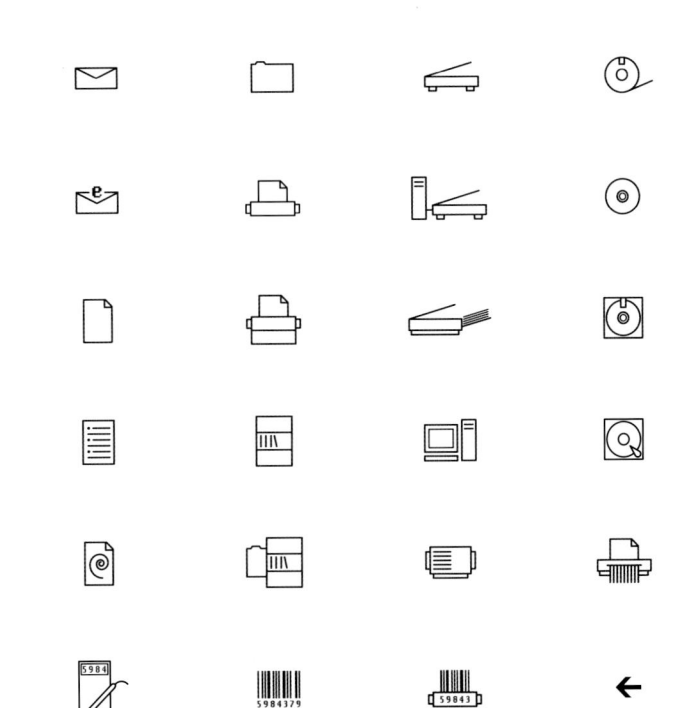

Masood Bukhari [USA]

52

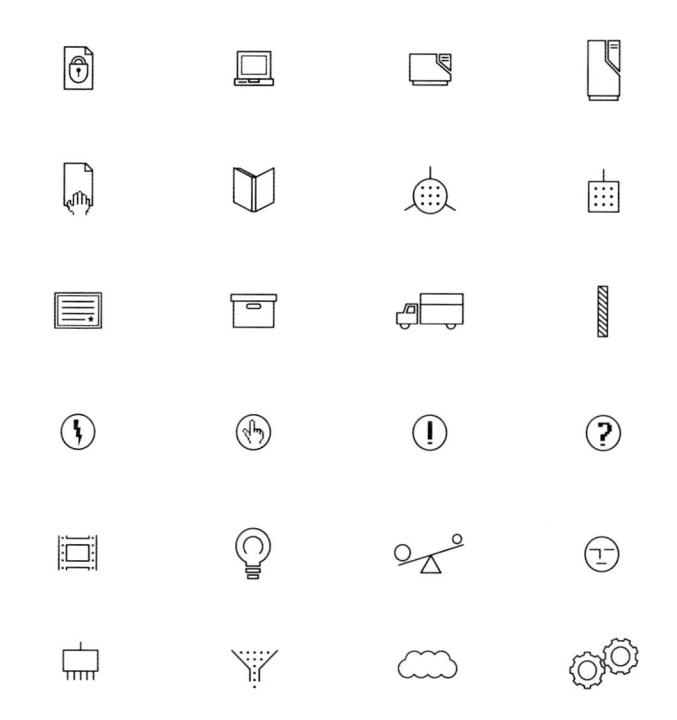

{ paintings }   { mirrors }   { lamps }

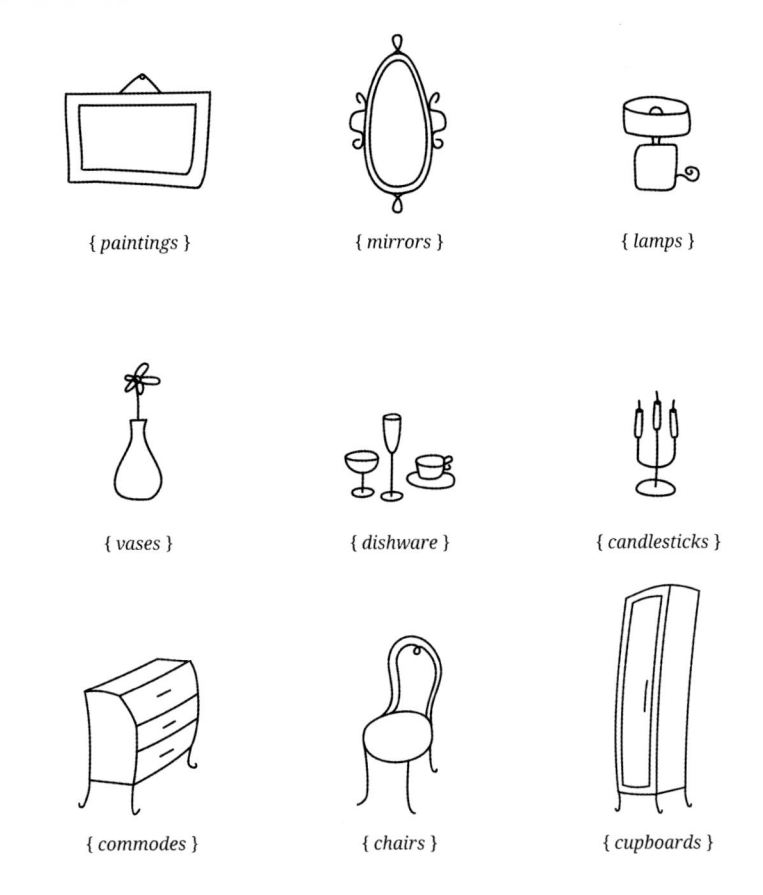

{ vases }   { dishware }   { candlesticks }

{ commodes }   { chairs }   { cupboards }

Bar	Cocktail Bar	Lounge Bar
Wine Bar	Sports Bar	Beach Bar

TECHNOLOGY

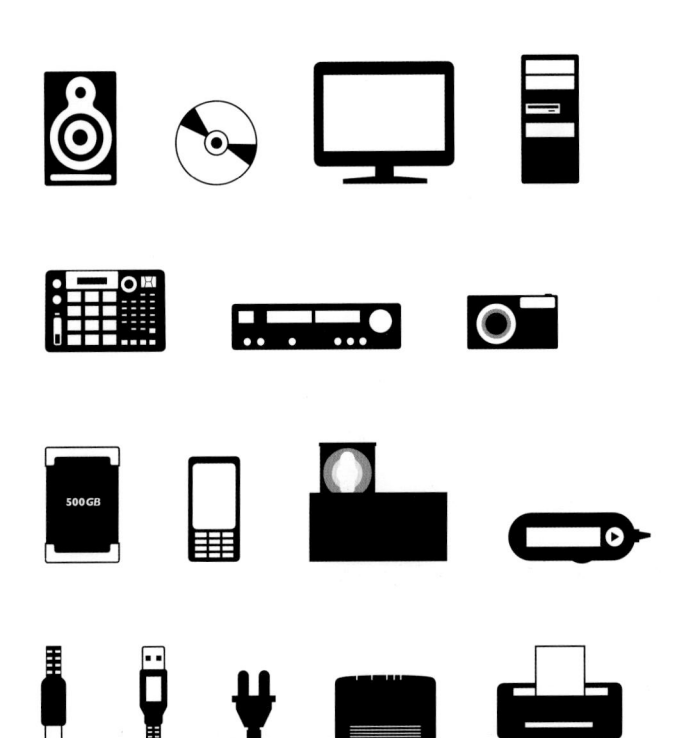

Lars Harmsen [GER] www.magmabranddesign.de

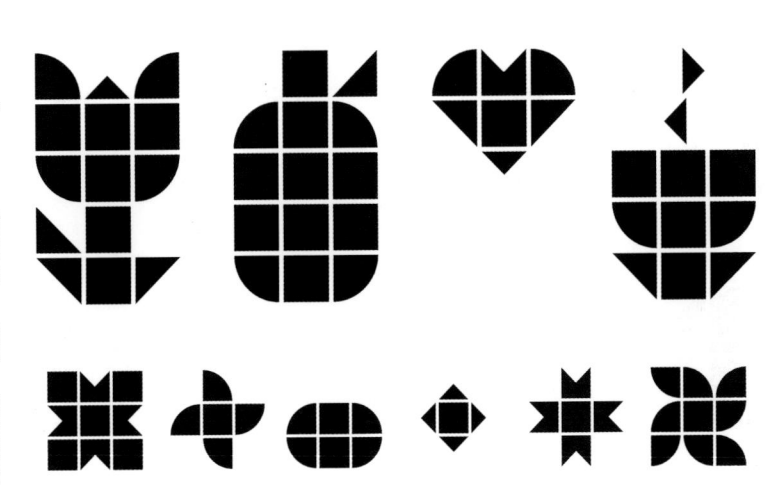

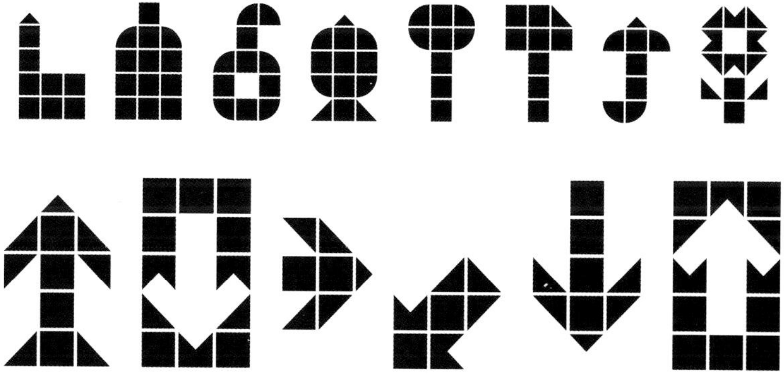

Lars Harmsen [GER] www.magmabranddesign.de

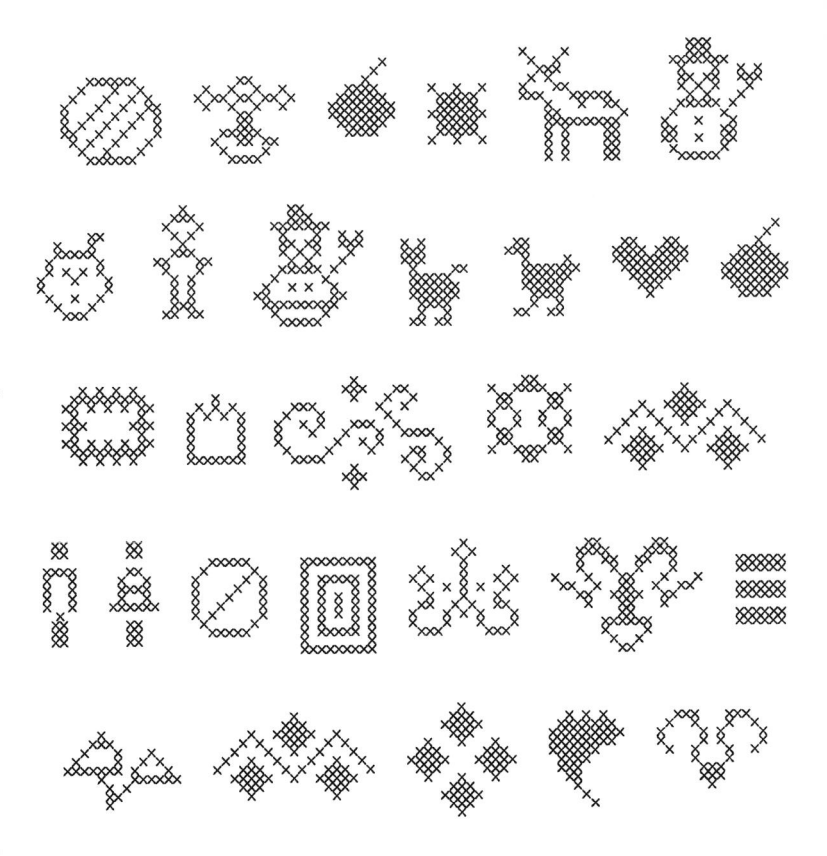

Deejay

Photo

Video

Alen Pavlovic [CRO] www.attra.hr

INFO	PORTAIKKO	VAATE-SÄILYTYS
VAATE-SÄILYTYS	→	←
KAHVI-AUTOMAATTI	TUPAKOINTI-PAIKKA	STOP LÄPIKULKU KIELLETTY

Jenni Kuokka [FIN] www.hahmo.fi

WC | WC | INVA-WC

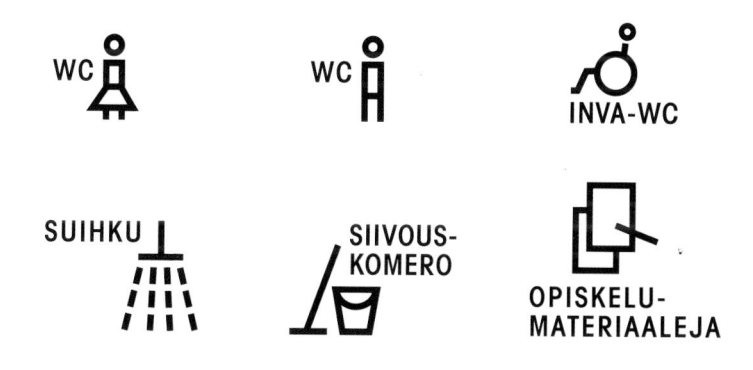

SUIHKU | SIIVOUS-KOMERO | OPISKELU-MATERIAALEJA

SALIT NEUVOTTELUTILAT

← **Tre** Oul **Pie** **Vii** **Lon** **Tal**
   Tku **Tor** **Kuo** **Lpr** **Kem** →

SALIT

4
TOIMISTO/BACKSTAGE

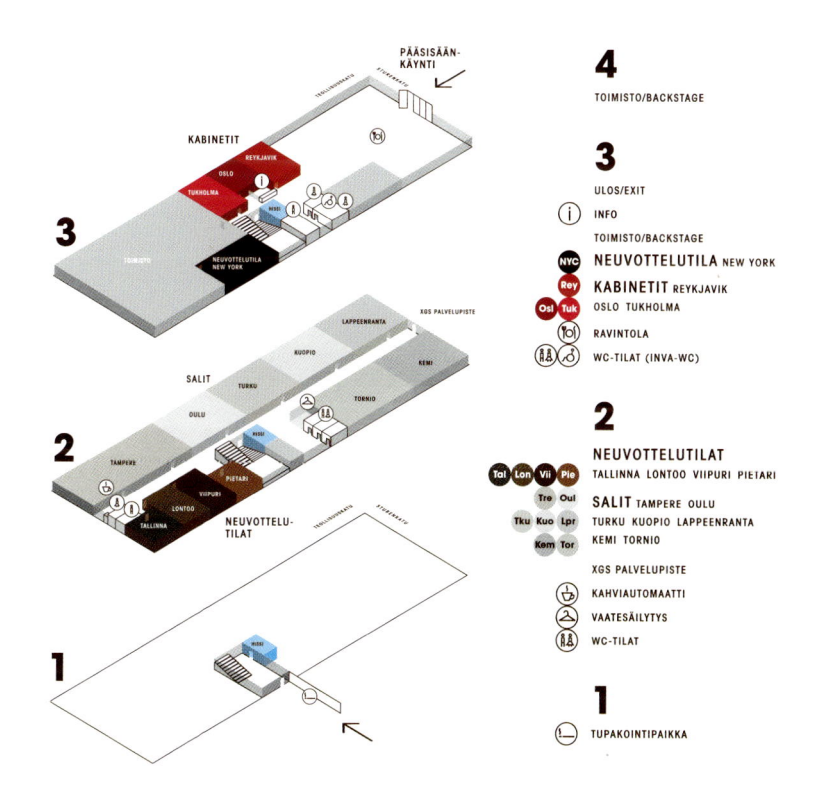

3
ULOS/EXIT
(i) INFO
TOIMISTO/BACKSTAGE
NYC **NEUVOTTELUTILA** NEW YORK
Rey **KABINETIT** REYKJAVIK
Osl **Tuk** OSLO TUKHOLMA
RAVINTOLA
WC-TILAT (INVA-WC)

2
NEUVOTTELUTILAT
Tal **Lon** **Vii** **Pie** TALLINNA LONTOO VIIPURI PIETARI
Tre **Oul** **SALIT** TAMPERE OULU
Tku **Kuo** **Lpr** TURKU KUOPIO LAPPEENRANTA
Kem **Tor** KEMI TORNIO

XGS PALVELUPISTE
KAHVIAUTOMAATTI
VAATESÄILYTYS
WC-TILAT

1
TUPAKOINTIPAIKKA

Map labels:
- PÄÄSISÄÄNKÄYNTI
- KABINETIT: REYKJAVIK, OSLO, TUKHOLMA
- TOIMISTO, NEUVOTTELUTILA NEW YORK
- SALIT: LAPPEENRANTA, KUOPIO, KEMI, TURKU, TORNIO, OULU, TAMPERE
- XGS PALVELUPISTE
- NEUVOTTELUTILAT: PIETARI, VIIPURI, LONTOO, TALLINNA

Richard Baird [GBR] www.richardbaird.co.uk

Sandra Mahn   [GER]   www.zweinullsieben.com

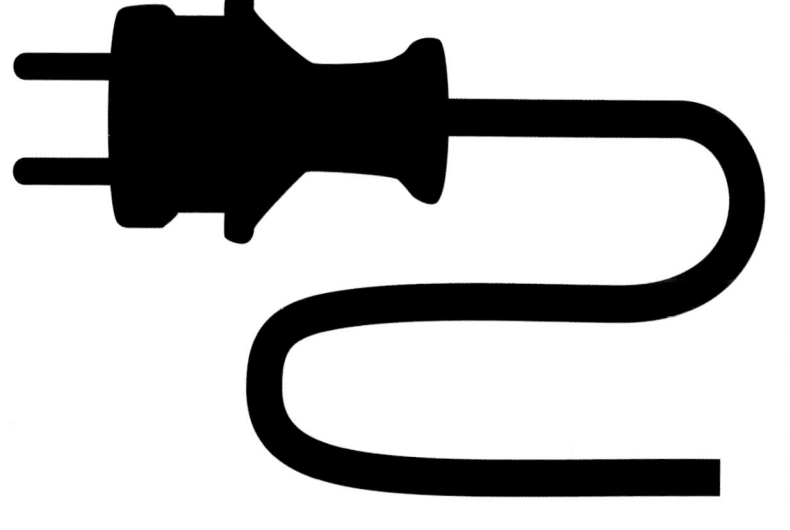

Archive Experts	Museum Experts	Students
Journalists and Editors	Scientists	General Public

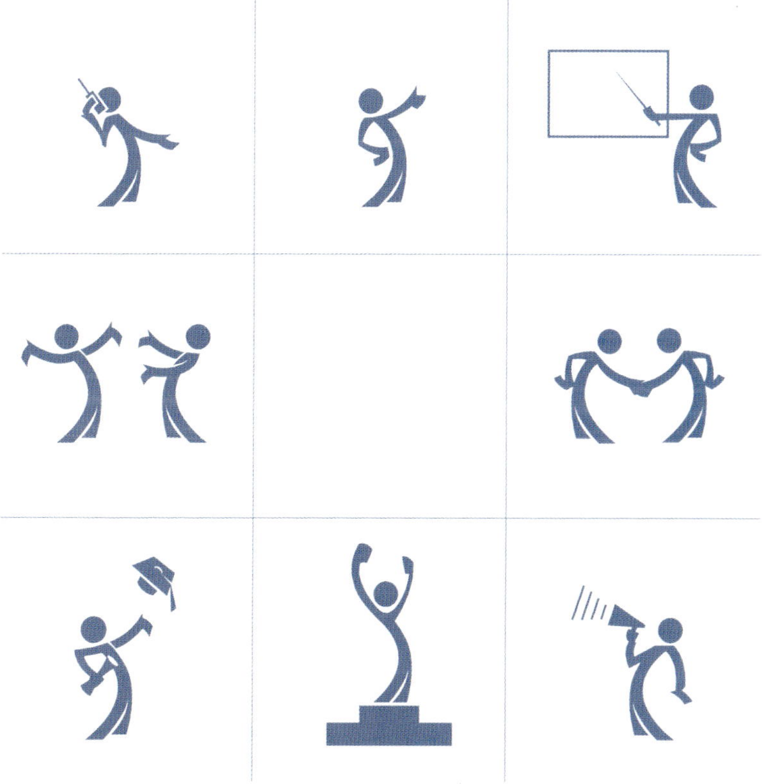

Bo Virkelyst Jensen (DEN) www.addsoul.com

STEFAN LANGE:
FRUCHTSALAT EP

REMIXES: MILD BANG
TUNES FOR FOOD
JAVIER FERREIRA
SOBAMONK

Sandra Hofacker [SUI] www.apfel-z.de

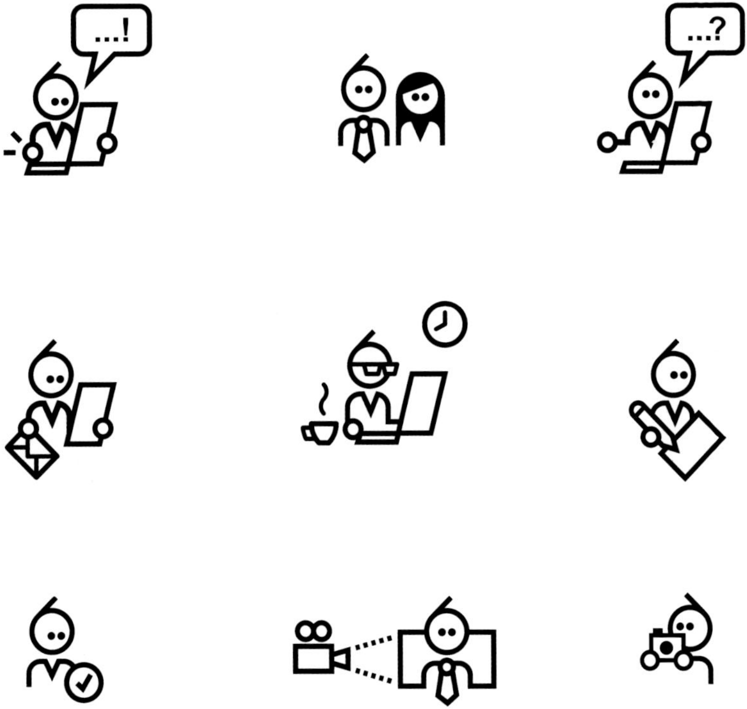

end user	software developer
device vendor	remote supporter

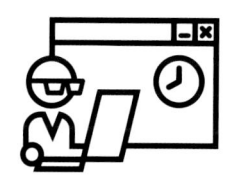

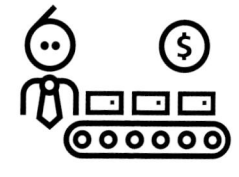

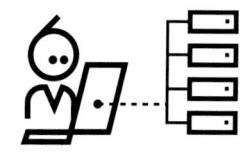

Bo Virkelyst Jensen [DEN] www.addsoul.com

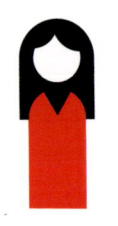

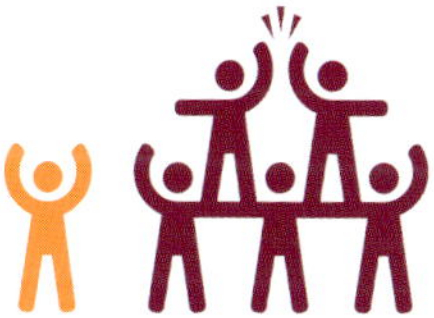

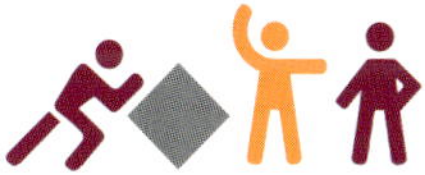

—yes—

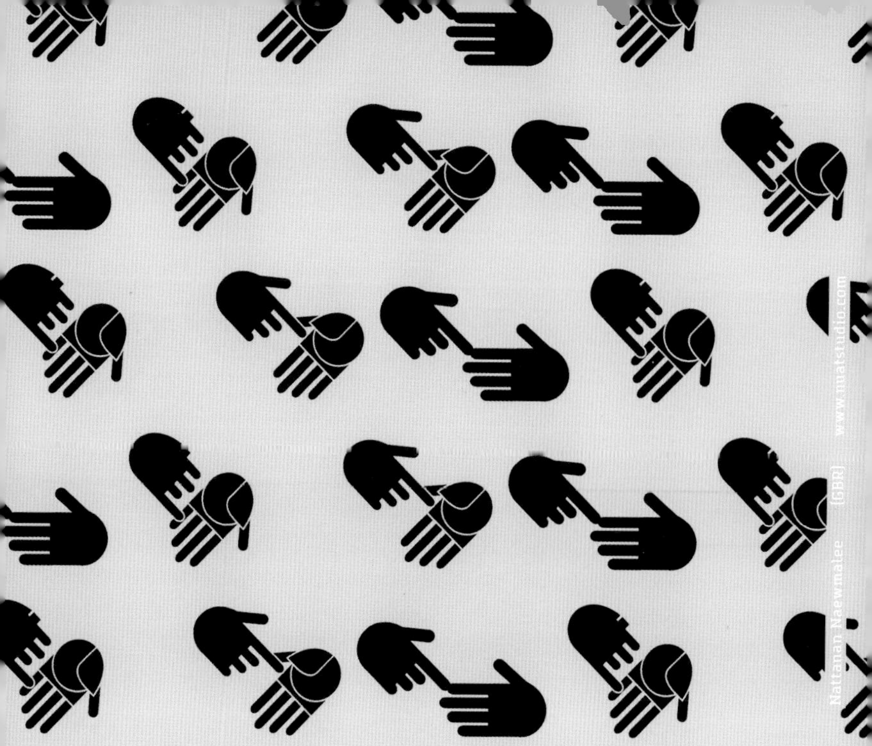

Nattanan Naewmalee (GBR) www.nuatstudio.com

Pictogram design with uniform set
for international hand signals and sign language

79

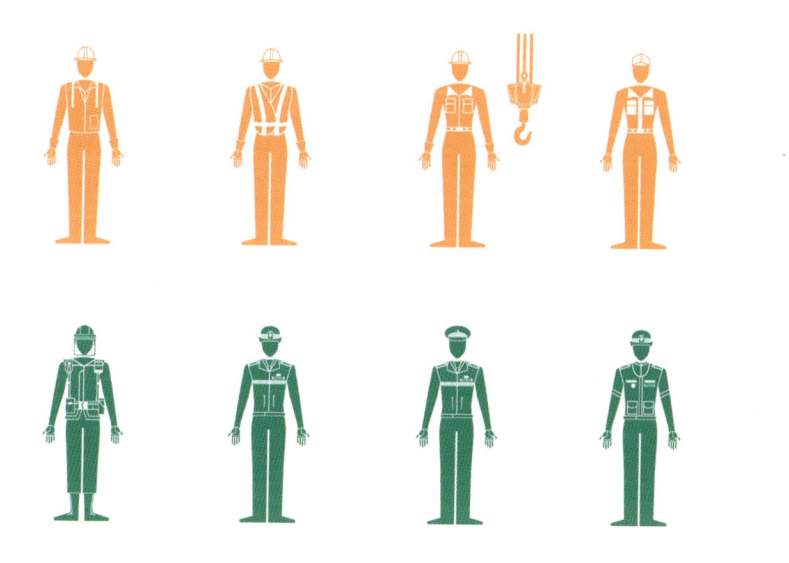

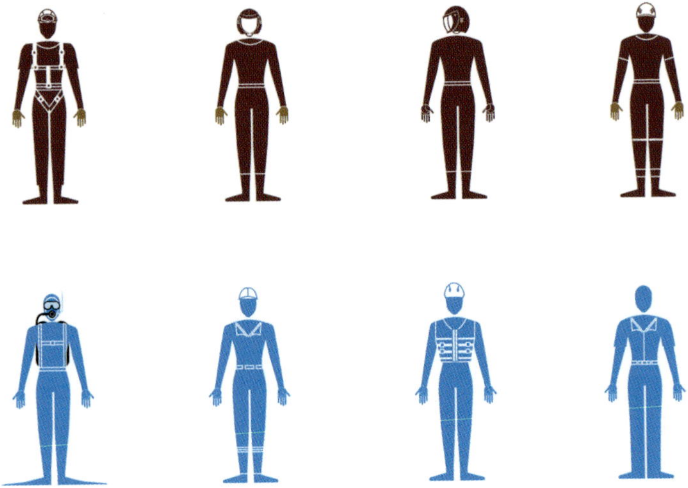

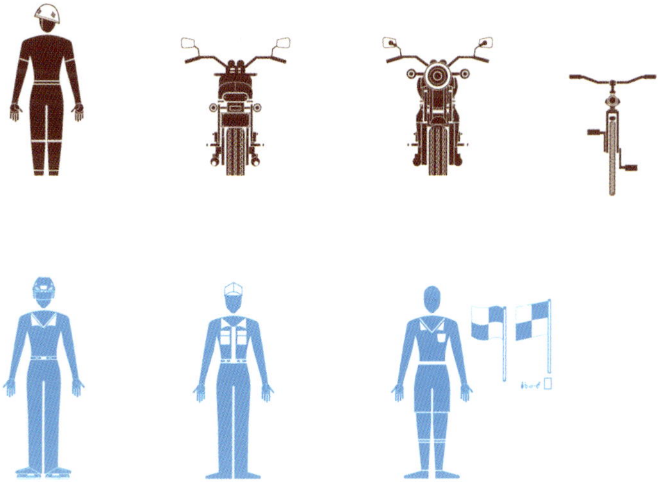

Nattanan Naewmalee (GBR) www.nuatstudio.com

The collection of
HANDS SIGNALS
of Traffics and Security by human movement

Strart your engines

Stop

Go ahead and pass me

Turn off your turn signals

Single riding

Left turn

Hazards on the road	Don't pass me	Stop your engine
Staggered riding	Right turn	Speed up

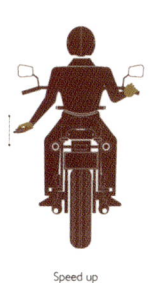

left turn

Alternate right hand

Right turn

Leave the front of the pace line and moving to the right

Leave the front of the pace line and moving to the left

Potholes or debris on the left side

Stopping or Slowing
using the light hand

Stopping or Slowing
using the right hand

Rail road crossing

Potholes or debris on the right side

Left arm and hand held up and
out to signals that bicyclist,
runners, skaters or vehicles are on the left

Left arm and hand held up and
out to signals that bicyclist,
runners, skaters or vehicles are on the right

Pick me up next

Hoist up

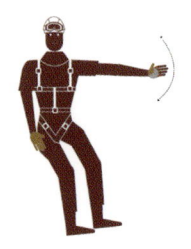

Hoist down

Ready / OK!

Cancel!

Take me that way

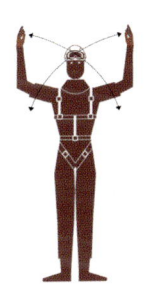

Abort / Go away

Stop!

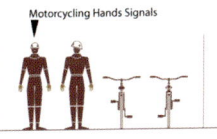

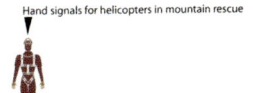

Bicycling Hands Signals

Motorcycling Hands Signals

Hand signals for helicopters in mountain rescue

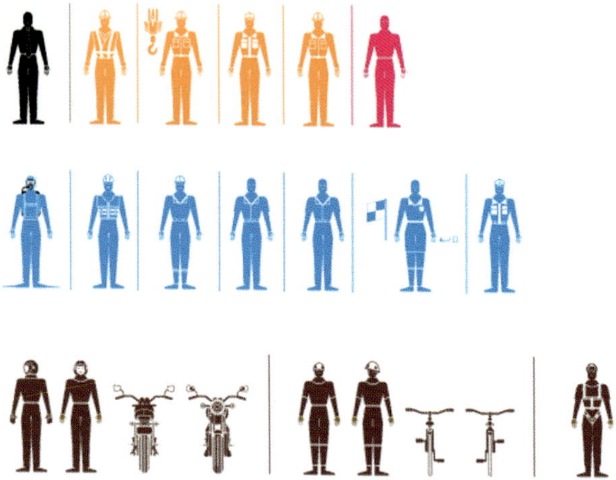

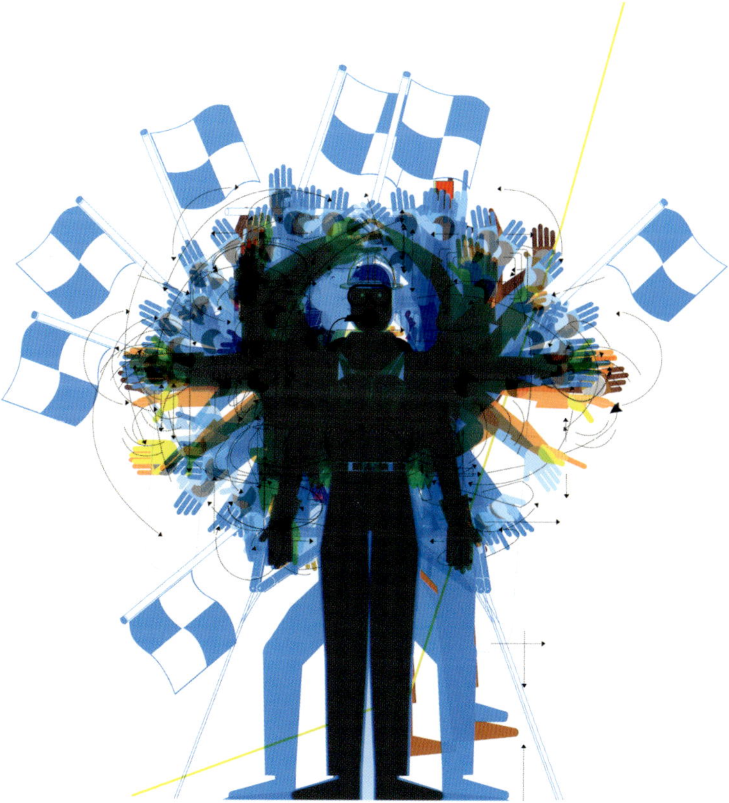

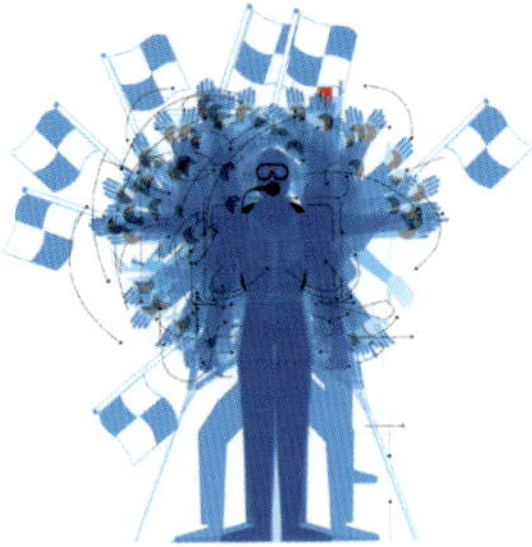

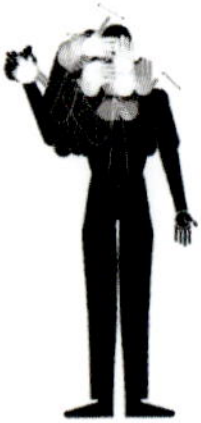

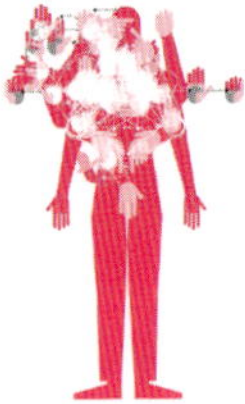

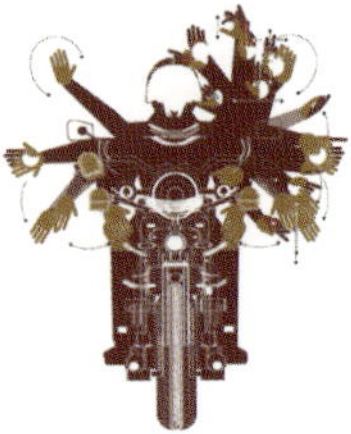

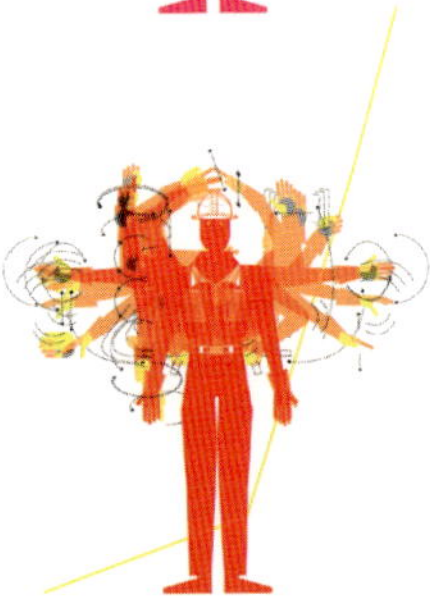

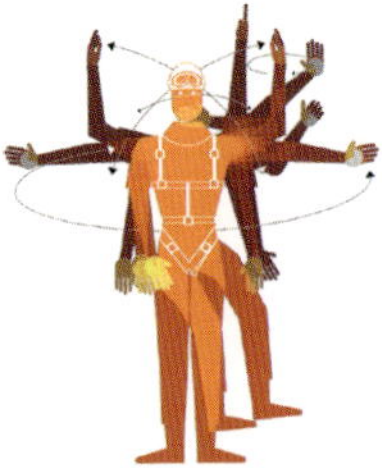

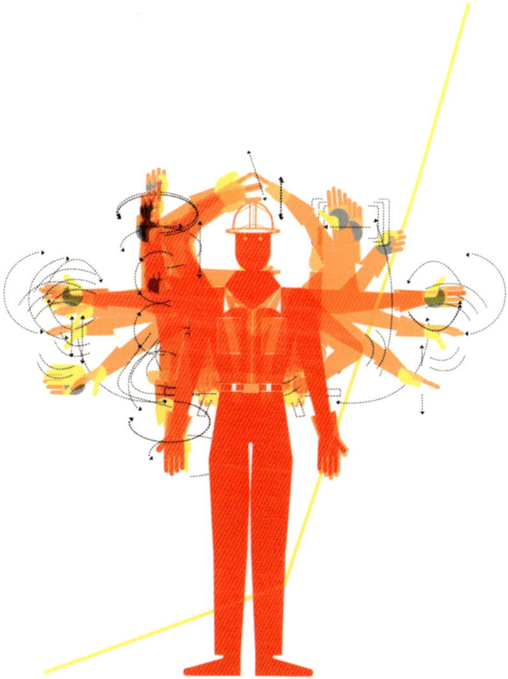

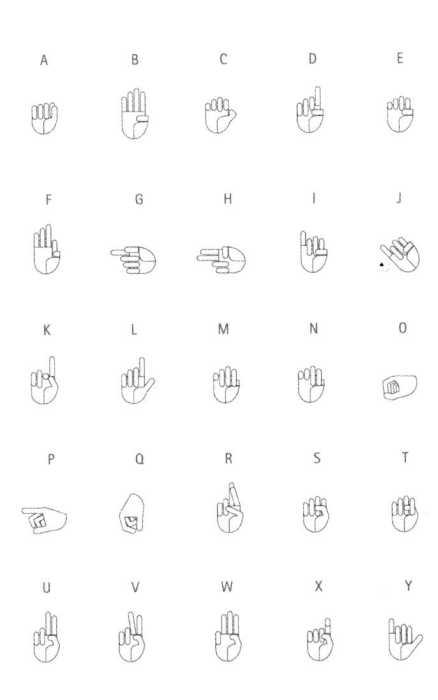

American Sign Language (ASL)

British Sign Language (BSL)

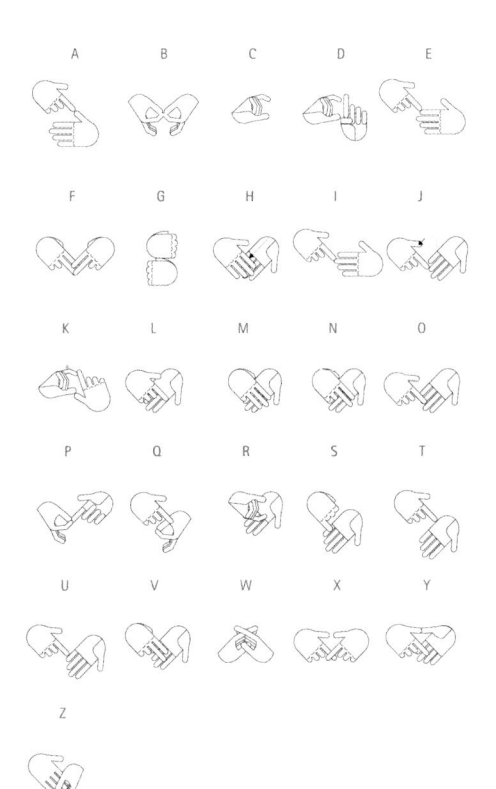

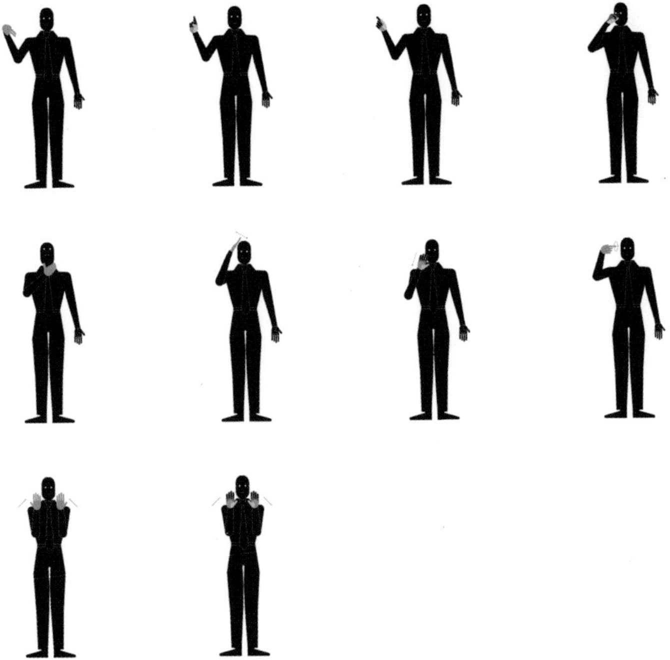

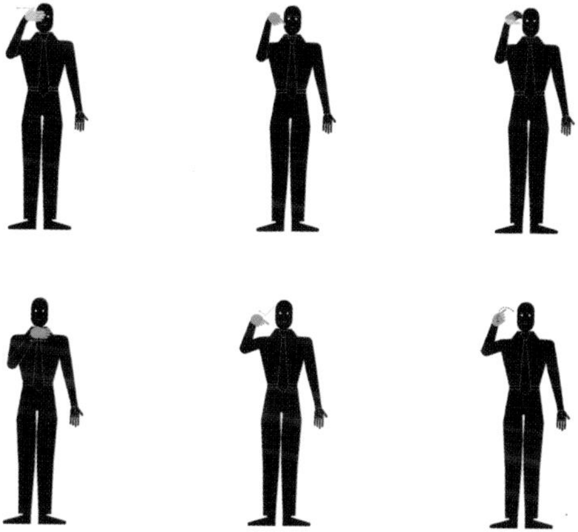

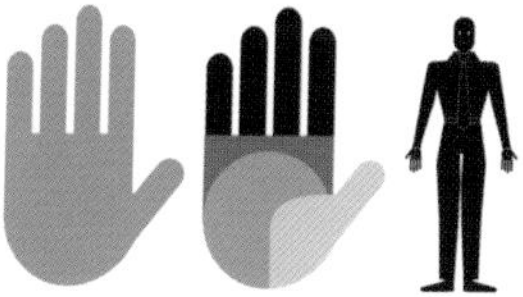

Alejandro Ovalles (VEN) www.jaoc.net

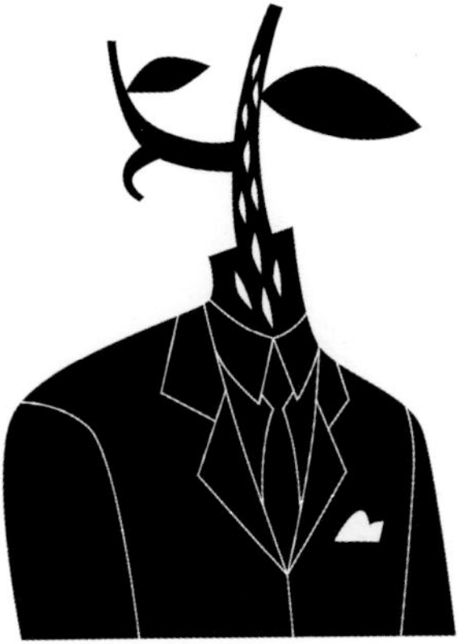

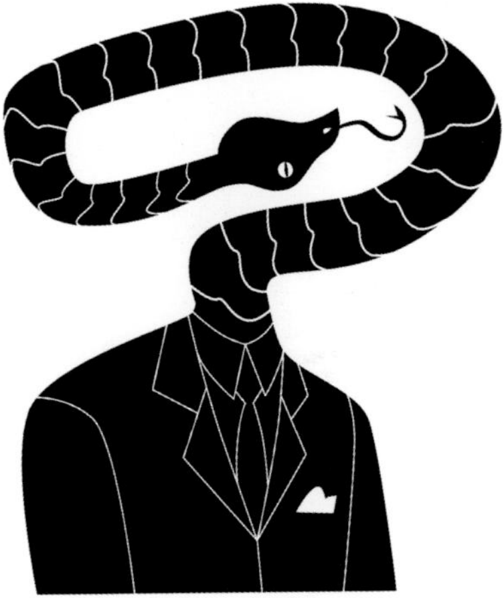

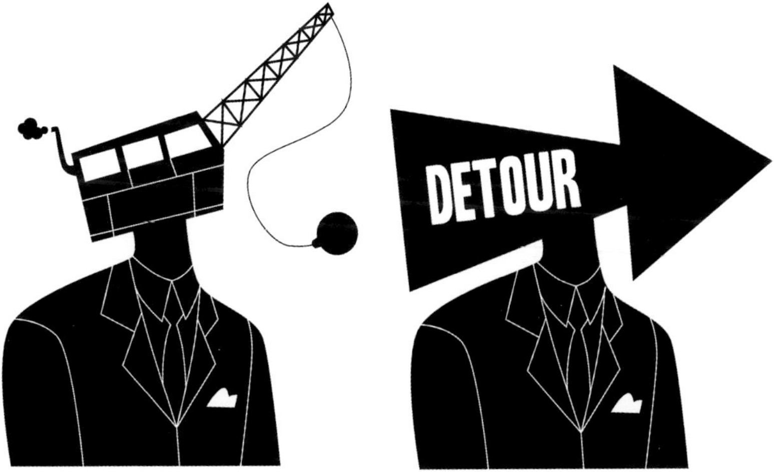
DETOUR

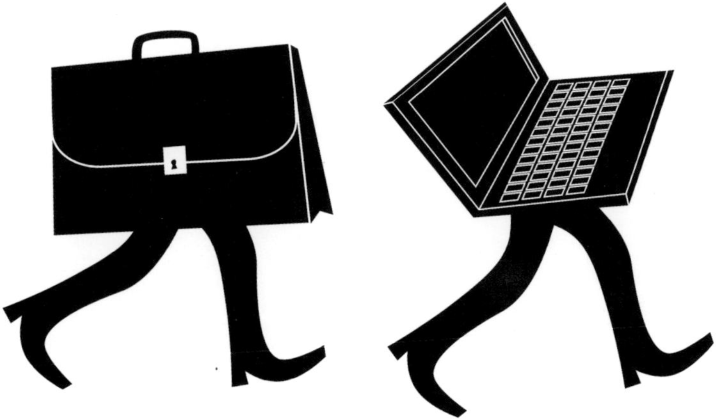

Alejandro Ovalles [VEN] www.jaoc.net

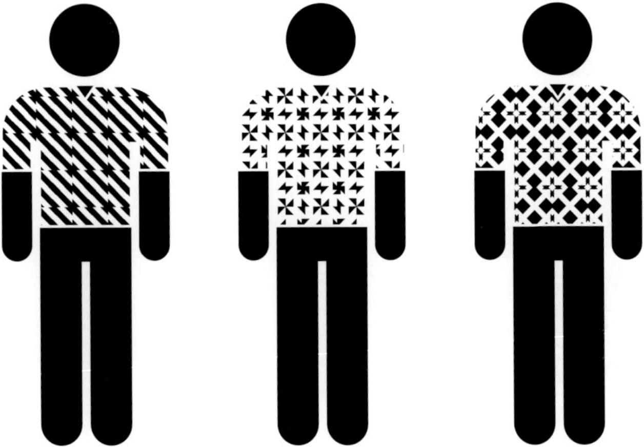

Peter Wölfel (GER)

Peter Wölfel (GER)

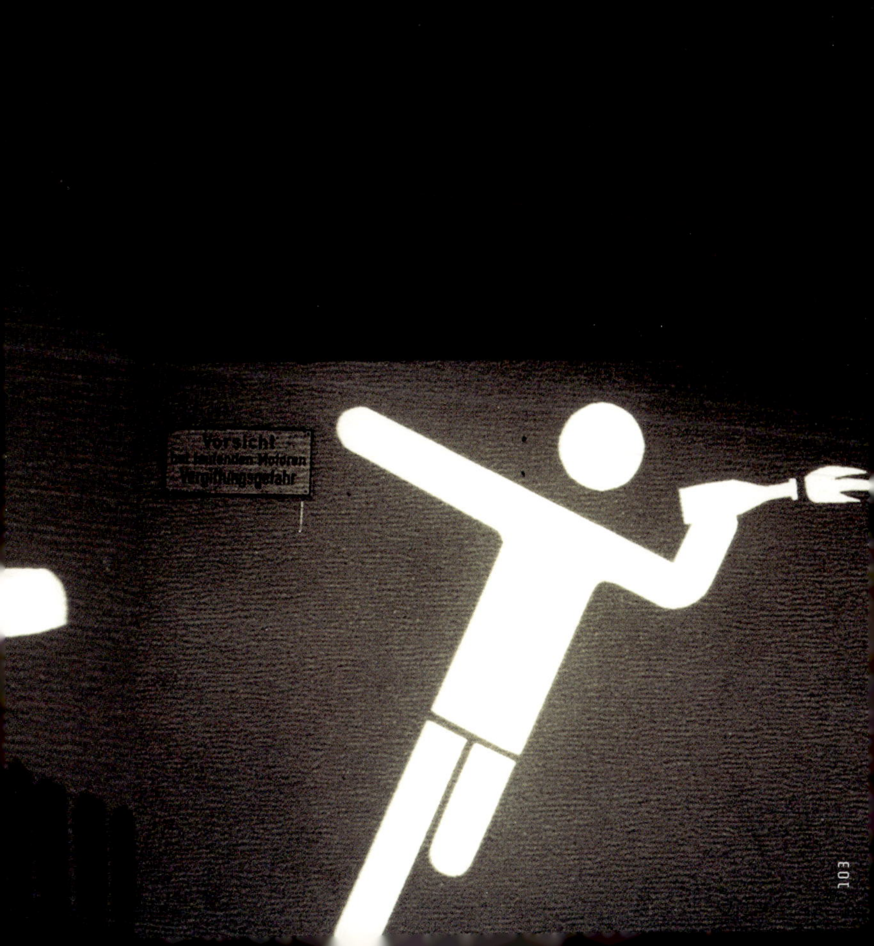
Vorsicht
bei laufenden Motoren
Vergiftungsgefahr

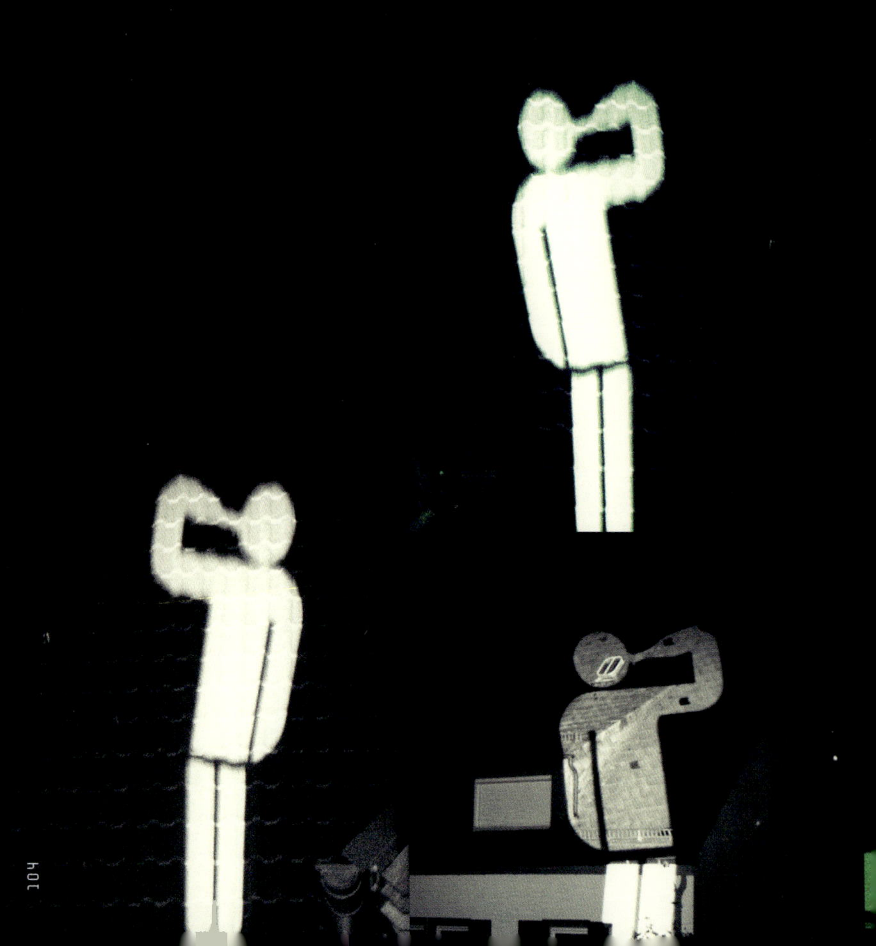

Peter Wölfel [GER]

105

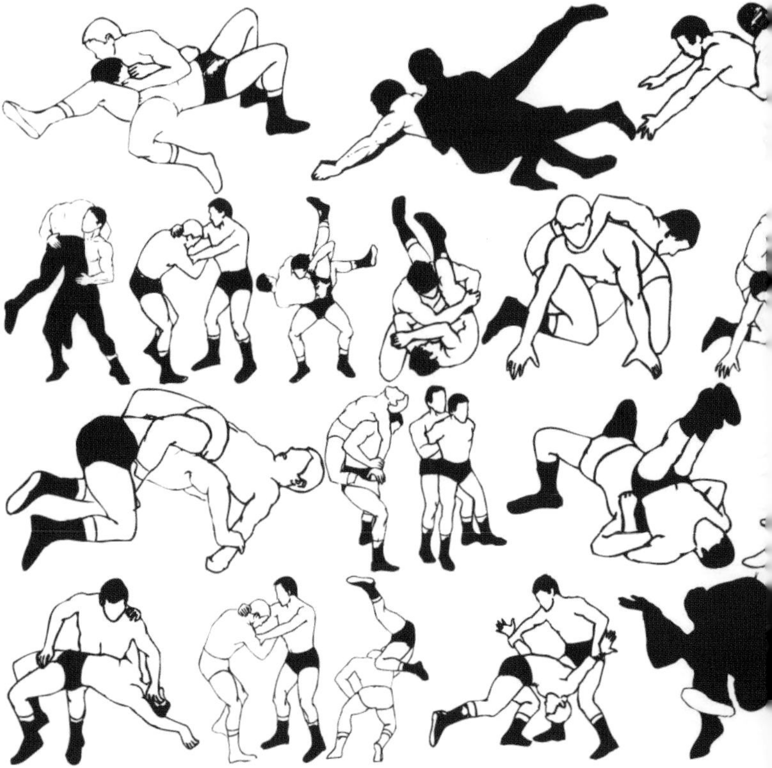

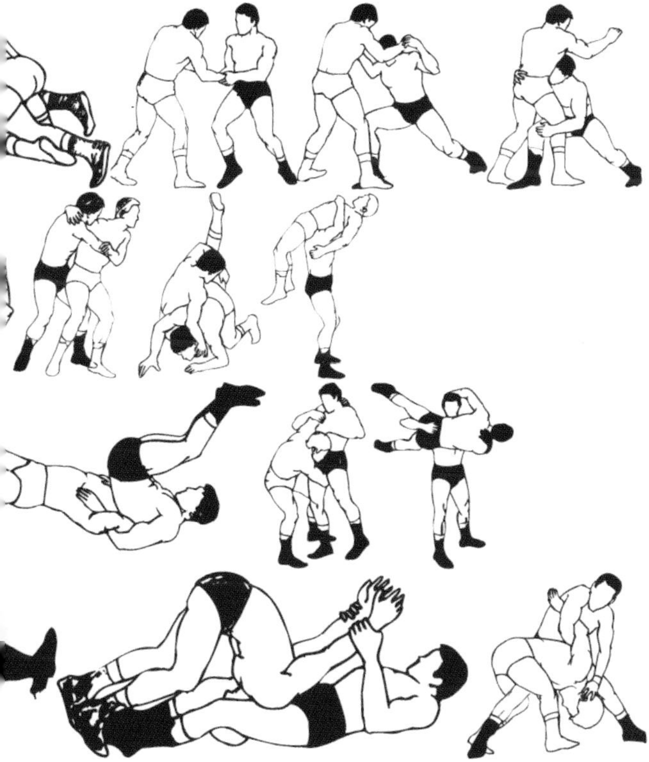

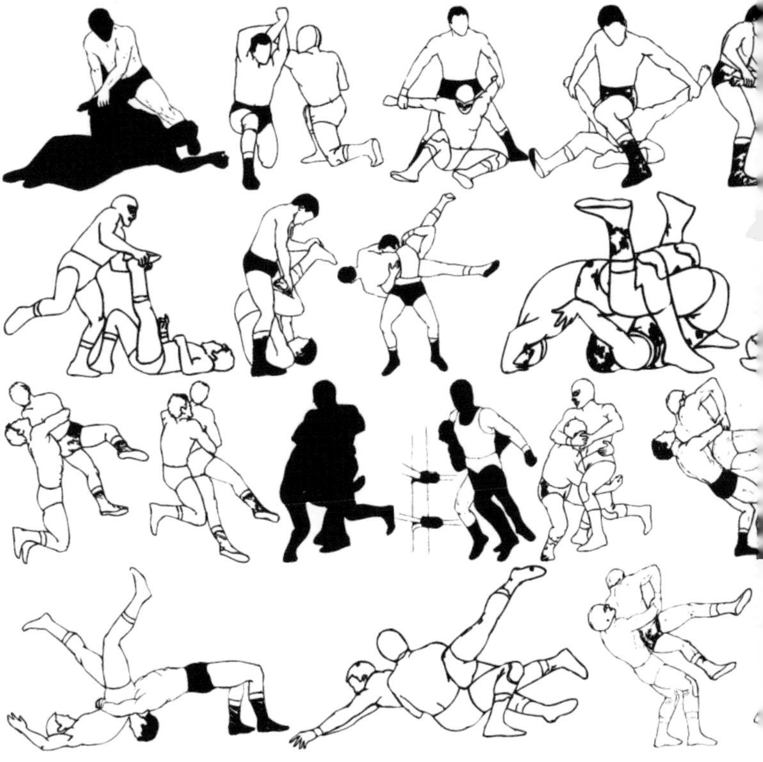

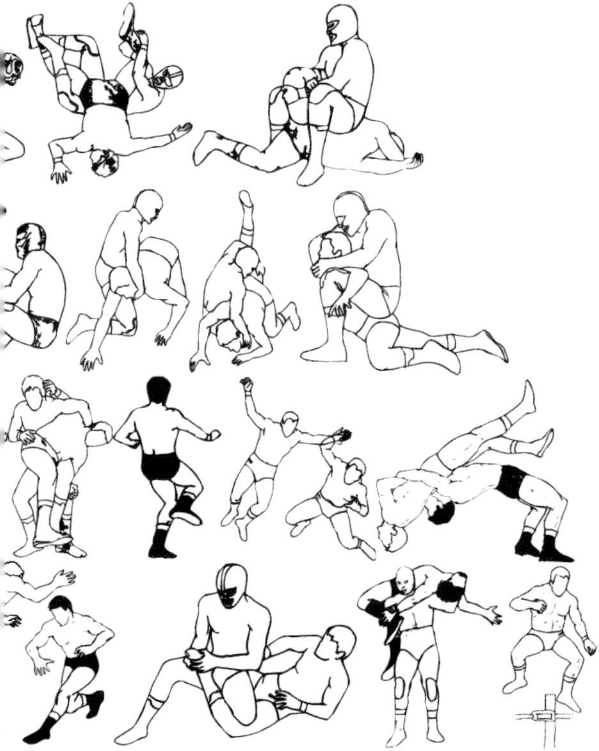

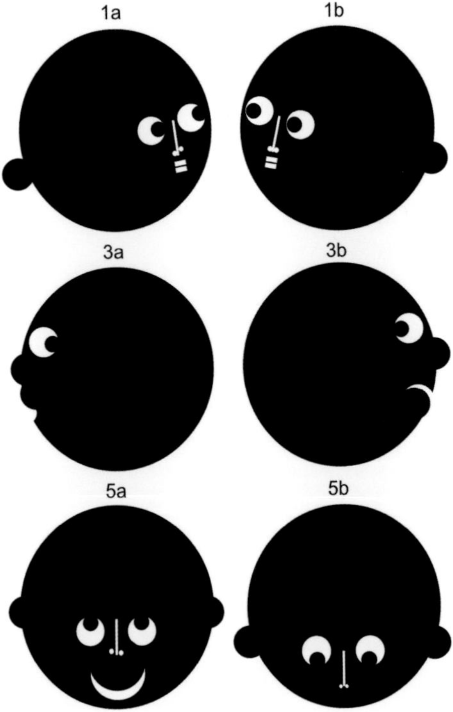
1a
1b
3a
3b
5a
5b

2a 2b

4a 4b

6a 6b

Kerstin Stephan [GER] www.kerstinstephan.com

Harri Lemke (GER) www.designbuero-lemke.de

Bo Virkelyst Jensen   [DEN]   www.addsoul.com

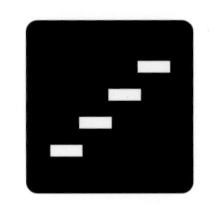

Miriam Figueras [ESP] www.cargocollective.com/mfigueras

Miriam Klobes [GER] www.mk-kommunikationsdesign.de

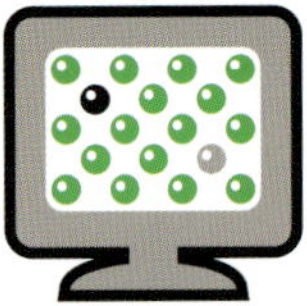
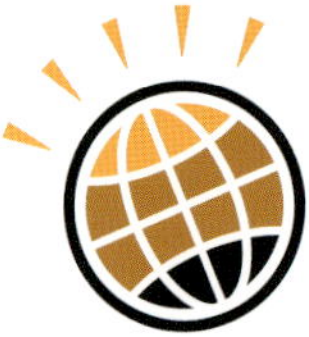
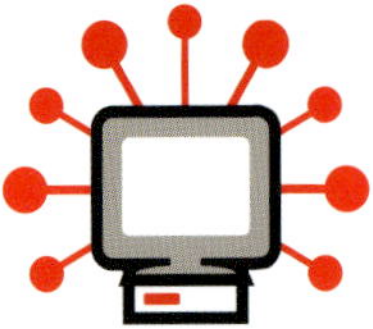
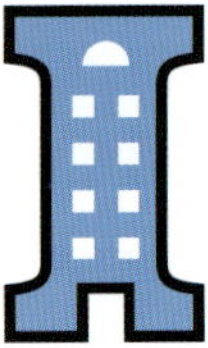
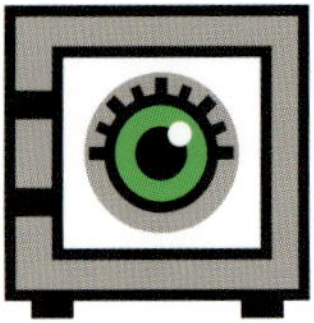
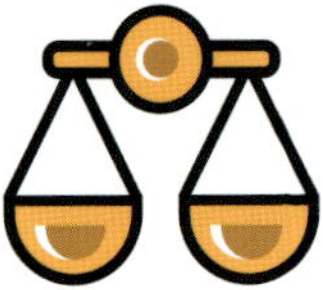

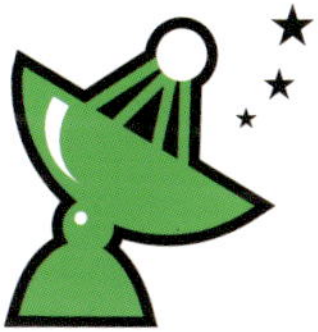
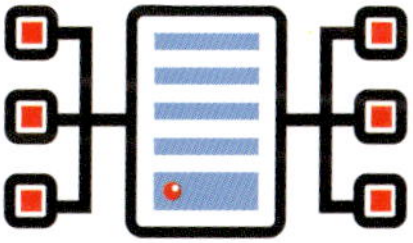
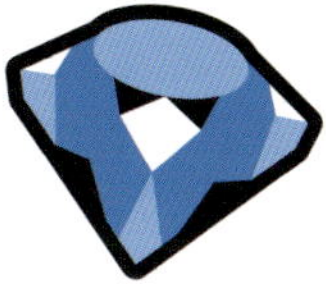

Puk Fenneman (NED) www.coolpuk.com

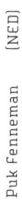

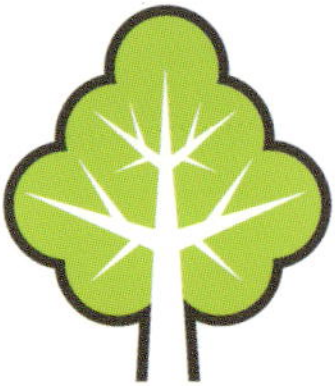

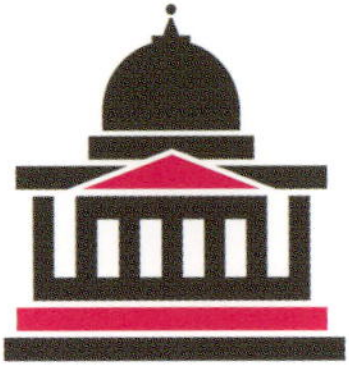
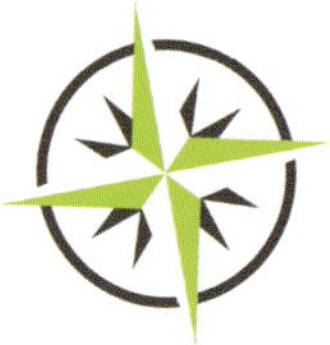
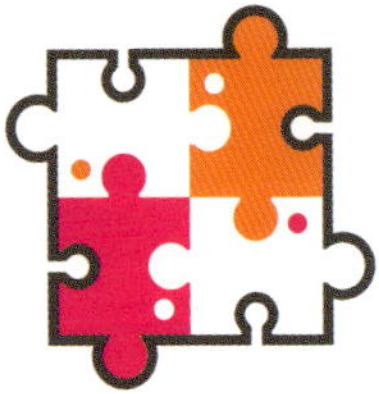

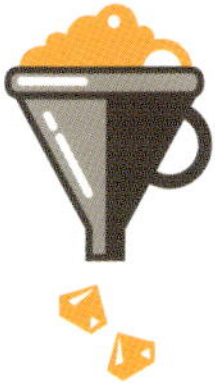

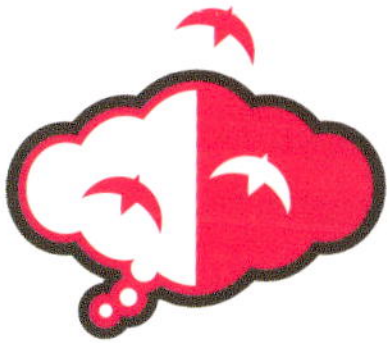

Puk Fenneman (NED) www.coolpuk.com

KÖLN

Harri Lemke [GER] www.designbuero-lemke.de

122

MÜNCHEN

Harri Lemke [GER] www.designbuero-lemke.de

STADTGEFLÜSTER
DUBAI
highlights | hotels | ausgehen | shoppen | sport | ausflüge | 24 stunden

125

STADTGEFLÜSTER DUBAI

highlights | hotels | ausgehen | shoppen | sport | ausflüge | 24 stunden

Harri Lemke [GER]   www.designbuero-lemke.de

127

Christopher Ledwig [GER] www.f1rstdesign.com

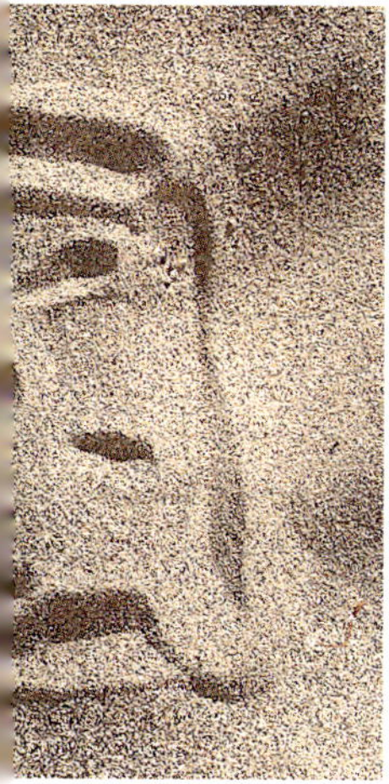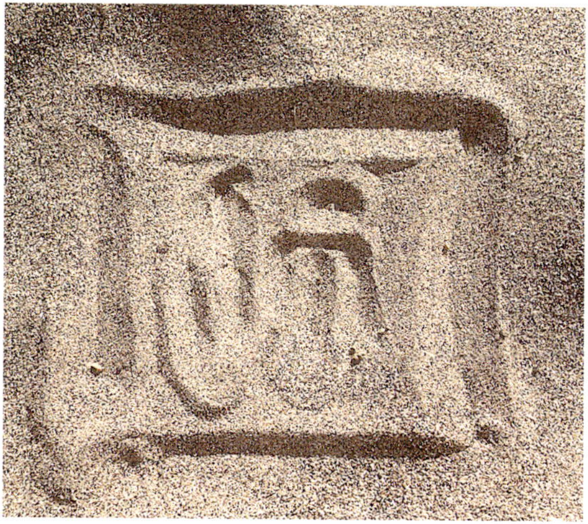

Julia Sysmäläinen [GER]

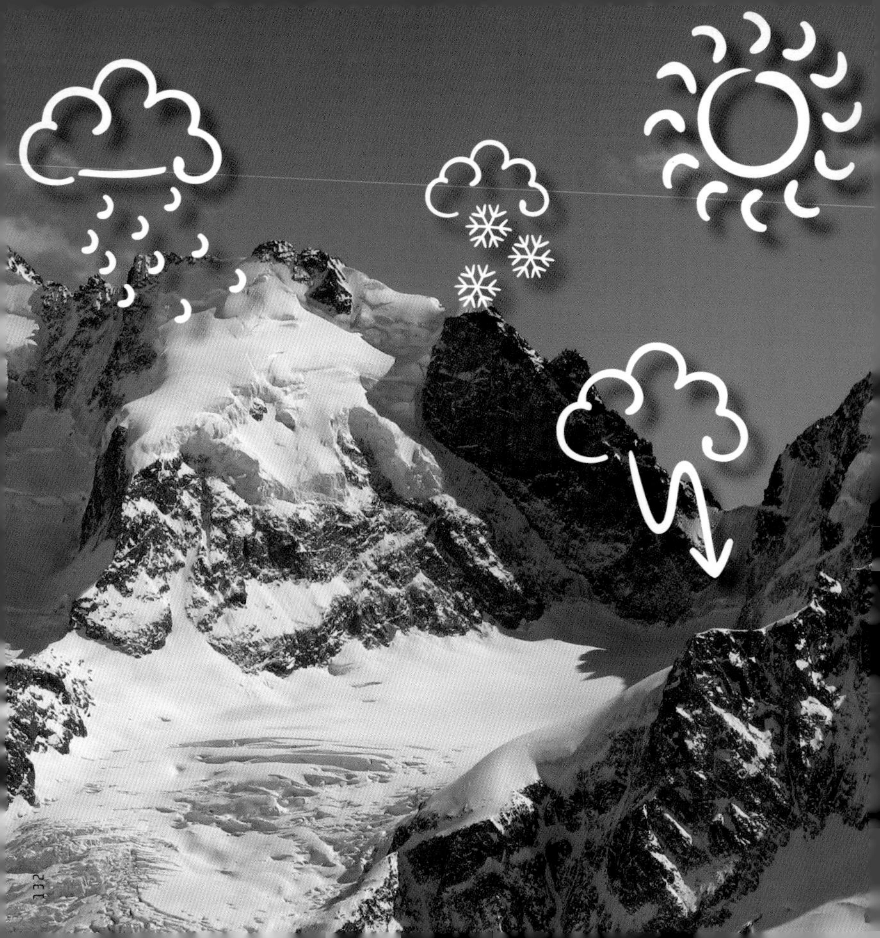

Julia Sysmäläinen (GER)

Daniel Bretzmann (GER) www.eyegix.com

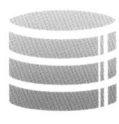

15

General	Youth unemployment	Non-working jobseekers
Economy (general)	Bankrupcies	Credit loans
Labor	Industial zones	Retail

Eyal Holtzman & Myrthe Stel [NED] www.2kilo.nl

136

Available vacancies

Social assistance

Investments comm. property

Offices

Tourism and leisure

Residences

House rental rates

The Hague city zones

Traffic

Population

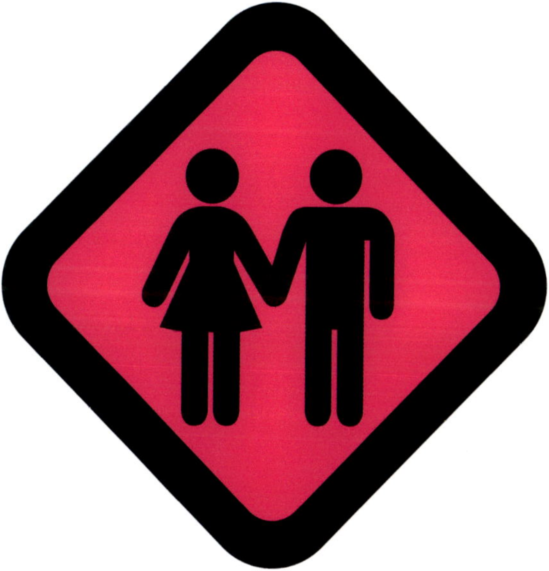

Eyal Holtzman & Myrthe Stel   [NED]   www.2kilo.nl

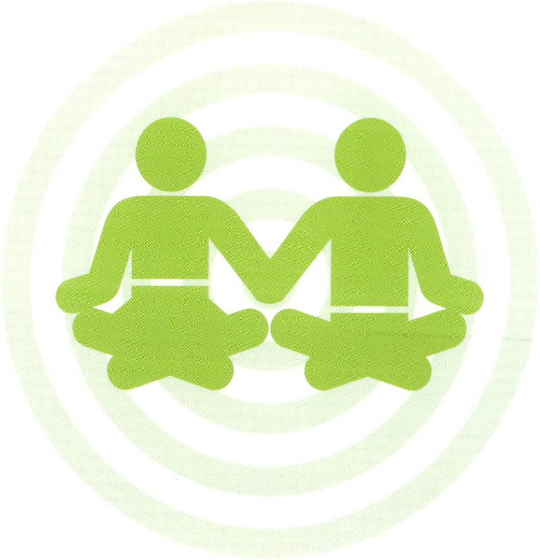

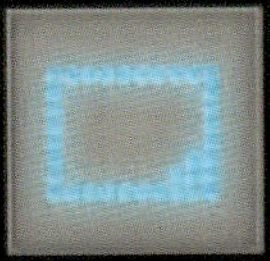

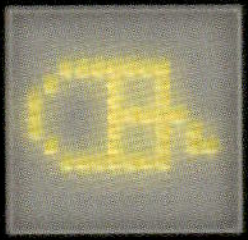

Andre Weier [GER] www.nalindesign.com

142

143

www.nalindesign.com

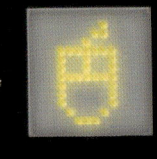

Andre Weier (GER)

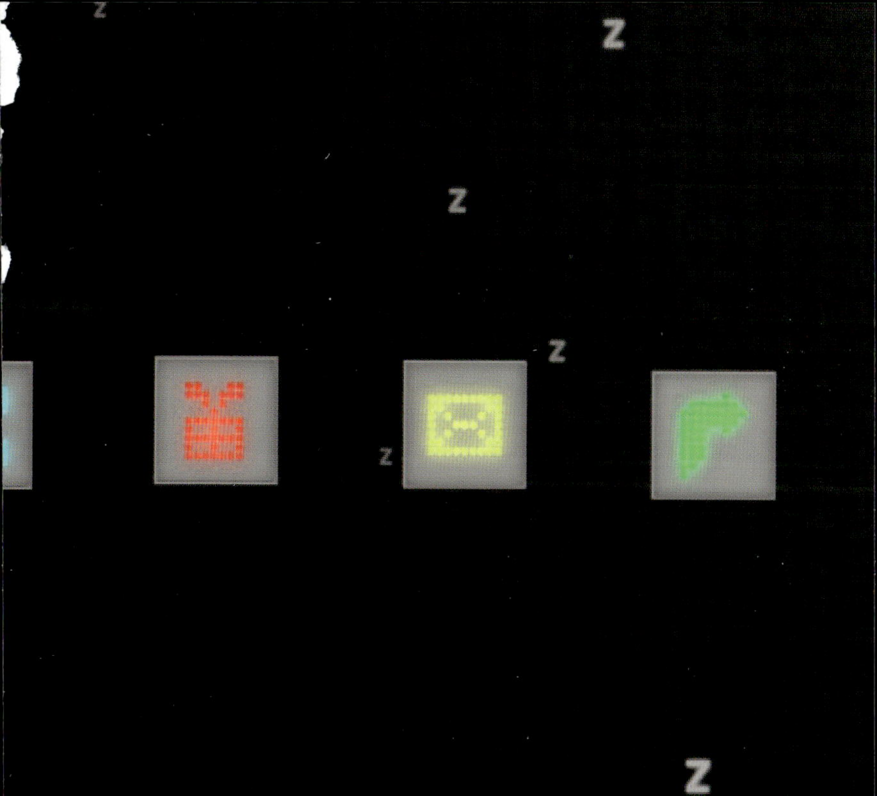
z
Z
Z
Z
z
Z

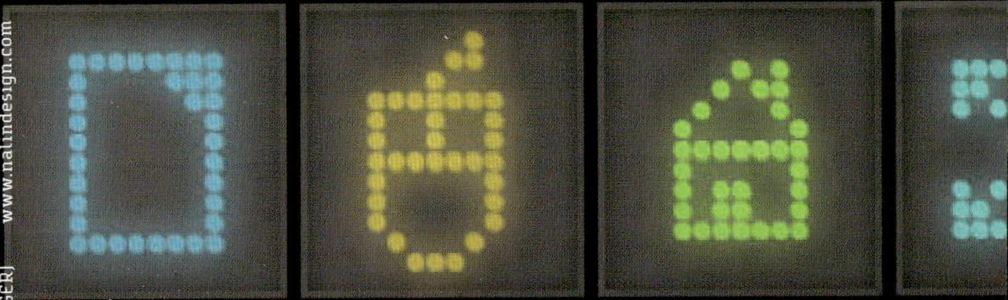

www.nalindesign.com

Andre Weier [GER]

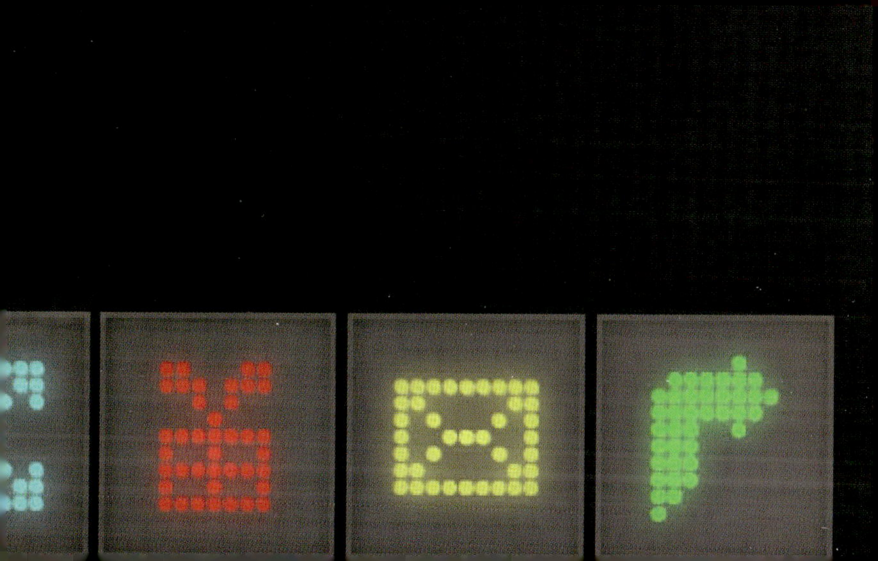

Feli Timmesfeld [GER] www.ergosign.de

€ 10,-

Feli Timmesfeld [GER] www.ergosign.de

PICTO /
NEIGHBORHOOD

Sergio Rodriguez Melo [COL] www.flickr.com/photos/garbagcolombia/

152

María Angélica Orjuela R.   (COL)

Marcel Weik [GER] www.mwkd.de

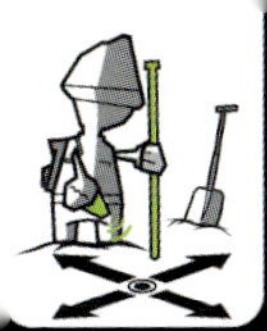
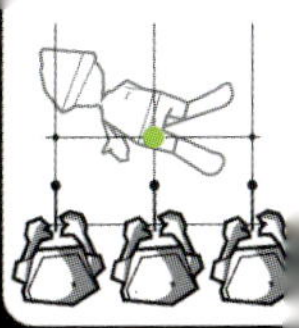
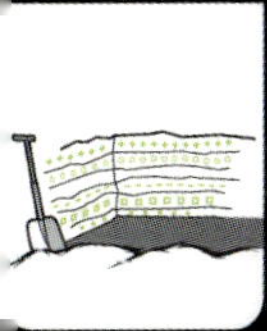
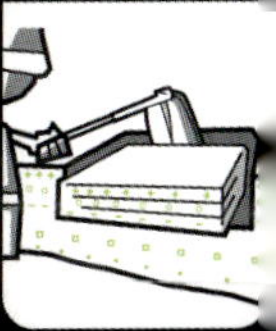
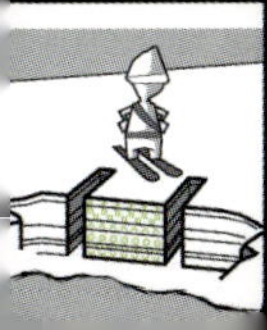
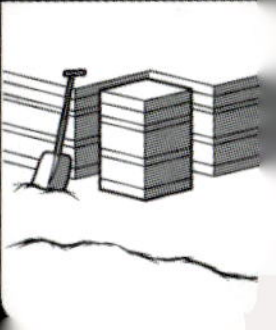

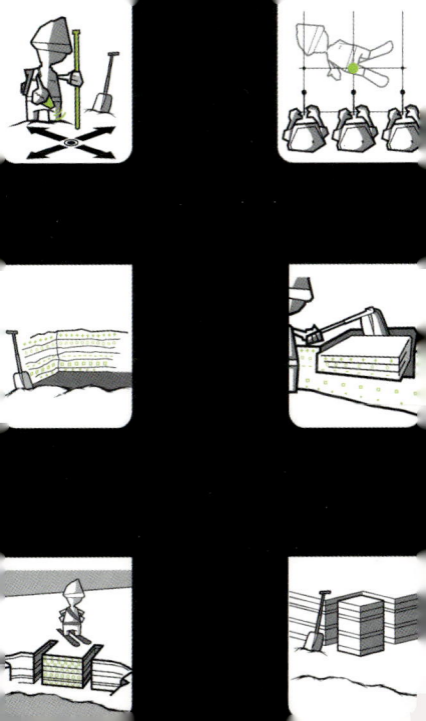

Marcel Weik [GER] www.mwkd.de

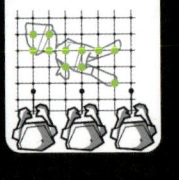

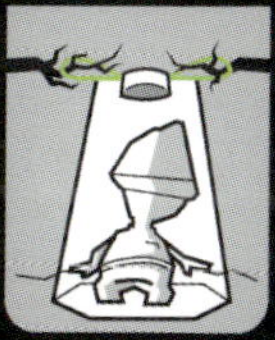

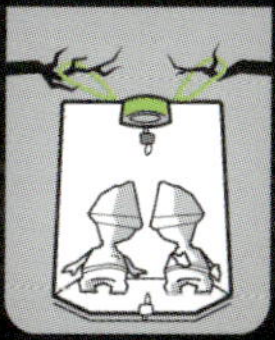

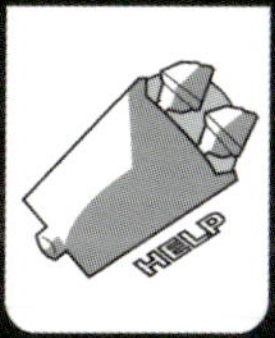
HELP

Simon Faerstain [DEN] www.faerstain.dk

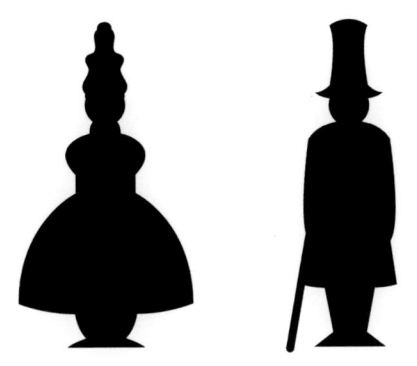

158

Simon Faerstain   [DEN]   www.faerstain.dk

Rachel Holmes (GBR) www.behance.net/Rachel_holmes

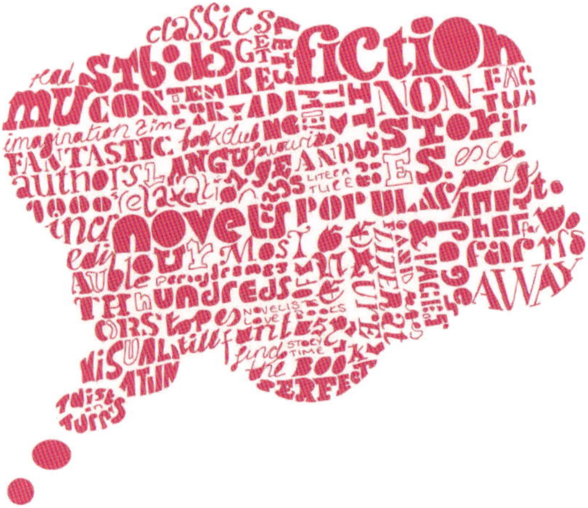

Fiction

⬆ ⬆

- ★ Bestsellers & new releases
- 🌿 Real lives & biographies
- Fiction
- 🪐 Science Fiction

- 🔴 Bargains
- 🟢 Local interest
- ❤ Romance
- 🔎 Crime

MAGA ZINES **Magazines**

🛈 Information

£ Pay desk

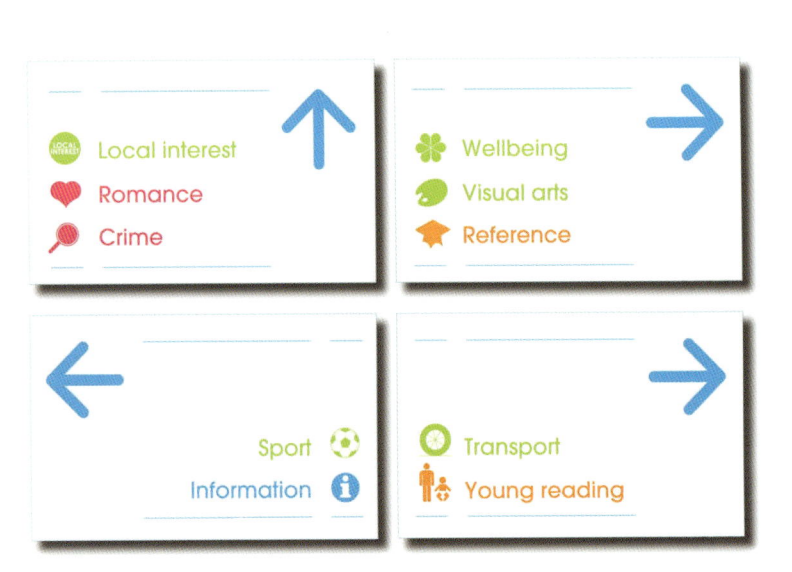

- Local interest
- Romance
- Crime

- Wellbeing
- Visual arts
- Reference

- Sport
- Information

- Transport
- Young reading

Factual books

Book Lists & Biographies

Other sectors
For those bits that dont quite fit into the other categories

Fictional books
Over 275,000 titles in this section covering all fictional novels from all genres, from love stories to period dramas to fantasy and mystery

Fiction

Local Interest

Lifestyle

Humour

Esoterism & Fairy Tales

Information £

Borders services
Always around happy to help with two help points in all stores

Science Fiction

Sport

Travel

Reference

Bargains

Pay points

Crime

Gardening

Visual arts

Young reading

Audiobooks

Romance

History & Politics

Nature

Music and Film

Magazines

Lower floor
Bestsellers & new releases
Bargains
Magazines
Young reading

Real lives & biographies
Local interest

Fiction
Science Fiction
Crime
Romance

Paperbacks

Information
Payment

Upper floor
Humour
Reference
Music & film

Travel
Lifestyle
Sport
Wellbeing
History & politics
Visual arts

Starbucks

Information

Wishlist:
Why not use this section to record titles you or a friend may be interested in.

Parent and toddler group
Every Tuesday
10.30am

National storytime
Every Saturday and Sunday
2.30pm
Children's department

Creative writing group
Every Monday
5.30pm

Quiz
Every Sunday
7.30pm
In Starbucks
All welcome

Mon-Fri	9am-9pm
Starbucks	9am-8.30pm
Sat:	9am-8pm
Starbucks	9am-7pm
Sun:	11am-4pm
Starbucks	10.30am-4.30pm

Preston Borders store
Unit C1 (B)
Deepdale Retail Park
Blackpool Road
Preston
PR1 6QY
Tel: 01772 703656
www.borderstores.co.uk

Borders Preston is the place to shop this Spring. Why? You don't need to go traipsing round the high street because we've got the best selection of Books, CDs and DVDs all under one roof. Our booksellers are here to give you the best service around.

Fictional books
Over 275,000 titles in this section covering all fictional novels from all genres, from love stories to period dramas to fantasy and mystery

Fiction
We offer the largest and most popular fiction section around. We're positive that you'll be able to find the title you want along with a few you won't have thought of before. Come to this section for both the famous authors and the lesser known, have novels ranging from period dramas, to cutting edge stuff.

Science Fiction
As an extension from our fiction section we also offer a science fiction area. This is ideal for the trekkies of just anyone willing to look into the future, whether realistic or bizarre.

Crime
This section features all the mystery and thriller books. It offers a chance to test your detective skills trying to unravel murder mysteries, or 'whodunnit'. This is one of our largest and most popular sections so you're sure to find the title you are after.

Romance
If you're looking for a happy ending, star-crossed lovers or your boy meets girl stories along with a few surprises thrown in, then this is the section to come to. It houses romance tales from back in the day to the more contemporary novels.

168

Factual books

Real Lives & Biographies
Take a sneaky little peek into not only the lives of the rich and famous, but also those icons that you admire. This section is packed full of true stories of grit, determination, bravery, heartache, and most of all stories of success and triumph. Read all about race stars, sports stars, politicians and much much more.

Other sectors
For those bits that dont quite fit into the other categories

Local Interest
Whatever your location your local Borders store has a range of information on your culture, also all know how interesting it is to find out your history, where you came from, what your part of the world used to be like.

Lifestyle
This section includes everything you'll ever need to know on following the perfect cocktail party or getting those homes grown veggies all while keeping an ideal house.

Humour
This section is perfect for gifts or something just to brighten up your day. These books range from small pocket sized gems to full laughter packed novels. Warning: some items may cause offence.

Bestsellers & new releases
Here you'll find the books that have been rushing off our shelves in the past few weeks, so maybe you'll want them too. This section also houses all new releases, as soon as they have been published. As your options change, so do our shelves.

Information £
Help to offer a book, or ask for recommendations from one of our many information points in store.

Borders services
Always around happy to help with two help points in all stores

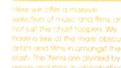

Sport
The active customers out here, we have a wide range of info on sports and transport, whether you're into football, swimming or cars, this is a perfect section for you to add to.

Travel ✈
Here we house everything you'll ever need to try trip travel, six stuck maps, tourist guides, language books, and you can also read up on the history of wherever you're visiting, or dreaming to go in the future.

Reference
For the more studious amongst you here we provide reference books on just about everything, from your standard English dictionary to advice on accounting and running your own business.

Bargains
This Borders bargains section houses all those hidden gems that can't be found anywhere else. It's the perfect place to pick up something that little bit different and all for a rock bottom price. This section contains a selection of all genres we have to offer, from books to CDs and DVDs to magazines.

Pay points ℹ
Purchase all your items here, including gift vouchers. Don't forget to ask about any upcoming events you may be interested in.

Wellbeing
If you're in need of a bit of relaxation this is the perfect place to retune you for nature. It's spiritual and mental wellbeing. It contains self-help books, and advice on everything from relationships to meditation.

Visual arts
In this section you will find everything from photography to fashion design, product design, fine art, illustration, graphic design and much more. We offer books for reference and for advice.

Young reading
Here you'll find everything for young readers, like story books ranging from learning to read to teen fiction. The area also has plenty of gifts and interactive activities to keep young readers active while you carry on with the rest of your browsing.

Audiobooks 🎧
Factual and fictional books on CD.

History & Politics
All figures on heritage from England to abroad.

Nature
Here you will find books ranging from animal habitats to keeping a tidy garden.

Music and Film 📀
Here we offer a massive selection of music and films and not just the chart toppers. We have a few of the more obscure artists and films amongst the stash. The items are ordered by genre and then in alphabetical order to make it easy if you know what you're looking for, and for easy browsing if you don't.

Magazines
The widest range of magazines on the high street.

---

www.behance.net/Rachel_holmes

Rachel Holmes [GBR]

169

LOCAL INTEREST

BARG AINS

MAGA ZINES

Visual arts

Rachel Holmes   [GBR]   www.behance.net/Rachel_holmes

Daniel Bretzmann [GER] www.eyegix.com

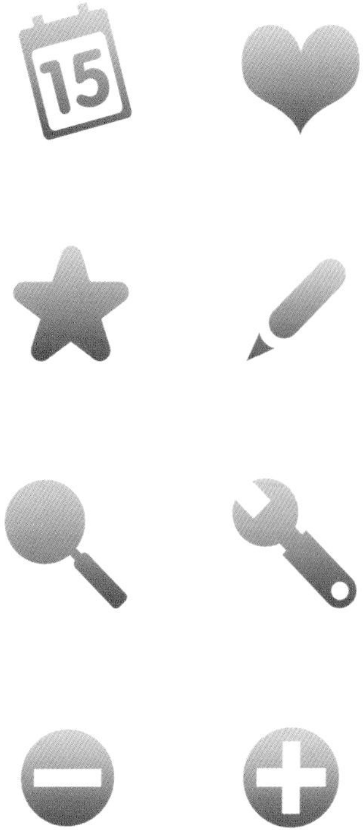

Arhuaco Tribe Bag

Carriel
Small leather satchel. typical
of the Antioquia region

Vallenato
Popular folk music

El Pibe
Colombia's most recognisable soccer player

Quimbaya precolumbian artpiece

Sombrero Vueltiao
Traditional hat

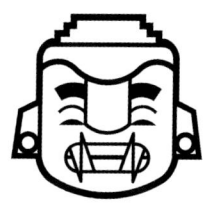

San Agustín
Pre-Columbian archaeological park
consider UNESCO World Heritage

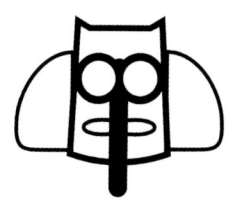

Marimonda
Character from the Barranquilla Carnaval

Aguardiente
Anise-flavoured liqueur derived rum sugar cane

La Chocolatera
Typical chocolate jar

The Baby Jesus
True venerated Religious image

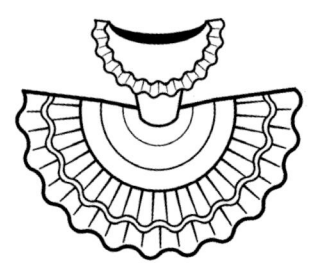

Cumbia
Musical style and folk dance

El Dr. J.E. Gaitán
Emblematic and charismatic political leader,
killed the april 9 of 1948

Sacred Heart
Catholic icon

Cartagena's National peagent

La Greca
Colombian emblematic coffee machine

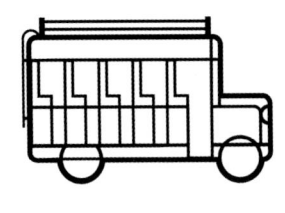

La Chiva
Typical colorfulled buses

The Beetles
Nickname for Colombian cyclists

The Bridge
Colombian jargon to define holidays

Orchid
National flower

El Pibe

Colombia's most recognisable soccer player

Hernan Berdichevsky & Gustavo Stecher (ARG) www.imagenhb.com

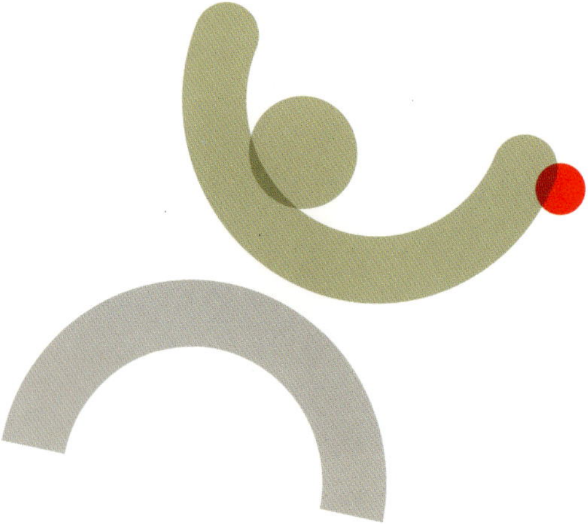

Hernan Berdichevsky & Gustavo Stecher   (ARG)   www.imagenhb.com

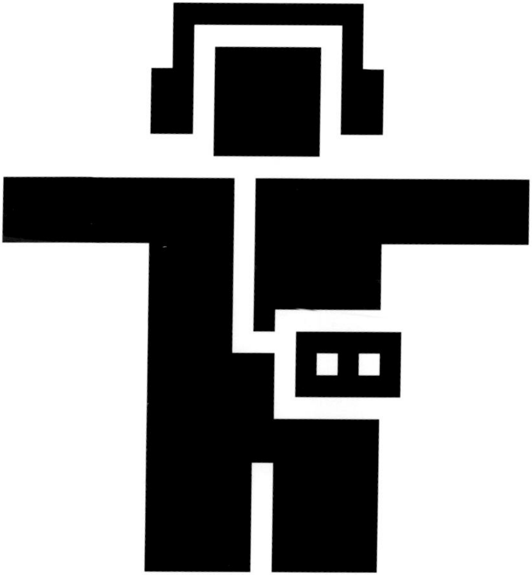

Bo Virkelyst Jensen (DEN) www.addsoul.com

salle de conférence

information

inscriptions

salle de dessin

graphisme

Marine Drouan [GER] www.portfolio.mixher.fr

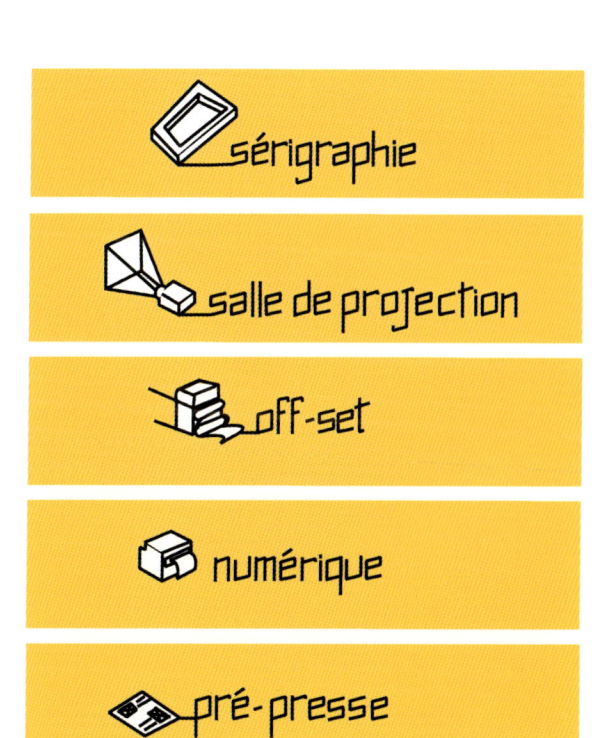

- sérigraphie
- salle de projection
- off-set
- numérique
- pré-presse

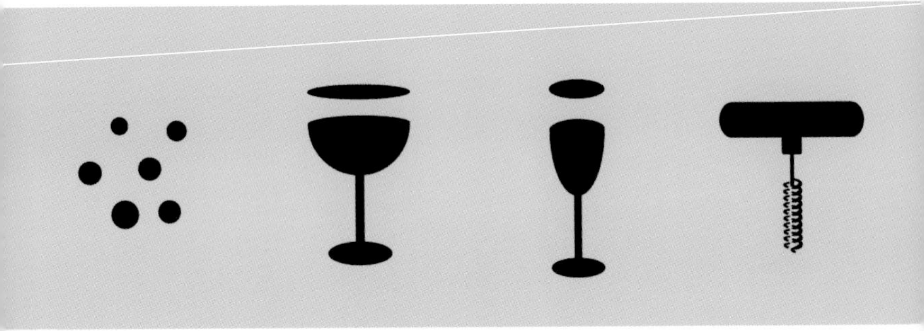

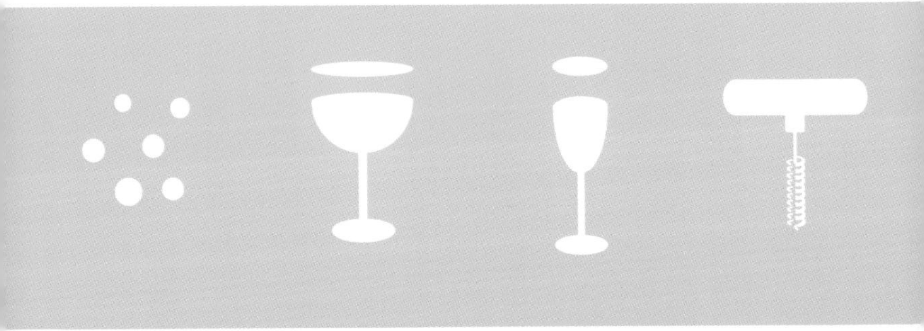

Marine Drouan 〉 (GER) www.portfolio.mixher.fr

Designgruppe Koop (GER) www.designgruppe-koop.de

190

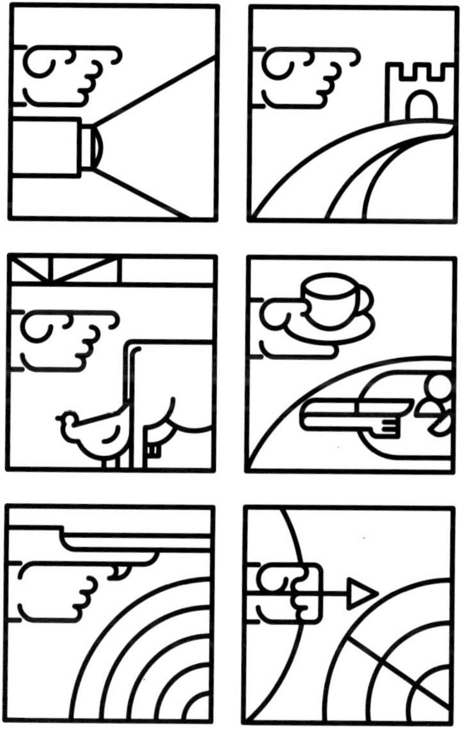

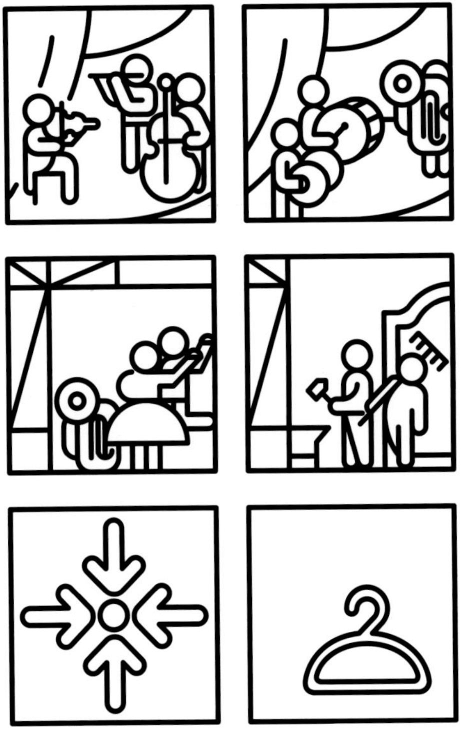

193

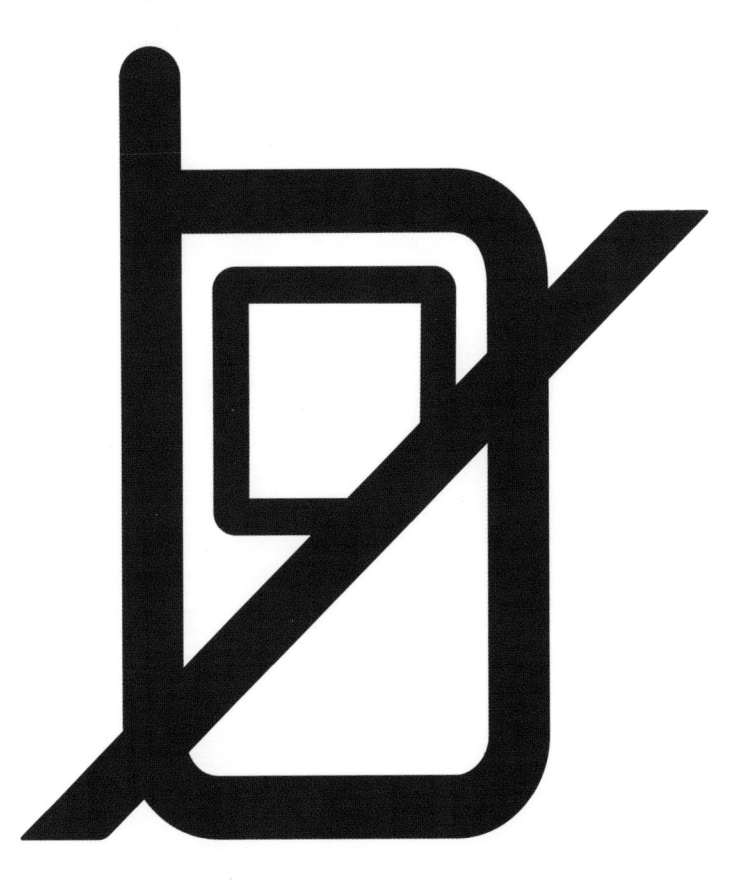

Designgruppe Koop [GER] www.designgruppe-koop.de

194

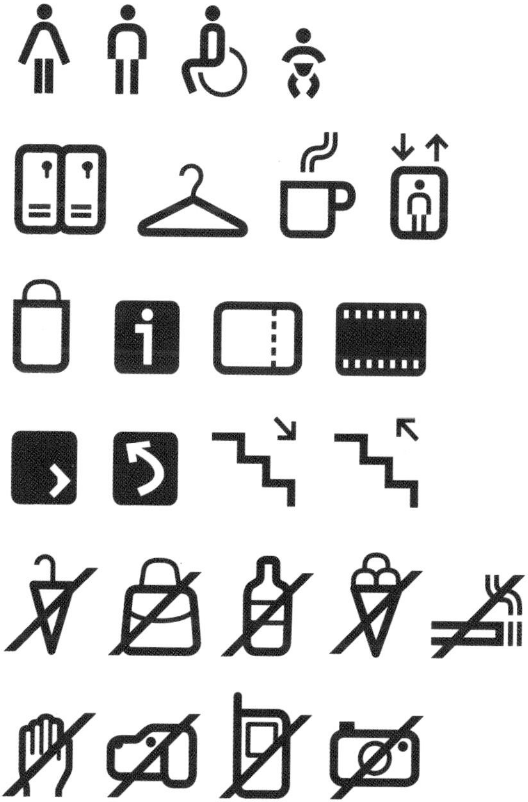
i

Designgruppe Koop   (GER)   www.designgruppe-koop.de

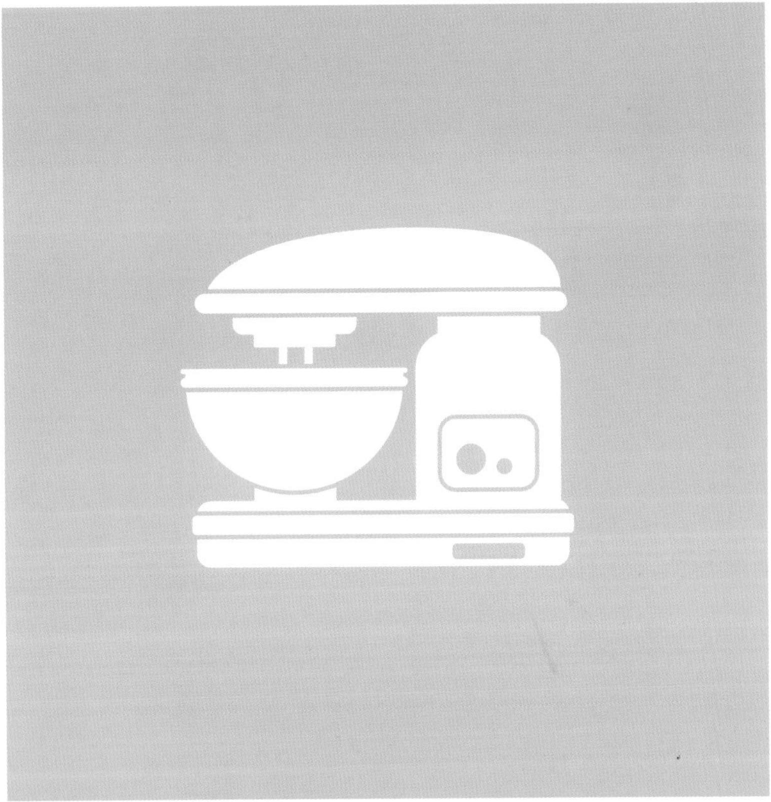

Andreas Dümmel (GER) www.pyruswerbeagentur.de

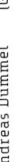

Harri Lemke [GER] www.designbuero-lemke.de

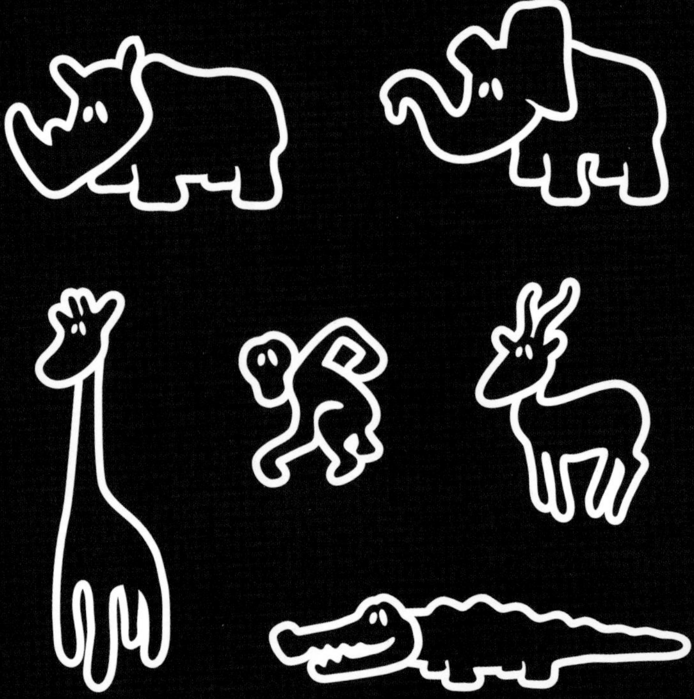

Bo Virkelyst Jensen [DEN] www.addsoul.com

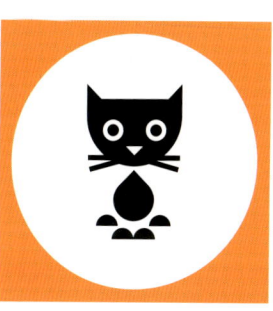

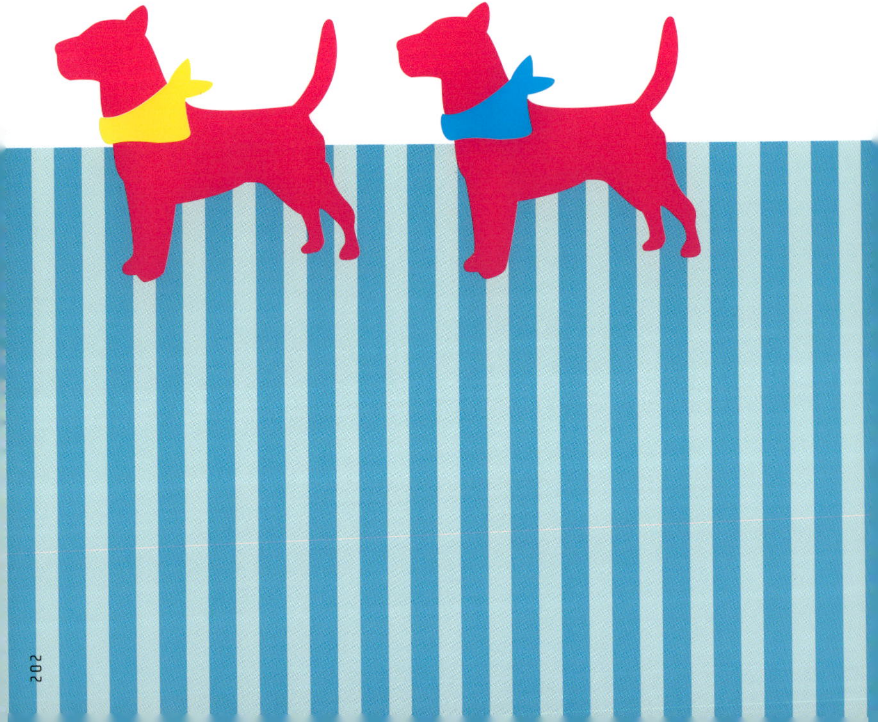

Jekaterina Fenzl [AUT]

203

Christopher Ledwig (GER) www.f1rstdesign.com

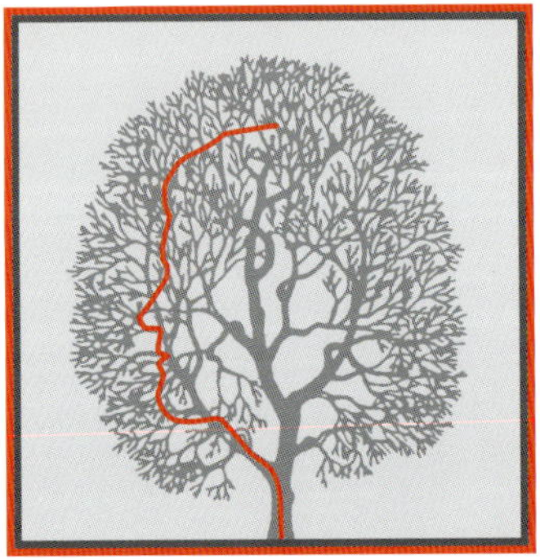

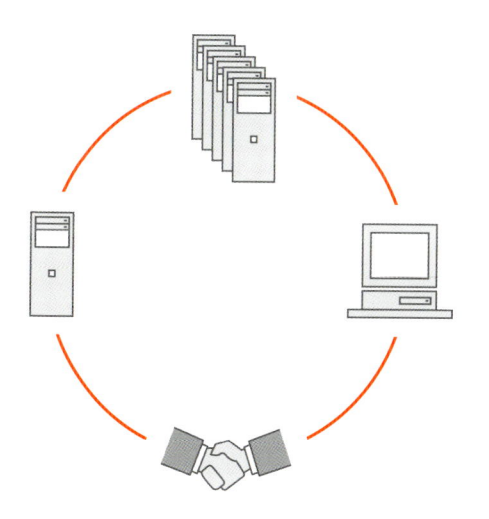

von **from** de **-40°C** bis zu **up to** jusqu'à **+230°C**

Christopher Ledwig (GER) www.f1rstdesign.com

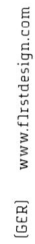

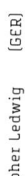

Infopunkt / Info point

Öffentliches WC / Public WC

Behinderten-WC / Disabled WC

Behinderten-Parkplatz / Disabled parking

Gastronomie / Restaurants

Café, Snack

- **Kinderspielorte /** Playgrounds
- **Bahnsteige Sonderfahrten /** Station extra tours
- **Busparkplatz /** Coach parking
- **Bus-Haltezone /** Coach pick-up/drop-off zone
- **RevierRad-Station /** Bike station

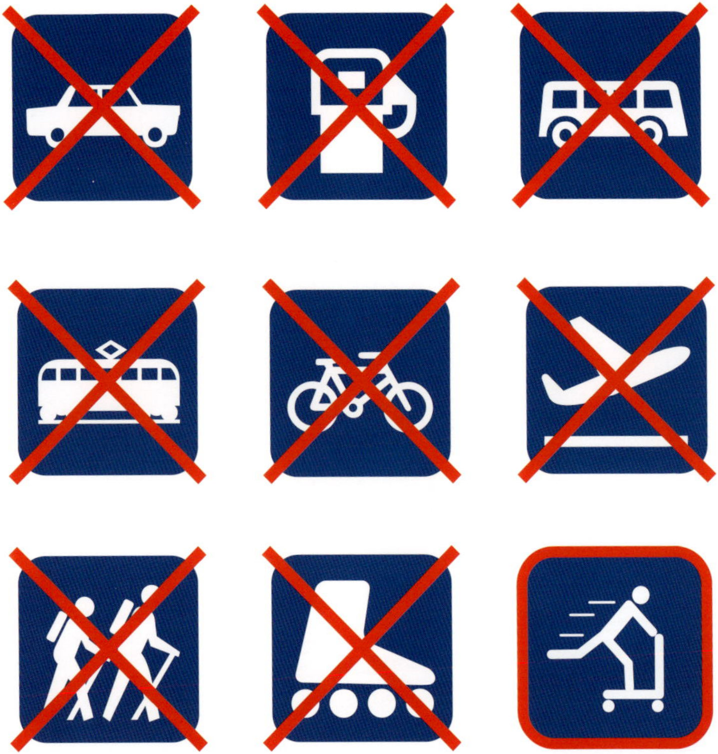

Christopher Ledwig [GER] www.firstdesign.com

Mode

Musik

Kunst

Christopher Ledwig   (GER)   www.f1rstdesign.com

Konzerte

Sport

Party

Tom Davie   (USA)   www.studiotwentysix2.com   214

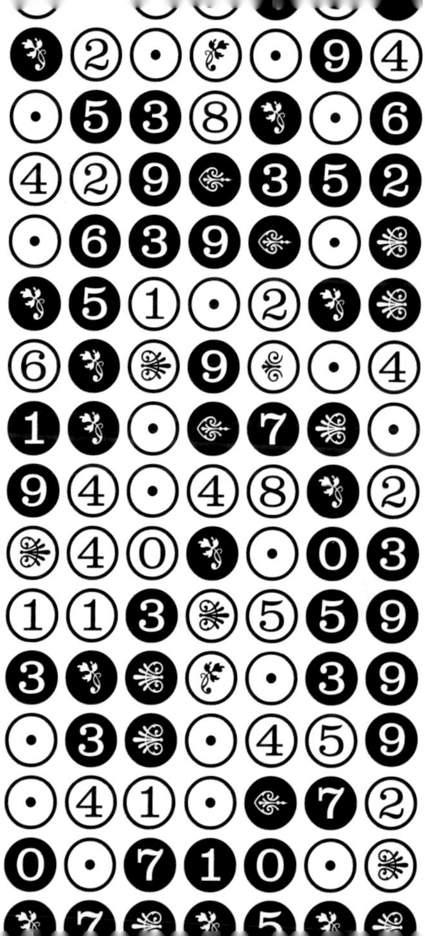

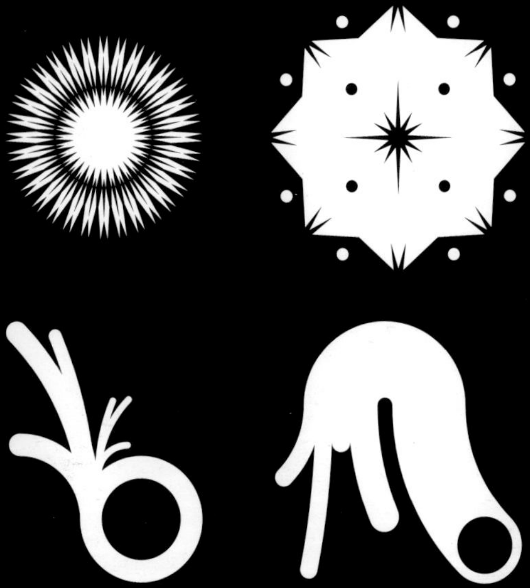

Lucas Rampazzo [BRA]

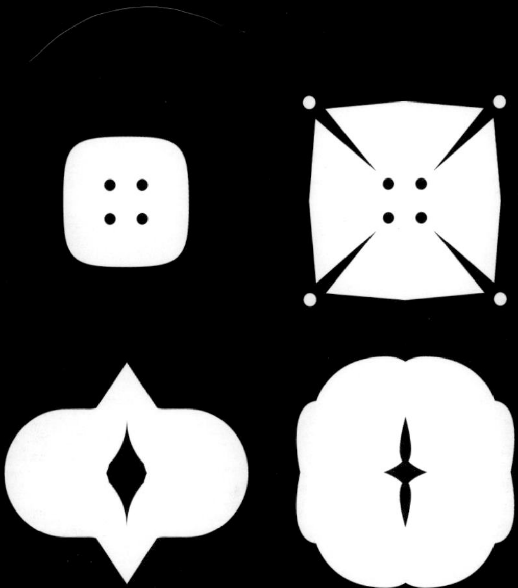

Lucas Rampazzo (BRA)

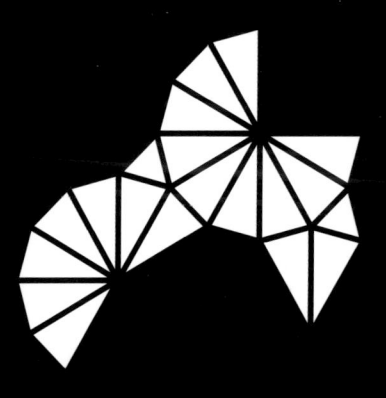

Sebastian Bade (GER) www.grafischerpool.de

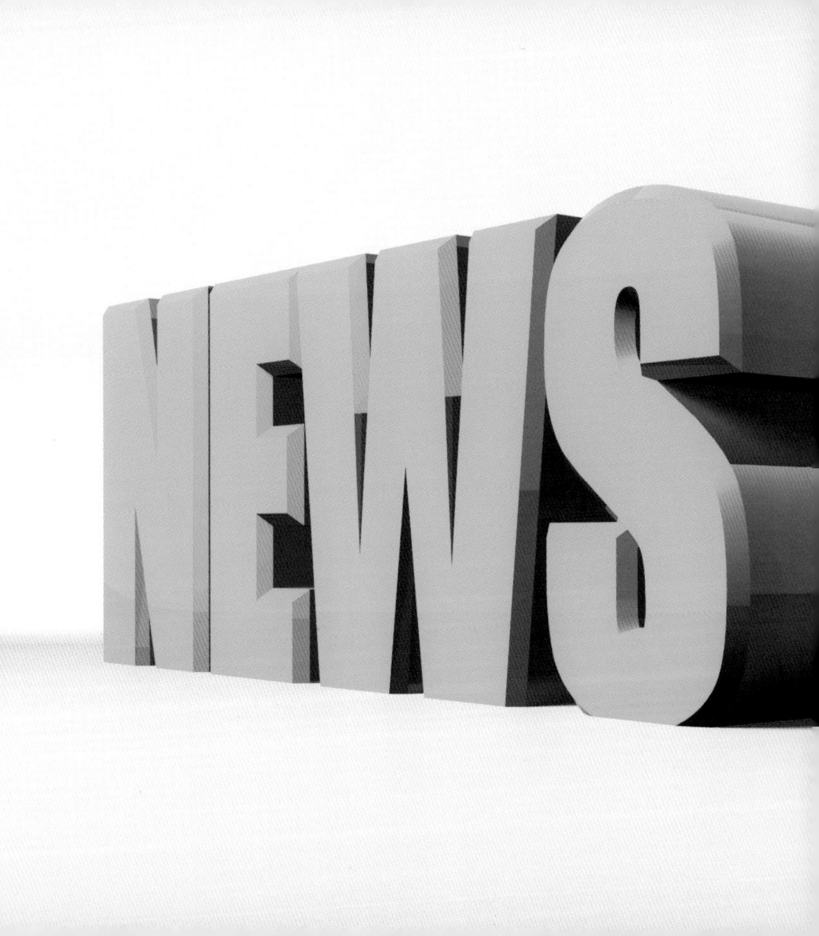

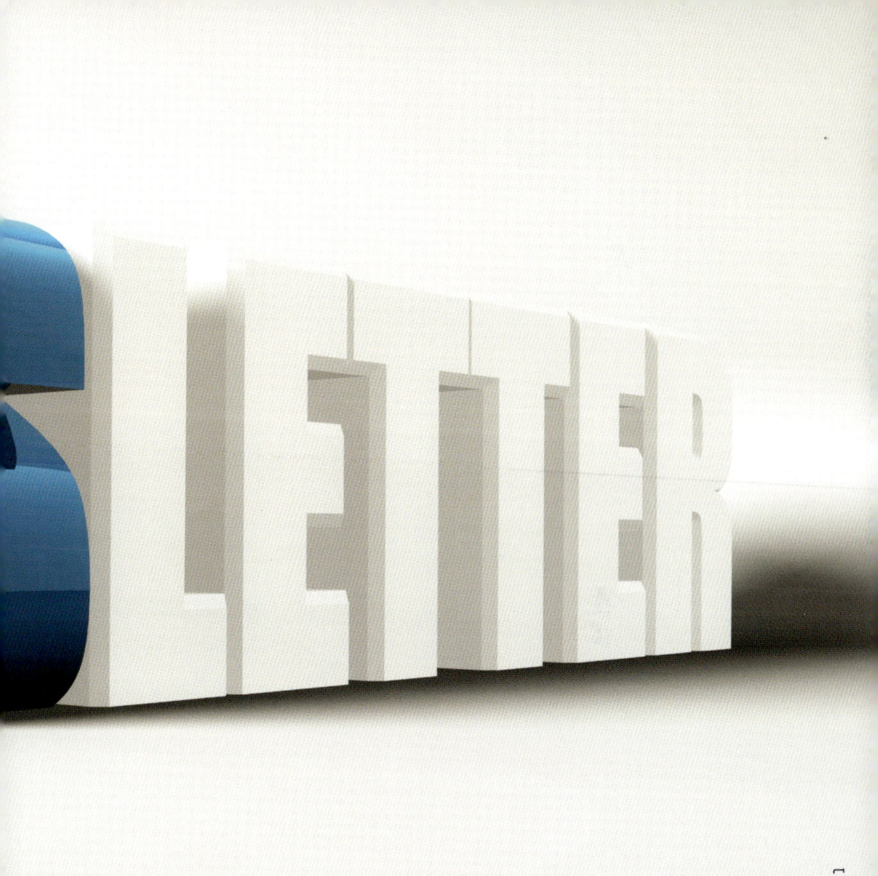
LETTER

Sebastian Bade [GER] www.grafischerpool.de

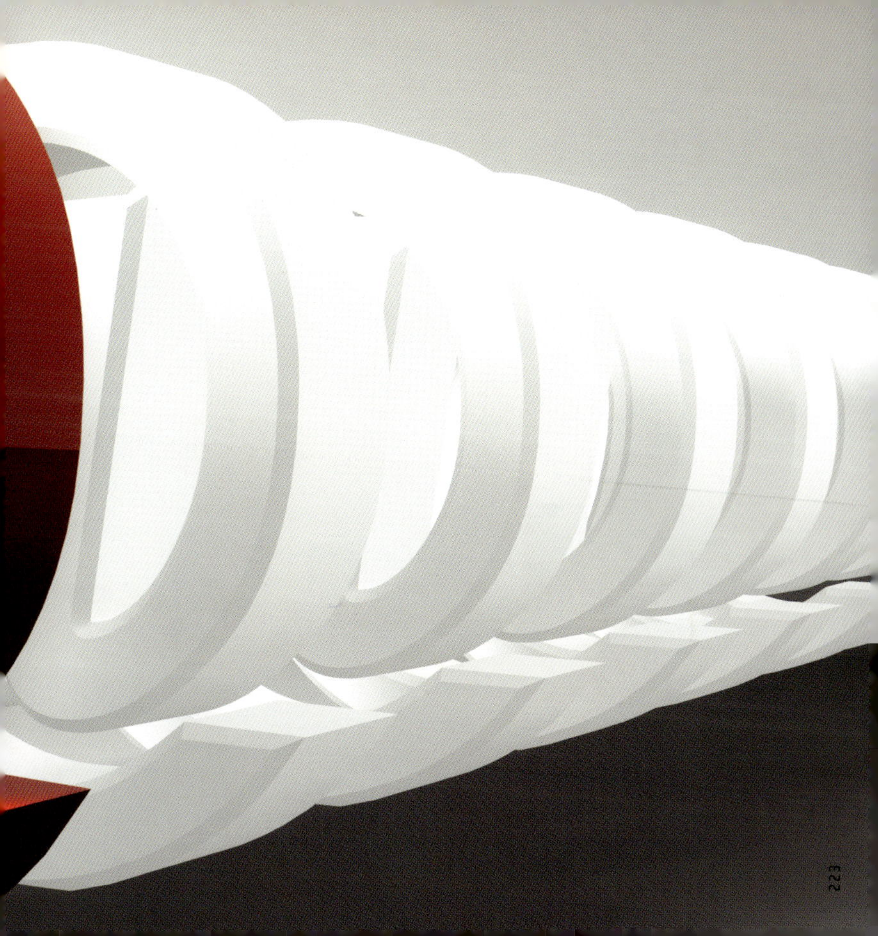

Christopher Ledwig   [GER]   www.f1rstdesign.com

224

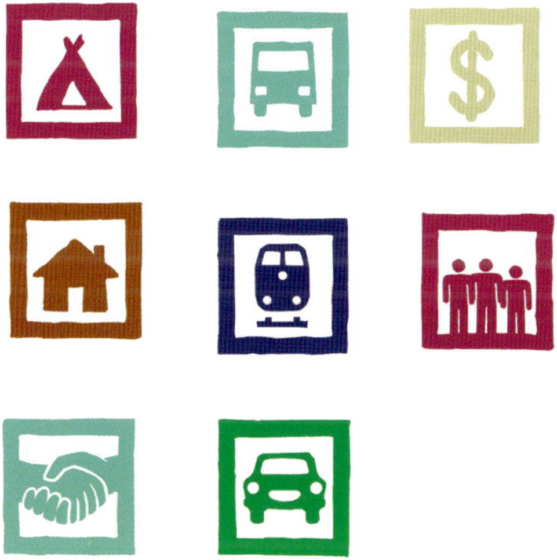

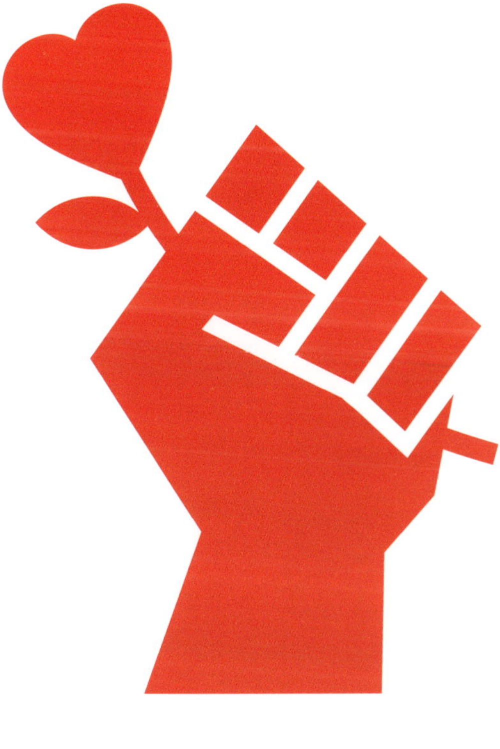

Steve Zelle [CAN] www.idapostle.com

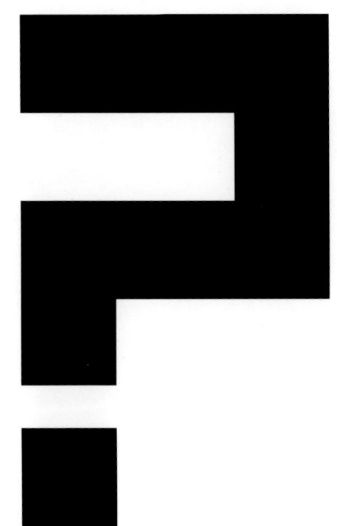

228

Sandra Vaz (ESP)

Freak

Andreas Eck [GER]   www.apfelgernhaber.de

Andreas Eck [GER] www.apfelgernhaber.de

232

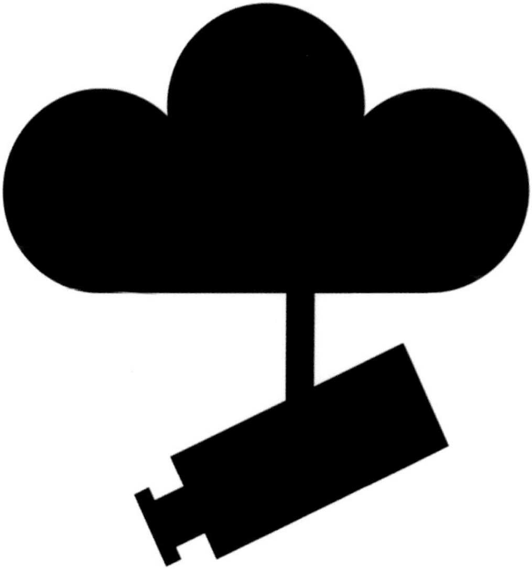

Gregory D'Addio (GBR) www.coroflot.com/greg_deAddio

Landscapes	**Vegetables**
Flowers	**Water**

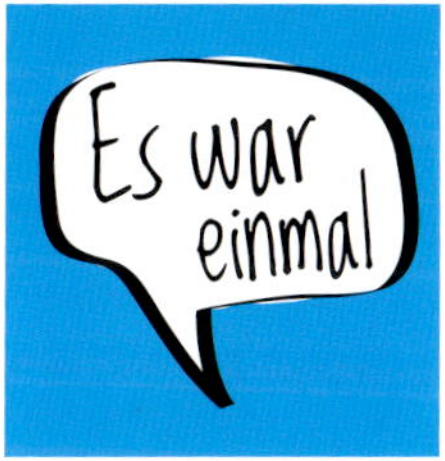
Es war einmal
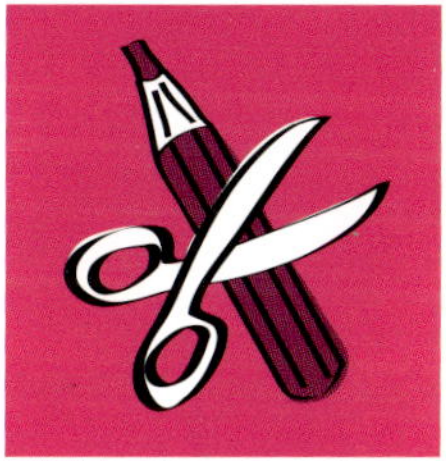
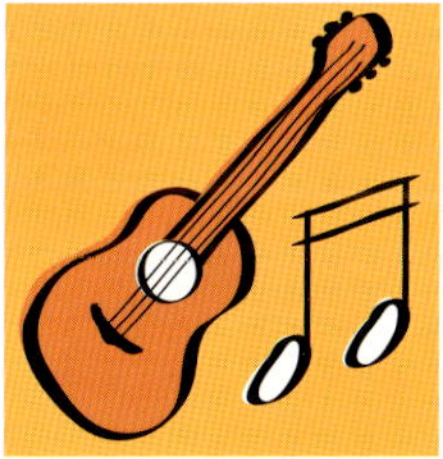
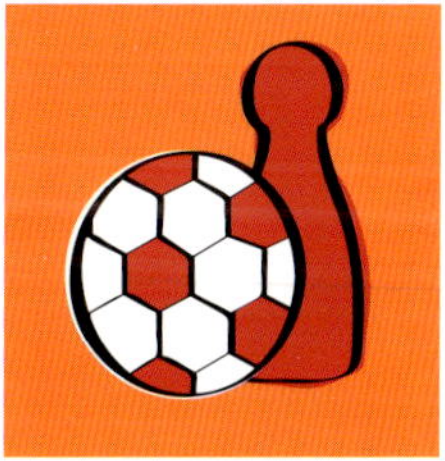
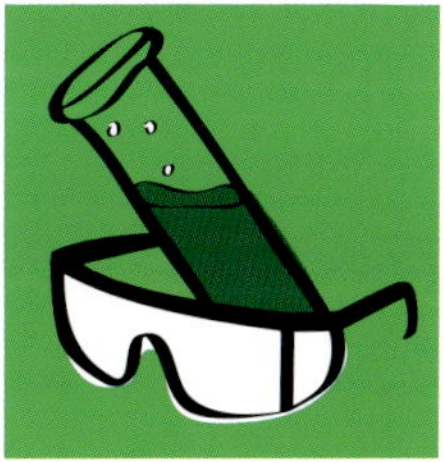
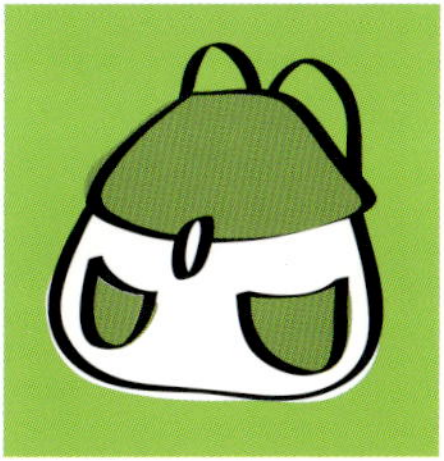

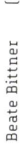

aA headphone

dD smashbox

gG speaker

bB walkman

eE tape

hH 909

cC radio

fF fm

il amp

jJ microfone

kK minidisc

lL band

Dominik Arenz [GER] www.stereoswebfunk.de

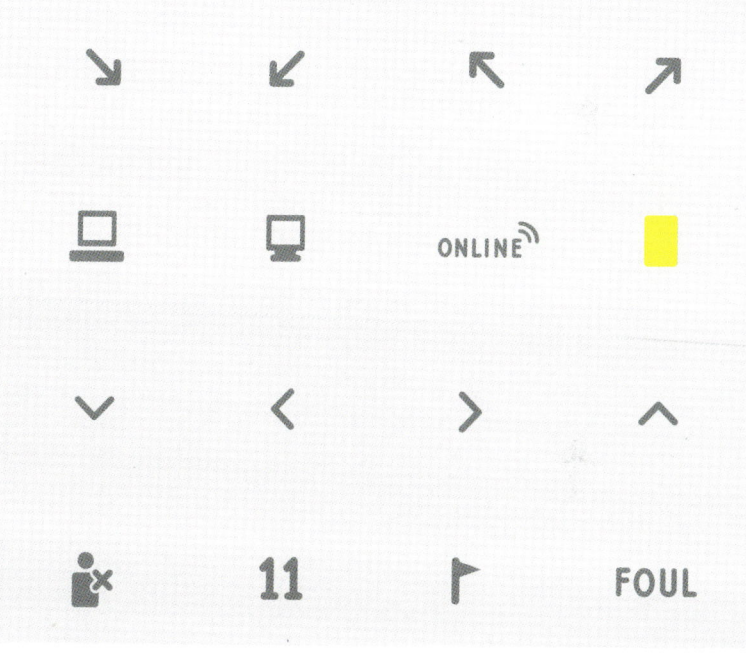

Dominik Arenz [GER] www.stereoswebfunk.de

242

Iconos Colombianos del Café
Icons of the best growing coffee regions in the word

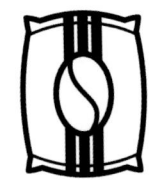

Oscar H. Correa C.   [COL]   www.correadesigns.com

TV

RADIO

SEARCH

NEWSPAPER

Unity

S2

Mission Apps

TransMail TE

Collaboration

TransMail

05_ FRAUENSEELSORGE
06 PROGRAMMHEFT

06_ FRAUENSEELSORGE
07 PROGRAMMHEFT

07_ FRAUENSEELSORGE
08 PROGRAMMHEFT

FRAUEN SEELSORGE

ALLGEMEINE FRAUENSEELSORGE

VERANSTALTUNGEN VON JANUAR BIS MÄRZ

01.01.2007 – 31.03.2007

Die Veranstaltungen bieten viele unterschiedliche Themen, die einladen zur Begegnung mit anderen und sich selbst.

FRAUEN SEELSORGE

ALLGEMEINE FRAUENSEELSORGE

VERANSTALTUNGEN VON JANUAR BIS MÄRZ

01.01.2008 – 31.03.2008

Die Veranstaltungen bieten viele unterschiedliche Themen, die einladen zur Begegnung mit anderen und sich selbst.

www.zweinullsieben.com

Sandra Mahn (GER)

FRAUEN SEELSORGE

Sandra Mahn [GER] www.zweinullsieben.com

STABILIZER **MORTAR** **BLOCKS**

PLASTER   **GLUE**

Yotam Hadar [ISR]

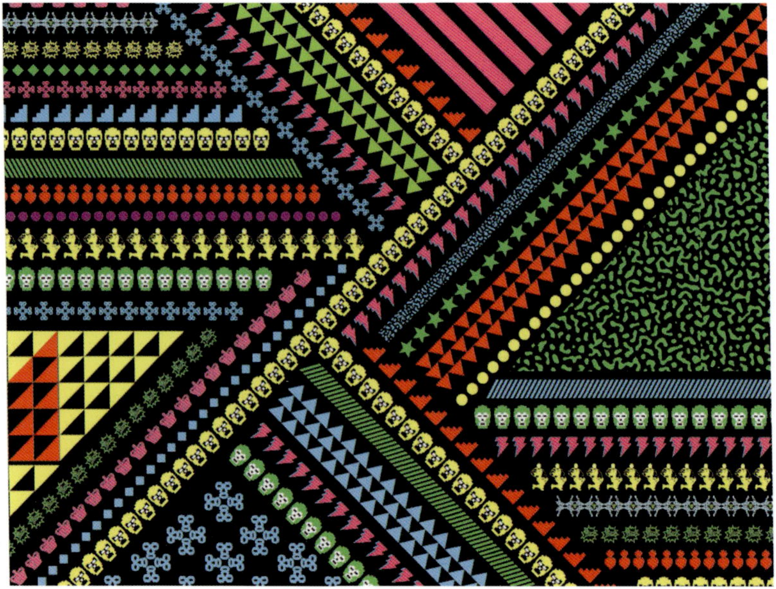

Escobas [MEX] www.escobas.com.mx

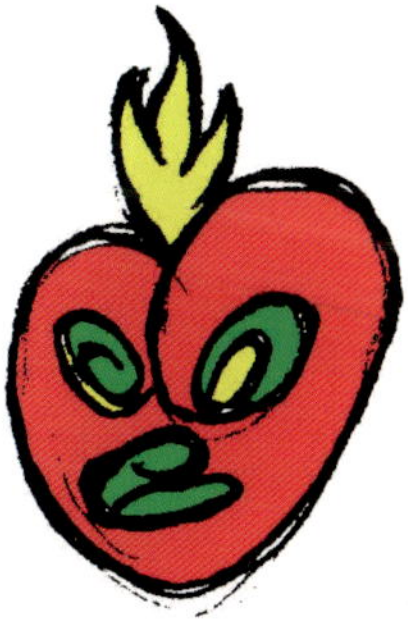

Escobas [MEX] www.escobas.com.mx

256

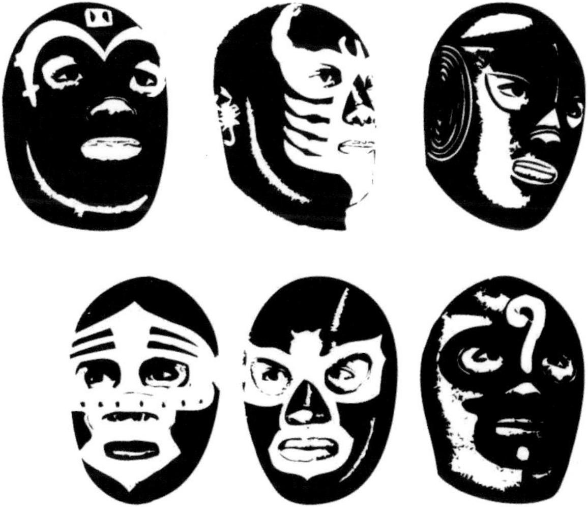

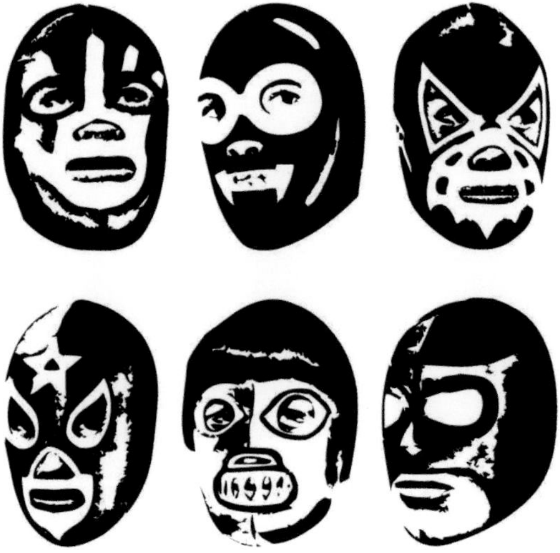

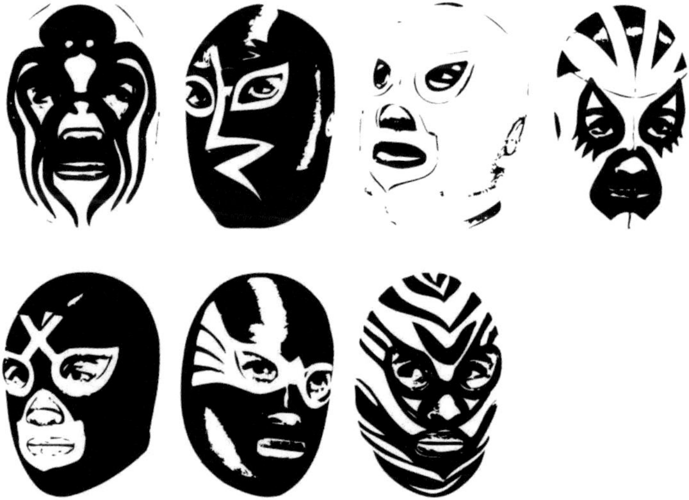

Escobas [MEX] www.escobas.com.mx

WATCH OUT!

NO TOUCH!

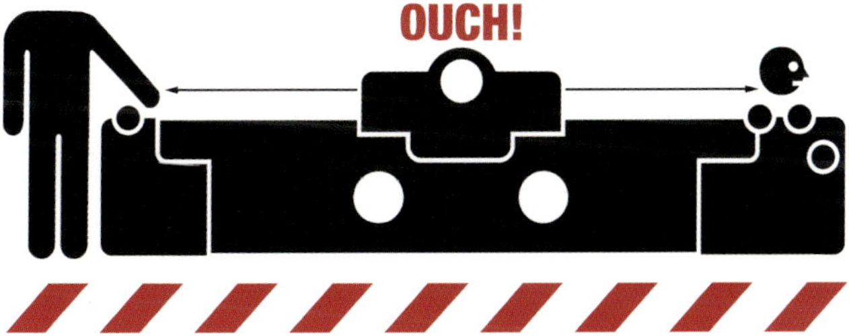

Marcus Melton [USA] www.marcusmelton.com

Sandra Hofacker [SUI] www.apfel-z.de

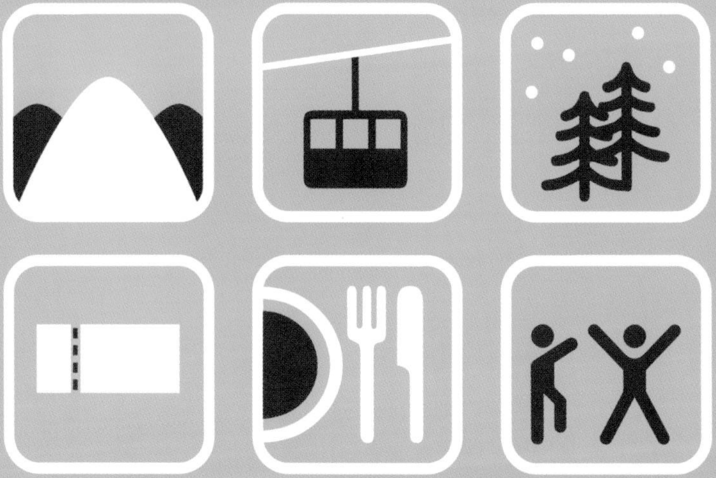

KLIMAFLEISCH

HITZEWELLE

URLAUBSWETTER

Sandra Marchionna [GER] www.gut-ding.com

WASSERSCHLACHT

KONSUMIDIOT

FLUCHTWELLE

EISBÄRKILLER

GRILLSAISON

Sandra Marchionna [GER] www.gut-ding.com

KLIMAANLAGE

Kerstin Stephan [GER] www.kerstinstephan.com

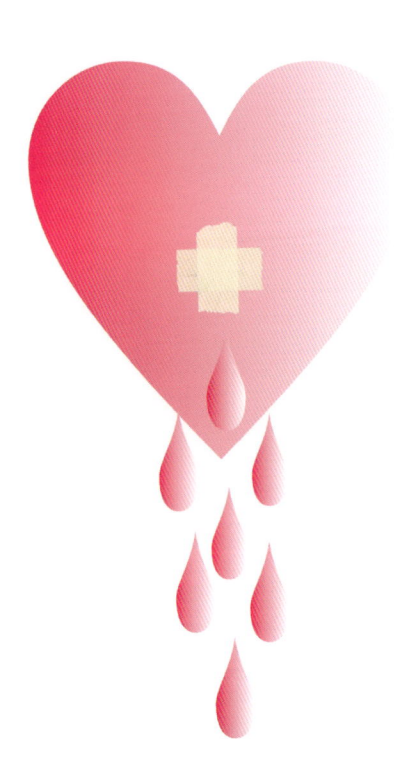

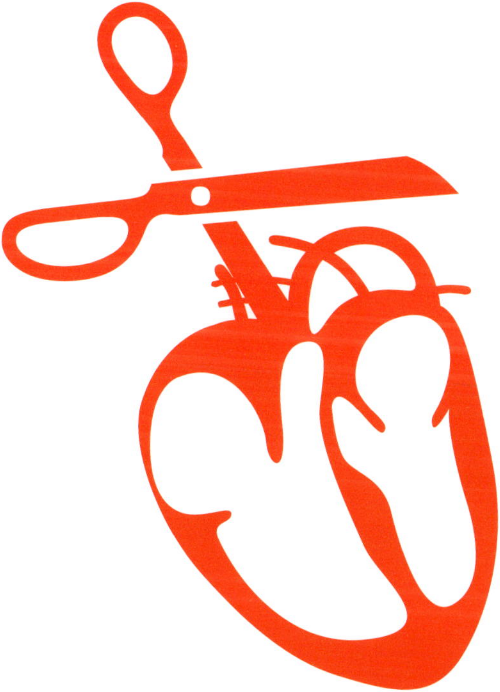

Davide Giulio Aquini (ITA) www.ad-g.it

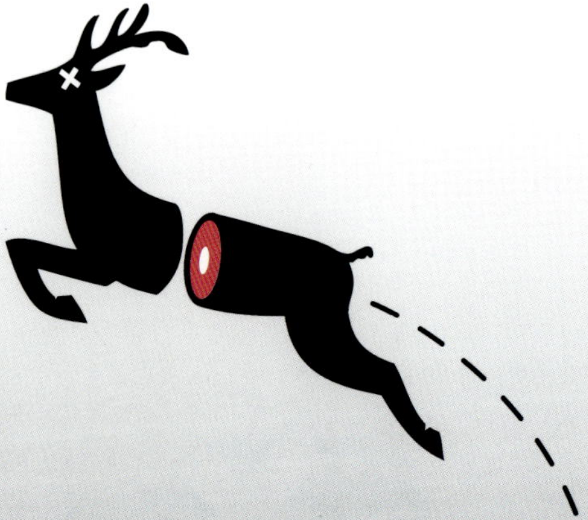

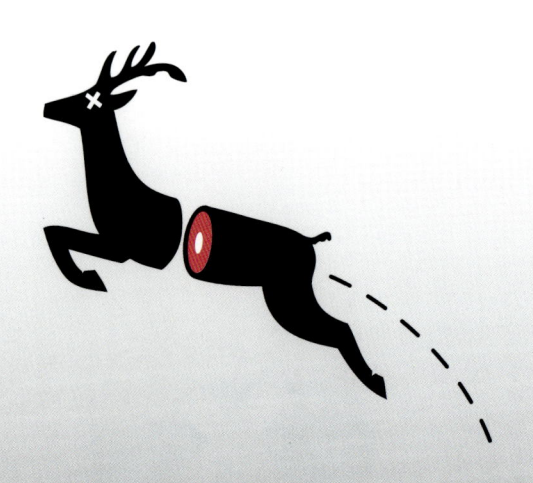

Matteo Neri [ITA] www.blackjackslab.com

Feli Timmesfeld (GER) www.ergosign.de

Design Workshop

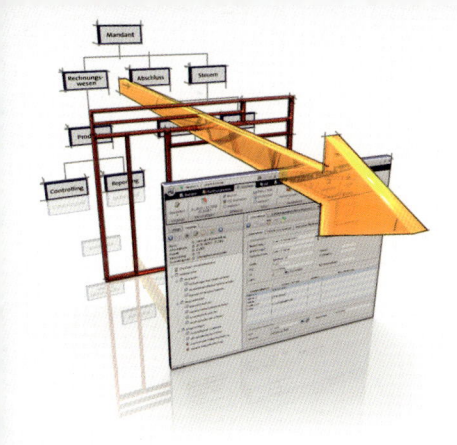

Today 10.00

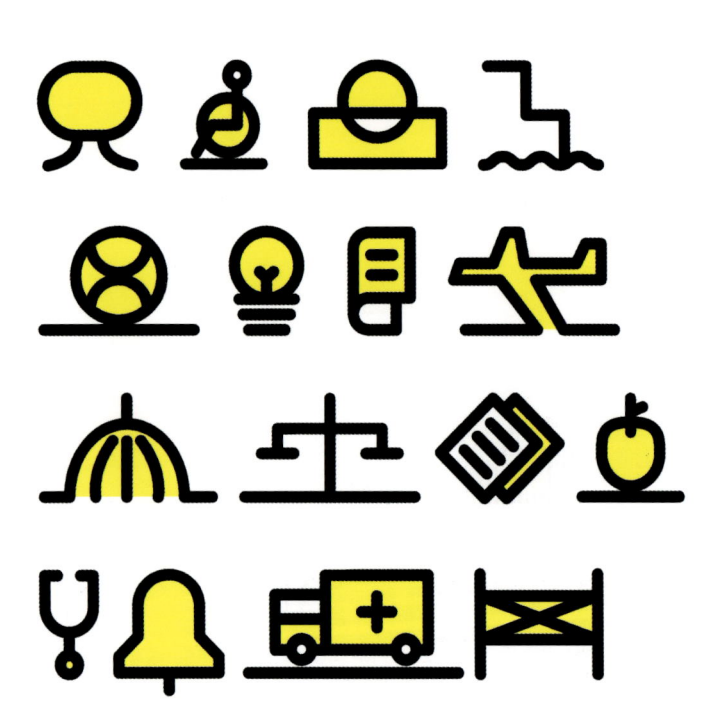

Hernan Berdichevsky & Gustavo Stecher (ARG) www.imagenhb.com

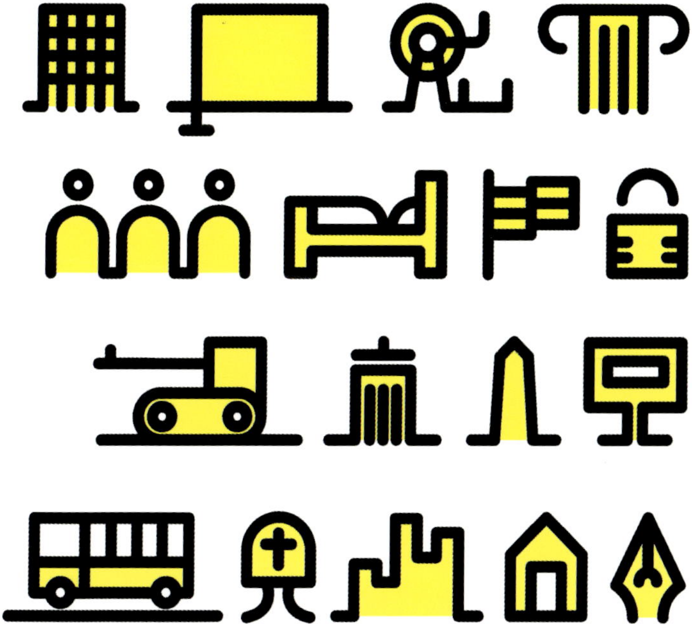

Richard Baird (GBR) www.richardbaird.co.uk

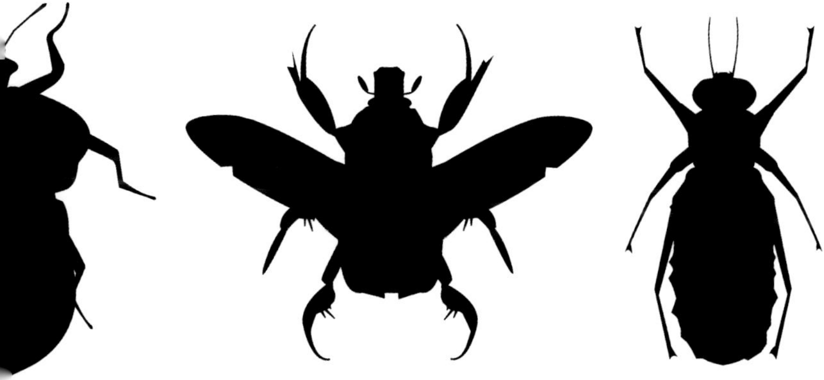

Richard Baird   (GBR)   www.richardbaird.co.uk   278

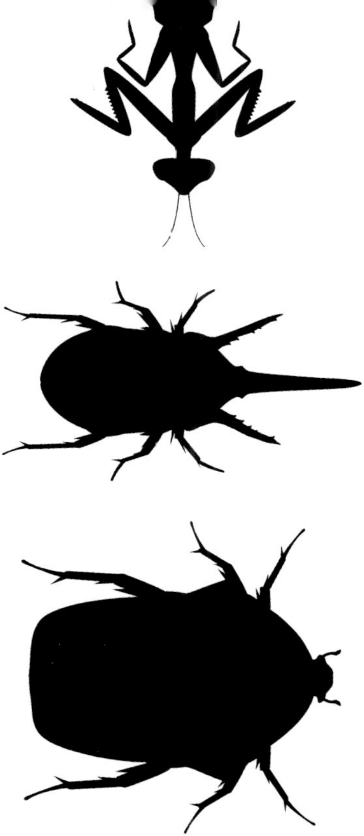

Richard Baird   (GBR)   www.richardbaird.co.uk

280

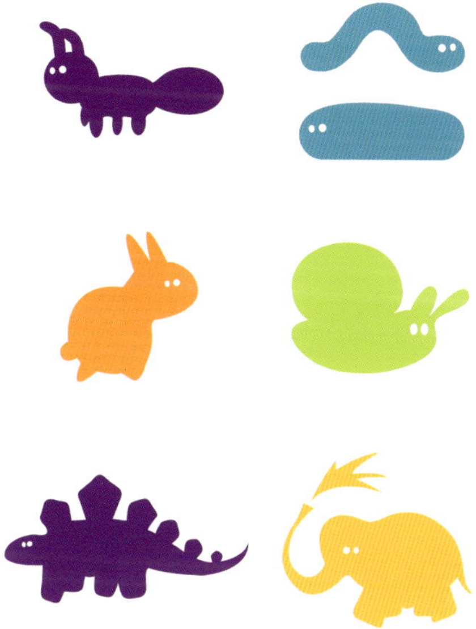

Richard Baird (GBR) www.richardbaird.co.uk

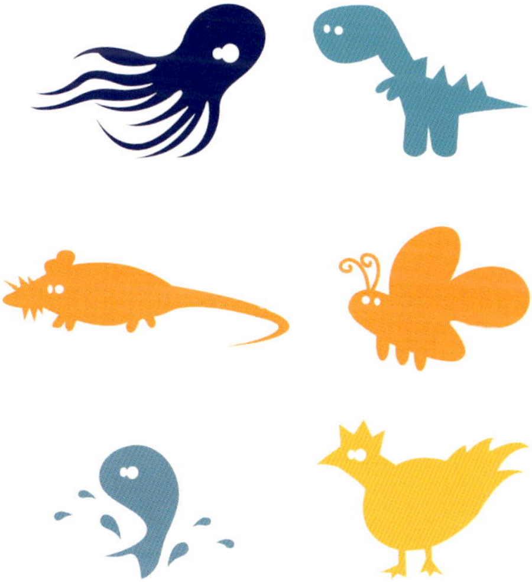

Richard Baird   (GBR)   www.richardbaird.co.uk

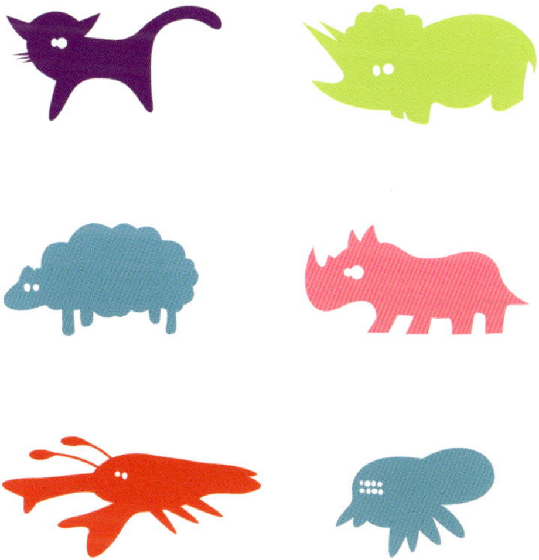

Richard Baird   (GBR)   www.richardbaird.co.uk

Lars Harmsen (GER) www.magmabranddesign.de

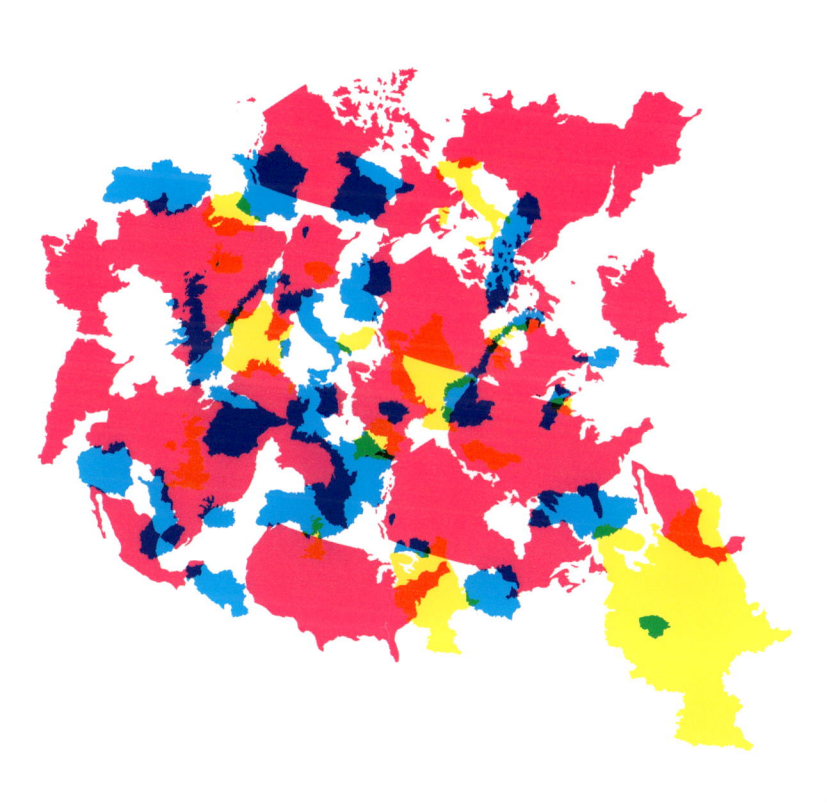

Mirco Kurth (GER) www.no28.de

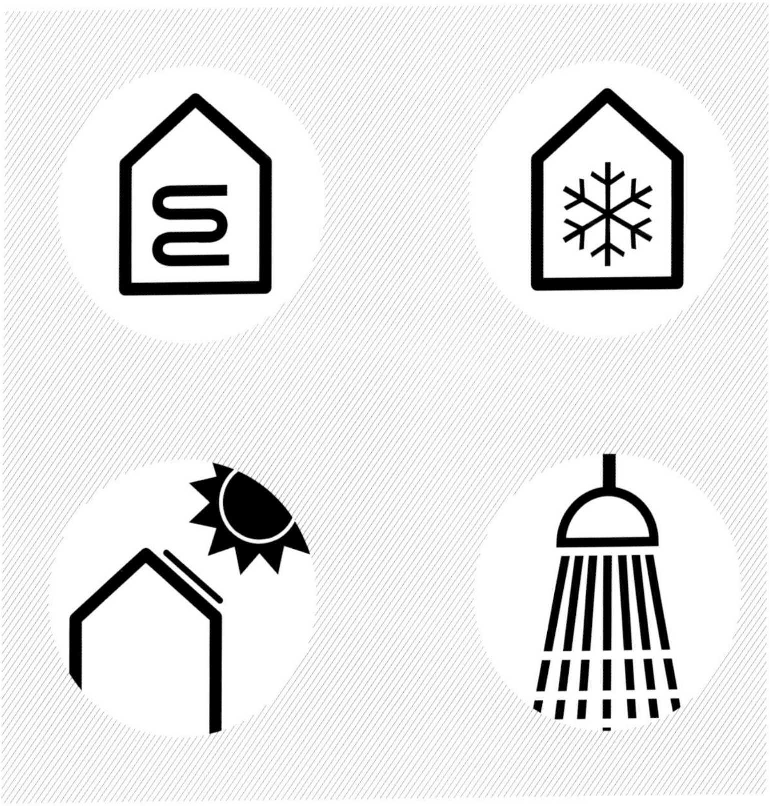

Matteo Neri   (ITA)   www.blackjackslab.com

Masood Bukhari (USA) www.masoodbukhari.com

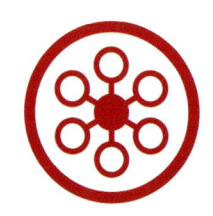

:(
;(
:)
;)

Marc Prien [GER] www.empegra.de

Beate Bittner [GER] www.glutrot.de

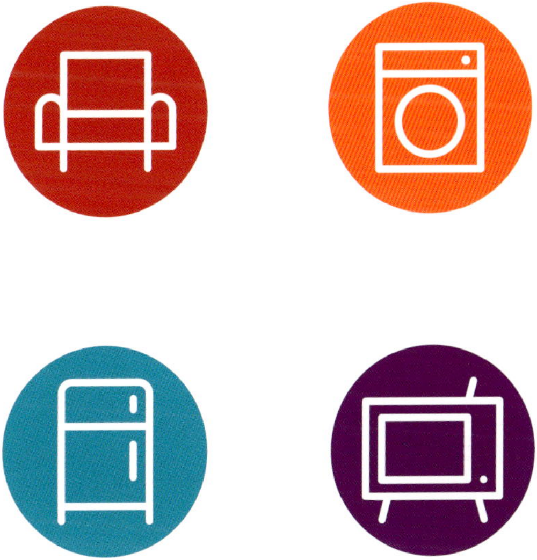

30°	23°	17°
MON	TUE	WED

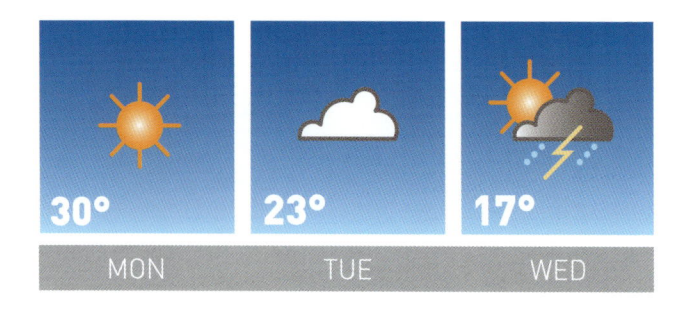

9°	11°	17°
MON	TUE	WED

19°	0°
THUR	FRI

19°	-3°
THUR	FRI

Switzerland

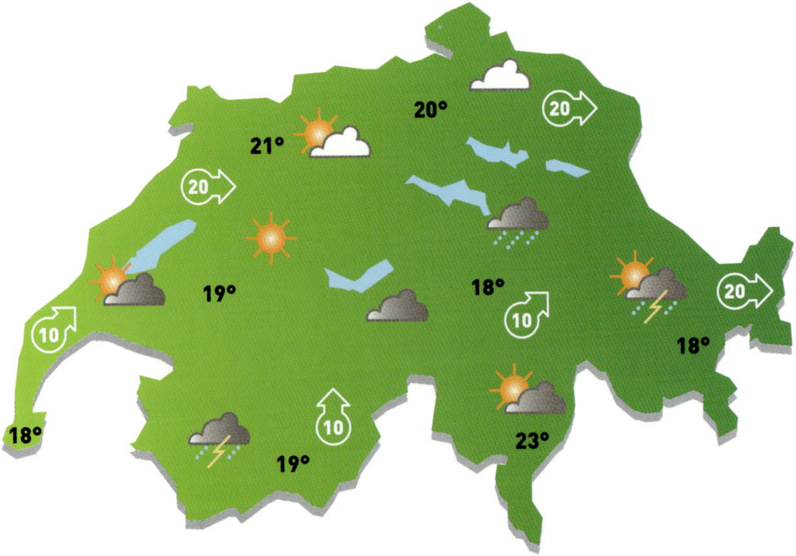

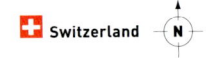

Masood Bukhari [USA] www.masoodbukhari.com

300

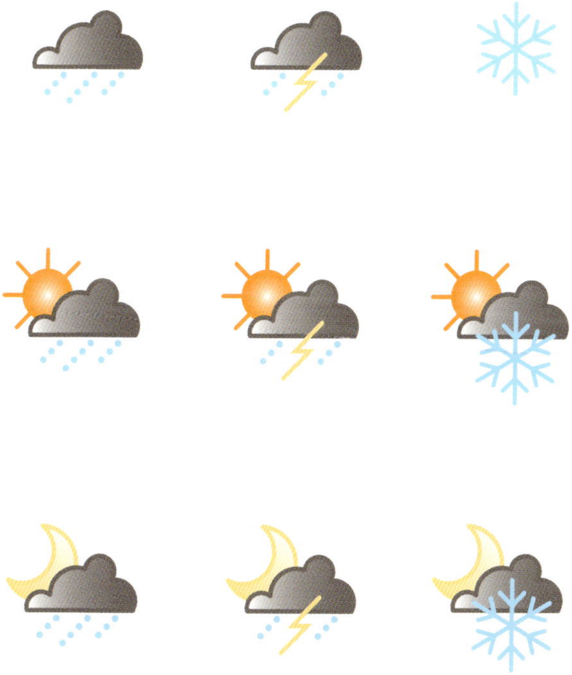

Jenni Kuokka [FIN] www.hahmo.fi

303

Jenni Kuokka [FIN] www.hahmo.fi

304

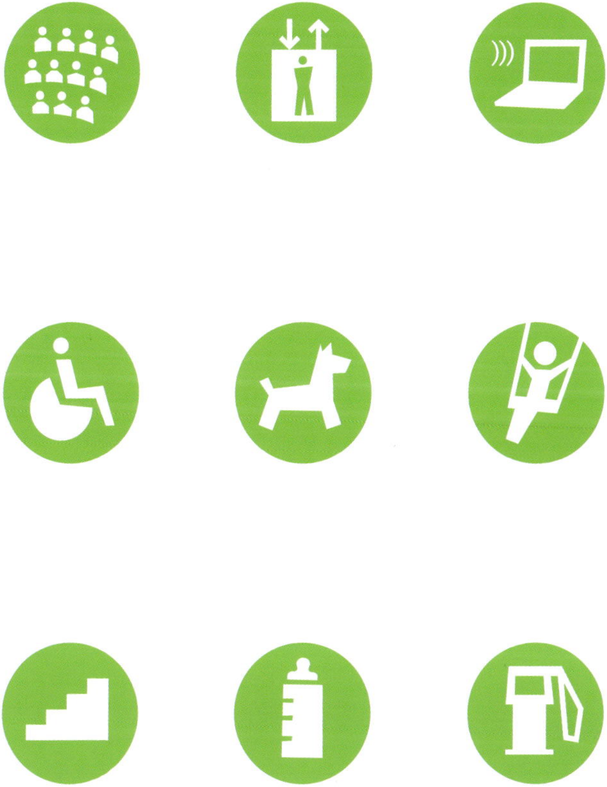

Jenni Kuokka [FIN] www.hahmo.fi

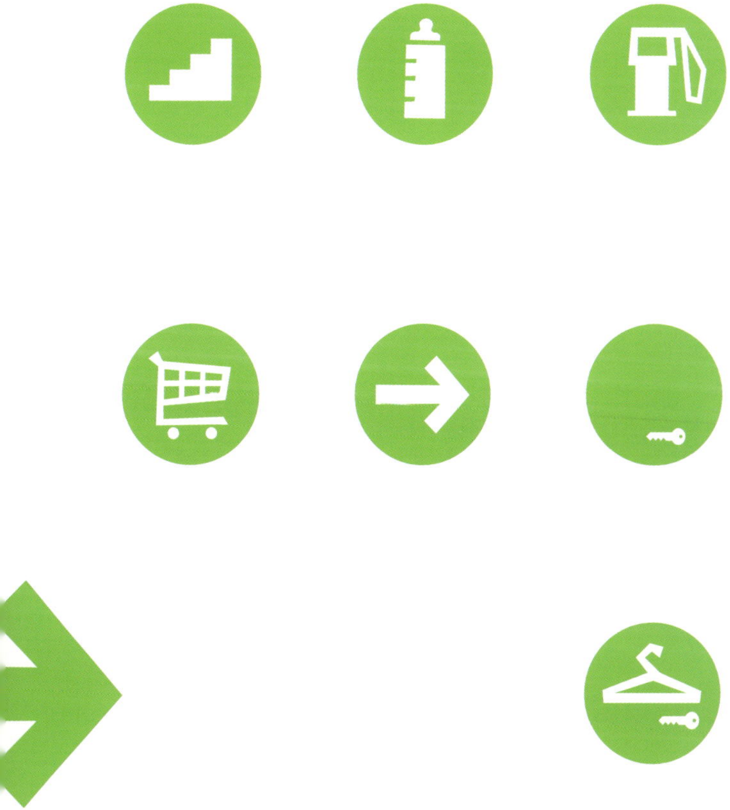

Erik Bertell & Pekka Piippo [FIN] www.hahmo.fi

Erik Bertell & Pekka Piippo (FIN) www.hahmo.fi

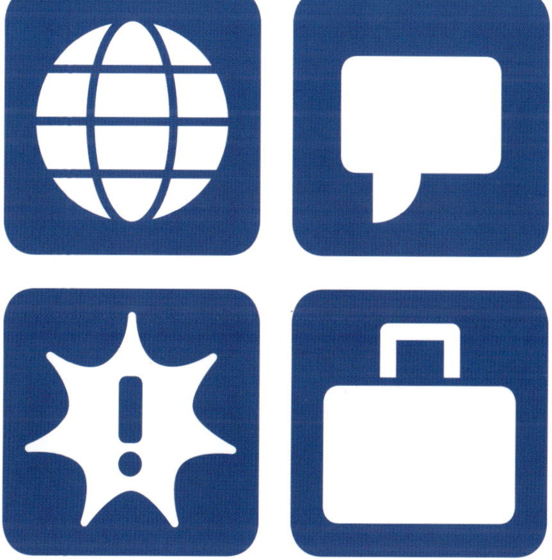

Erik Bertell & Pekka Piippo [FIN] www.hahmo.fi

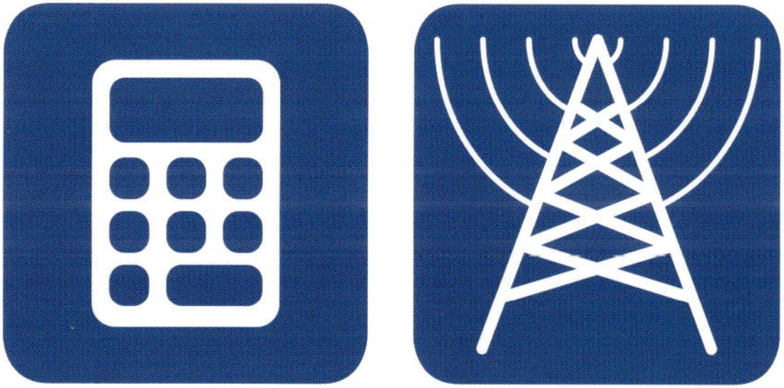

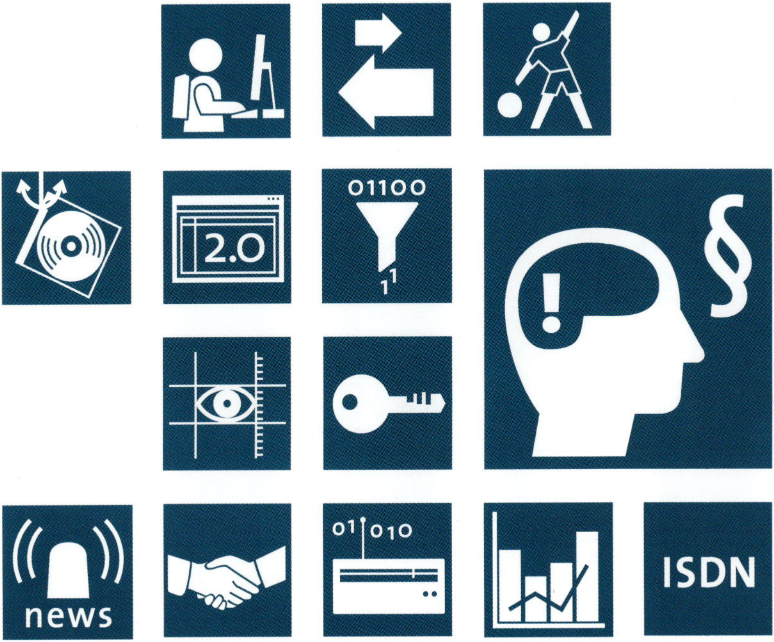
01100
2.0
news
01
010
ISDN

Frederike Wagner & Ann Katrin Siedenburg (GER)

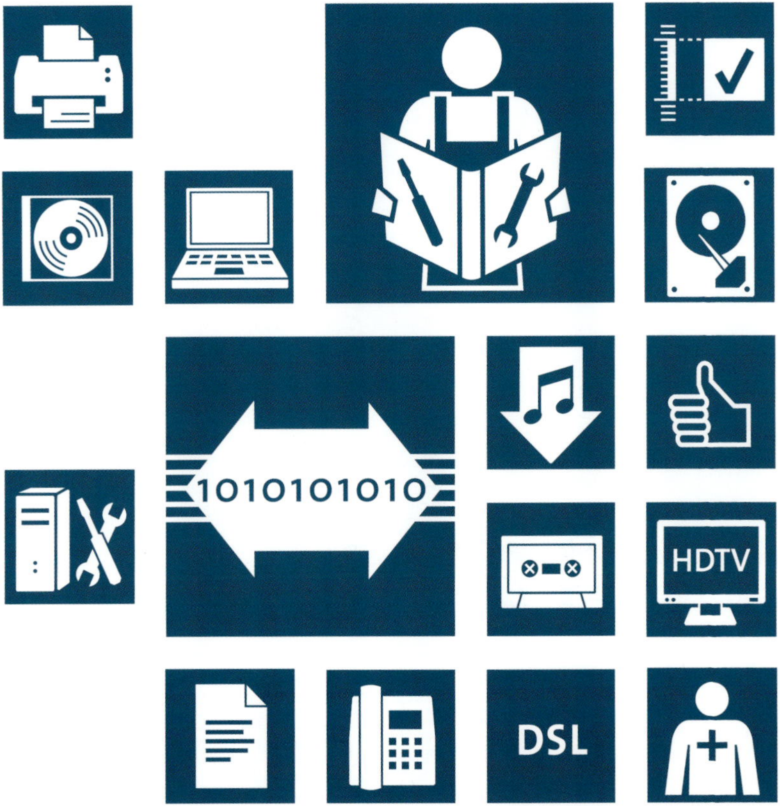
1010101010
HDTV
DSL

Frederike Wagner & Ann Katrin Siedenburg [GER]

Marcel Weik (GER) www.mwkd.de

Freie ARBEITEN

Auftrags ARBEITEN

www.buerodeluxe.com

Herzog [GER]

320

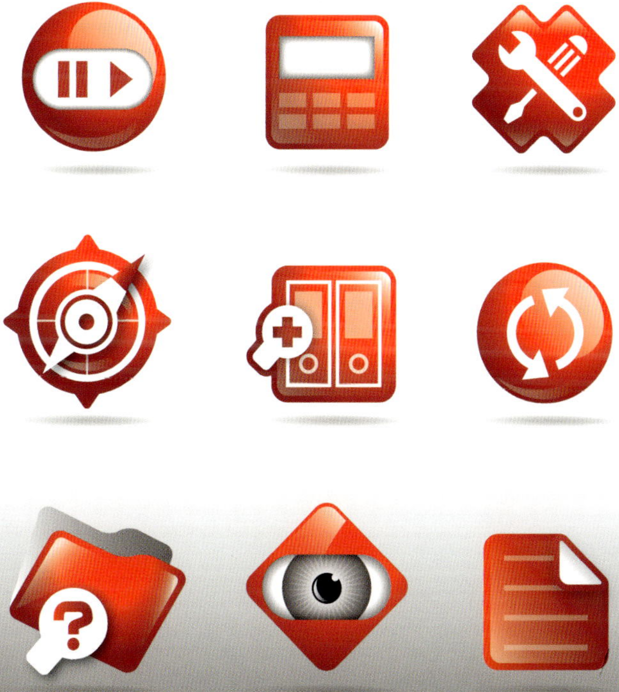

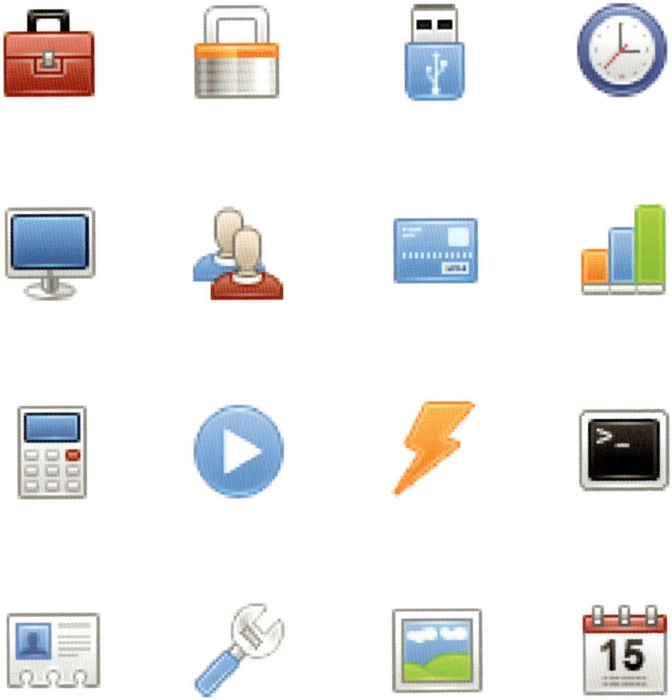
15

SUSTAINABILITY

Lanre Lawal [NGR]

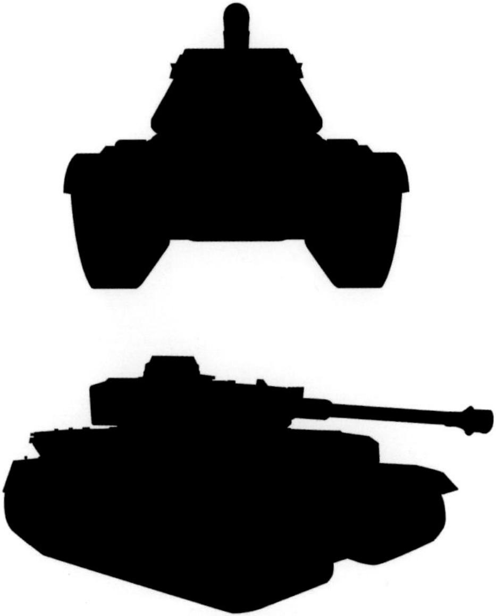

Florian Kettner (GER) www.rv20.com

Kai Schroeder (GER) www.artvanced-design.de

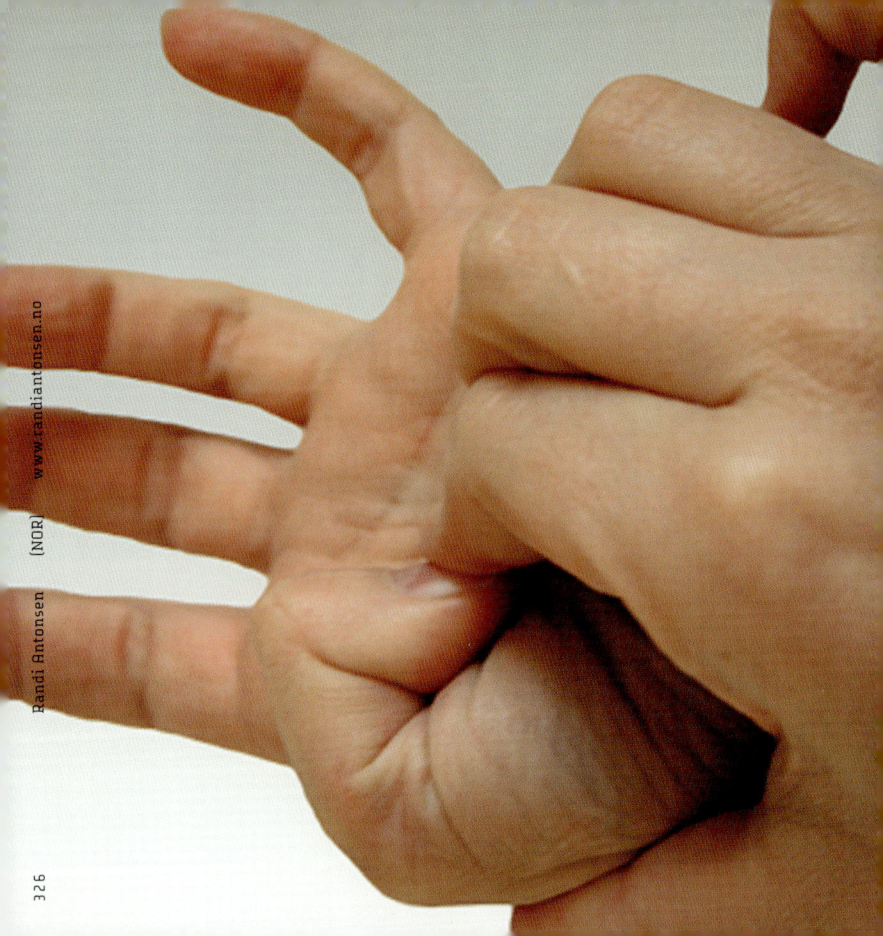

Randi Antonsen (NOR) www.randiantonsen.no

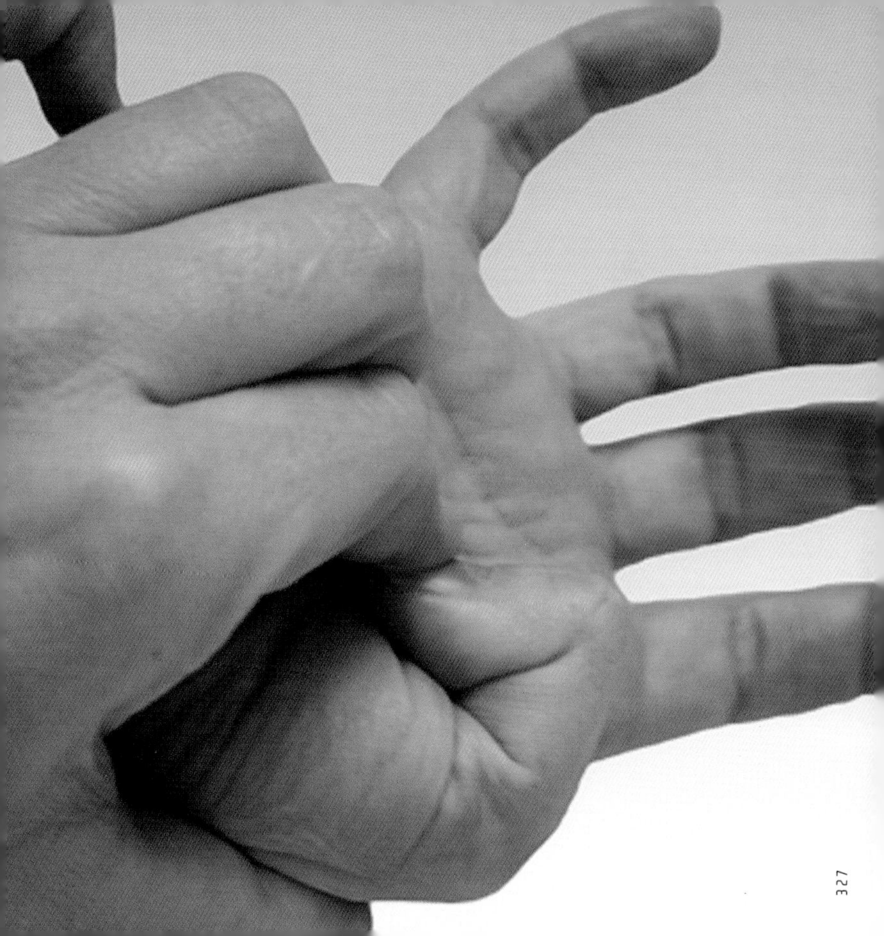

Randi Antonsen (NOR) www.randiantonsen.no

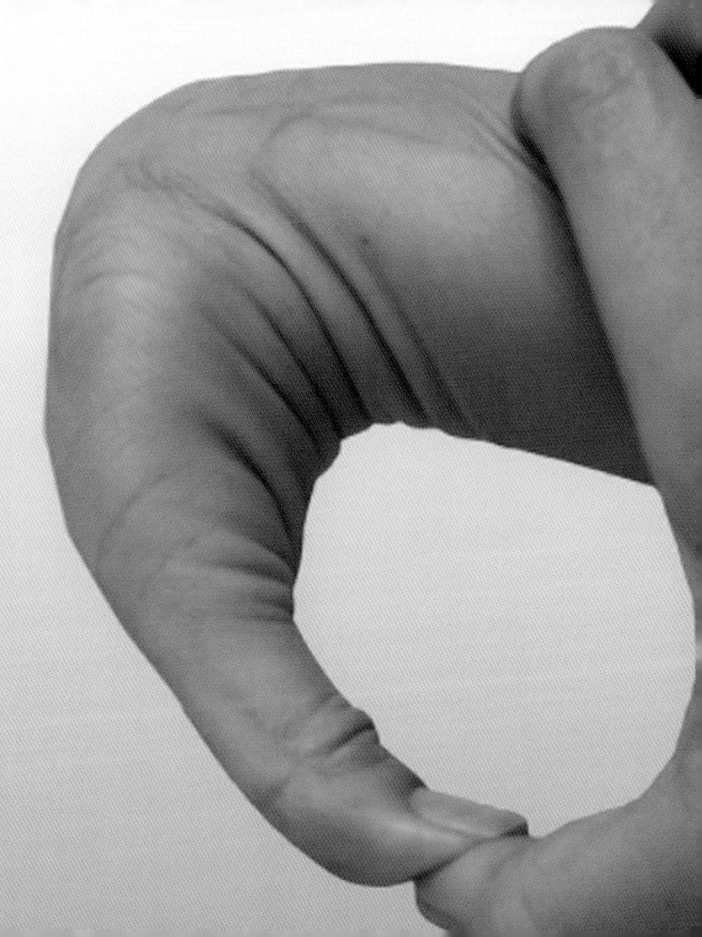

329

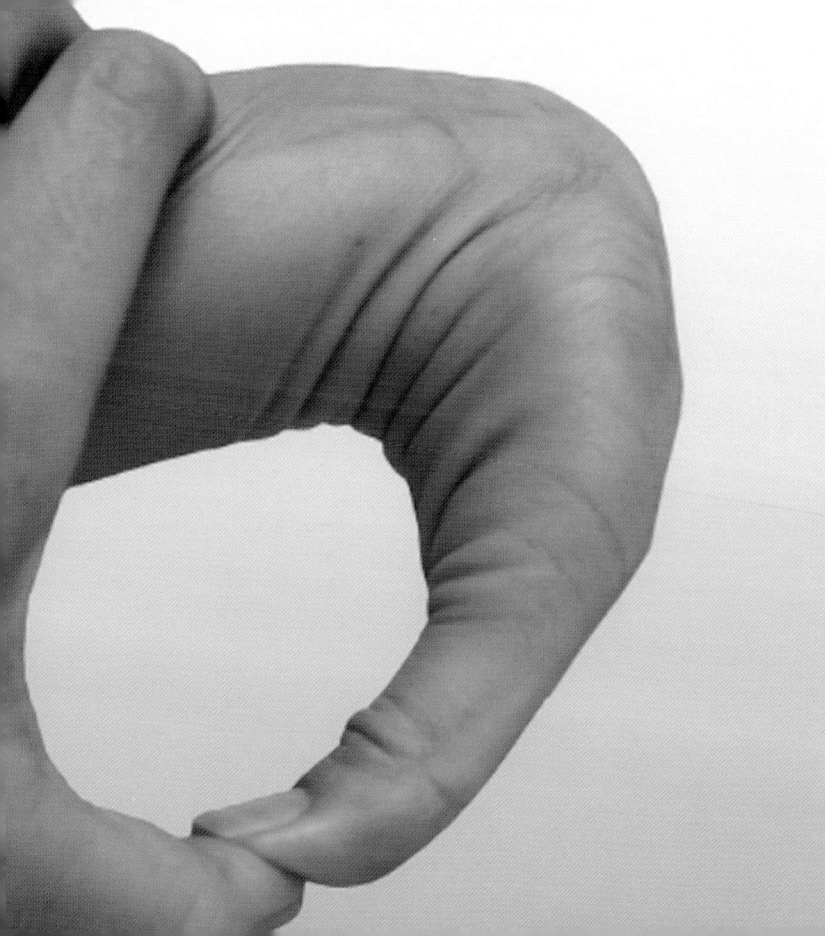

Randi Antonsen [NOR] www.randiantonsen.no

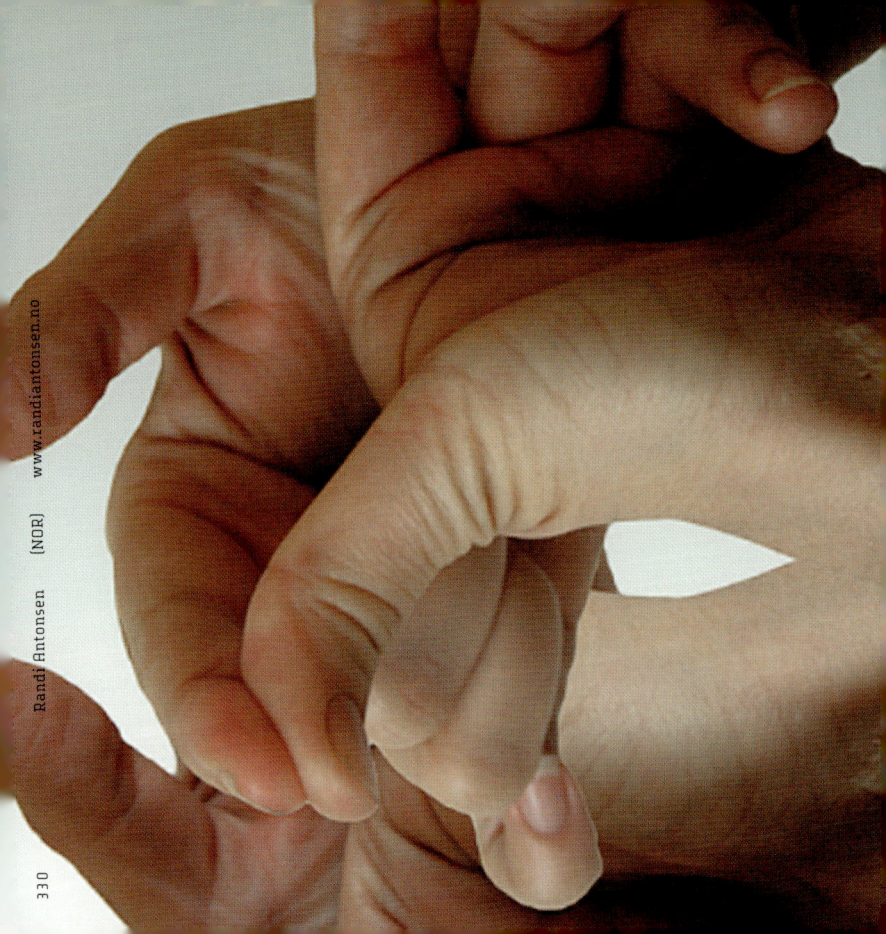

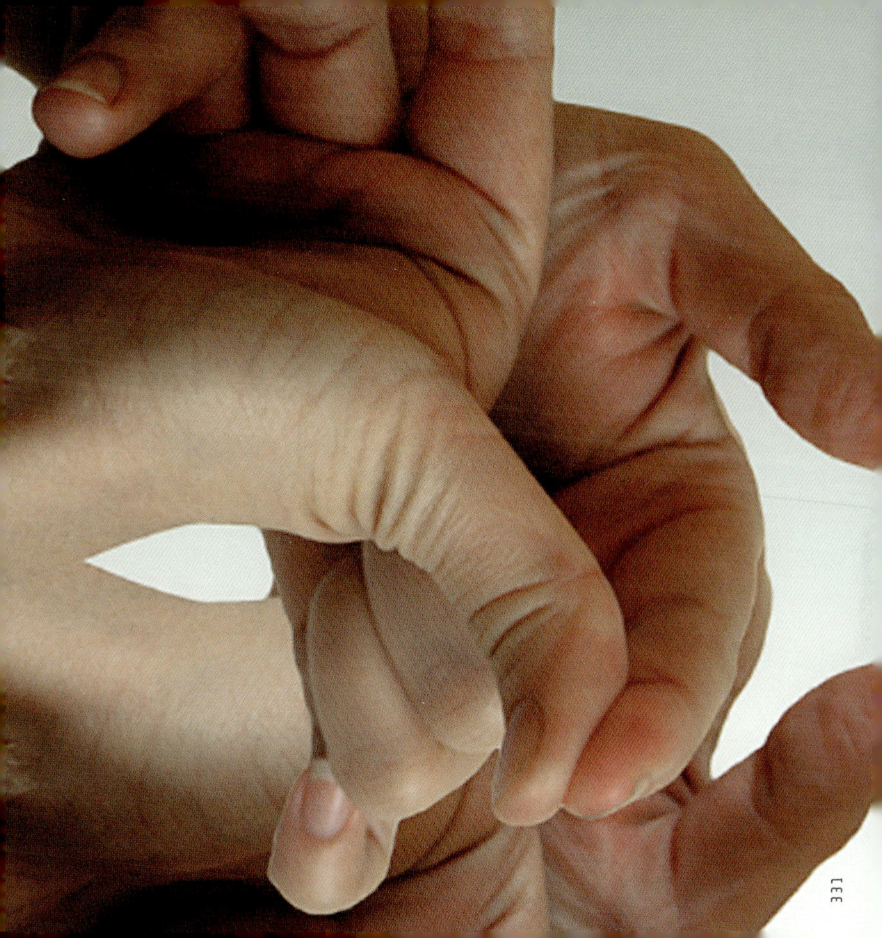

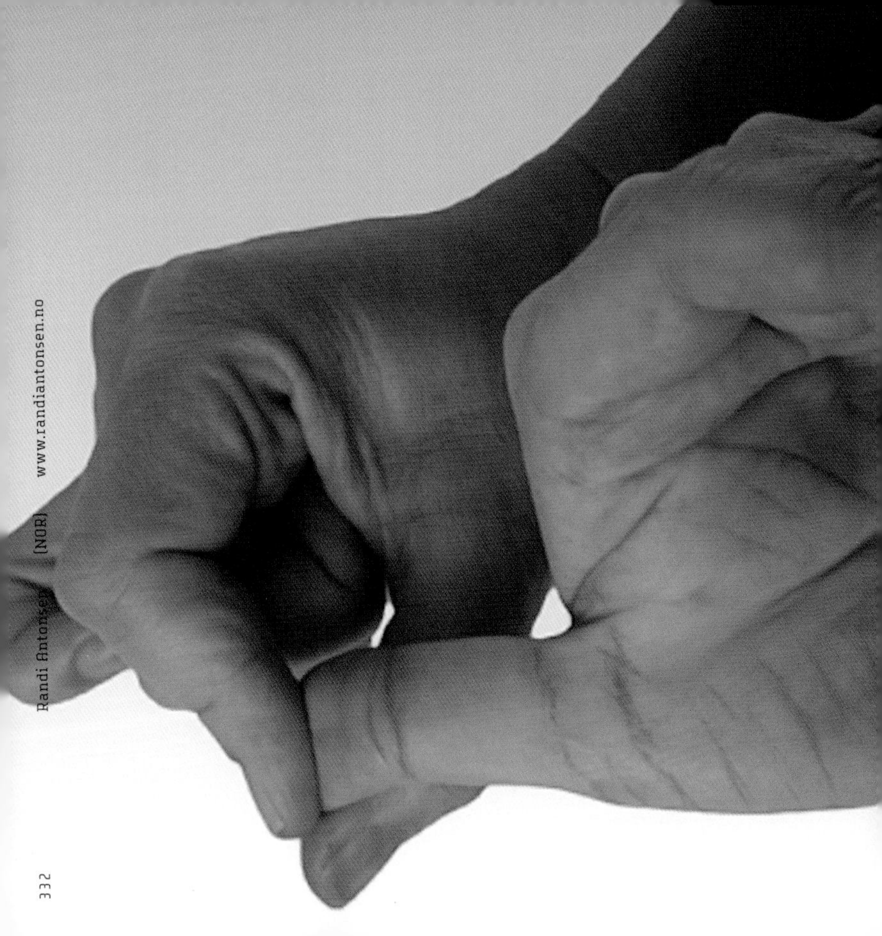

Randi Antonsen [NOR] www.randiantonsen.no

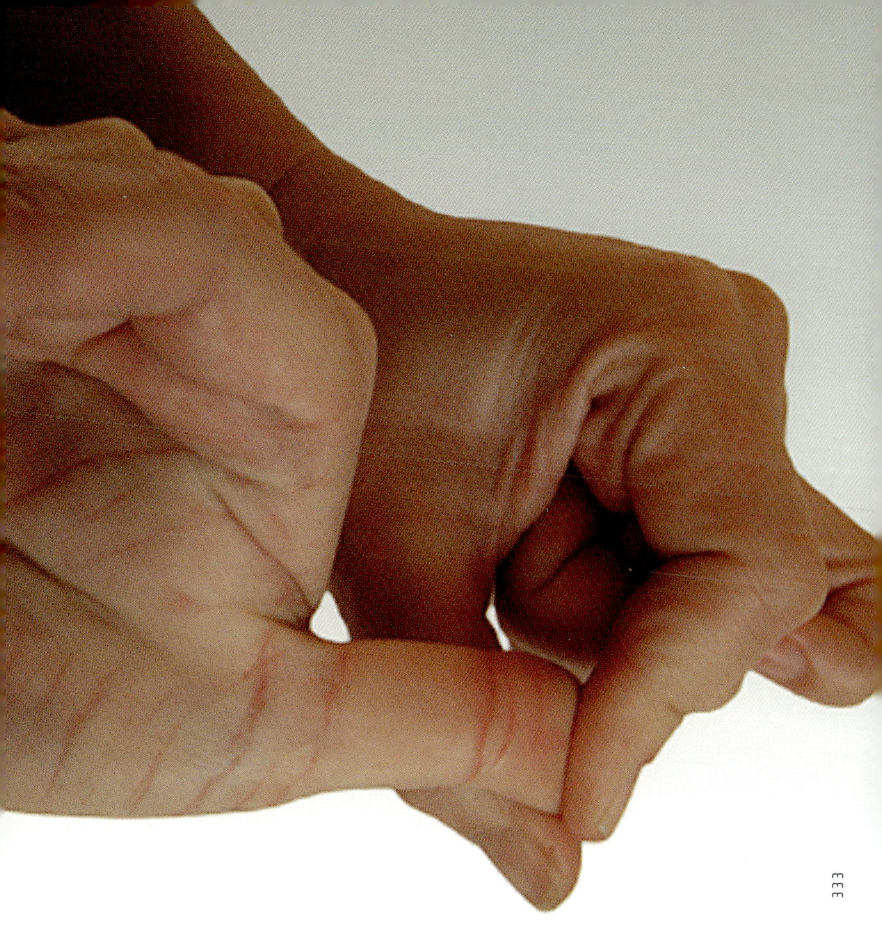

Randi Antonsen [NOR] www.randiantonsen.no

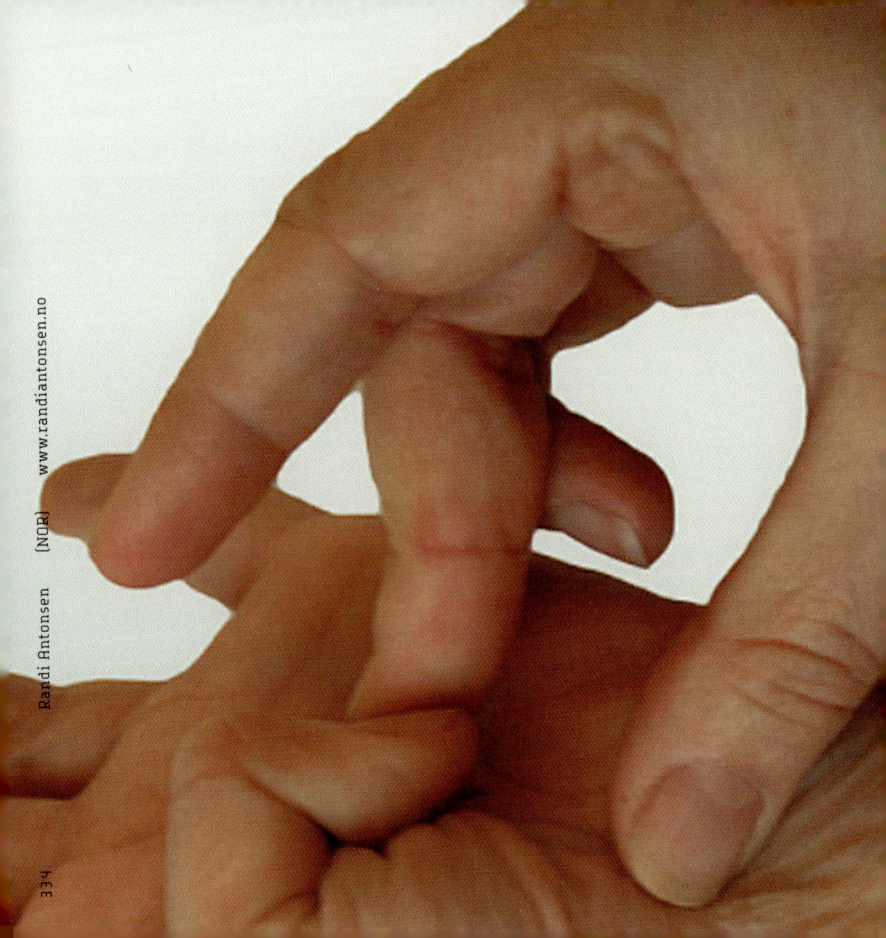

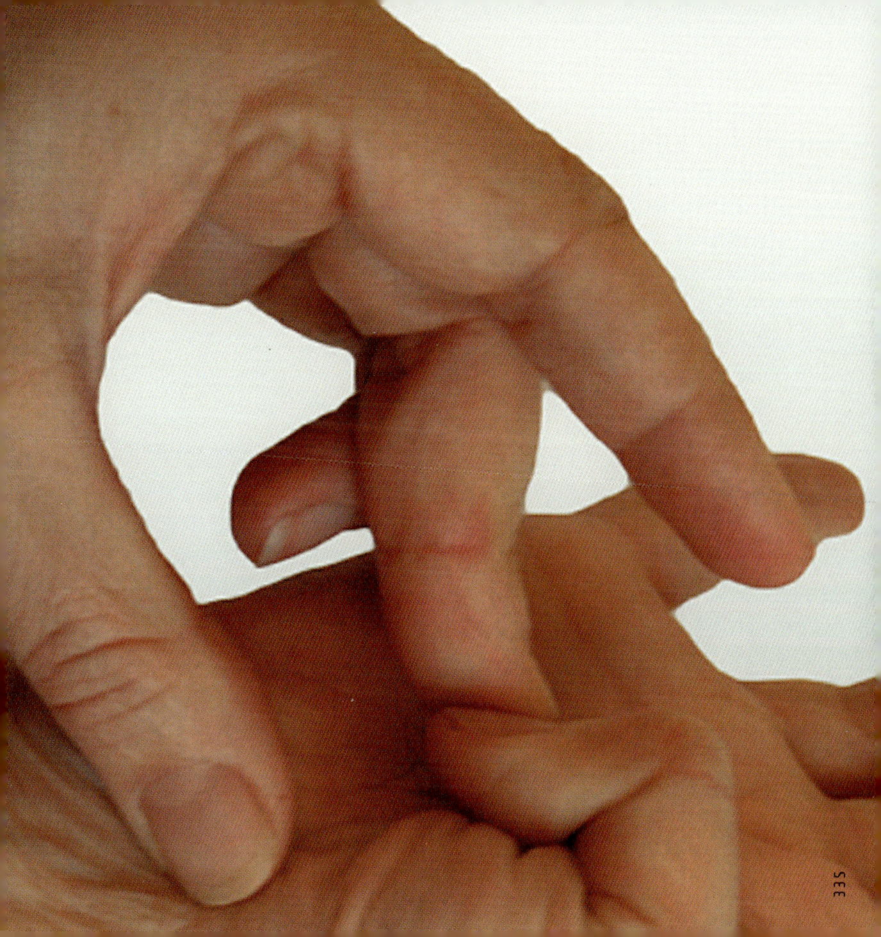

Michael Fetz   (GER)   www.michaelfetz.com

Landwirt-
schaftlicher
Verkehr frei

Schweinegg 0.3 km
Zell 2 km   Burgruinen 40 Min.

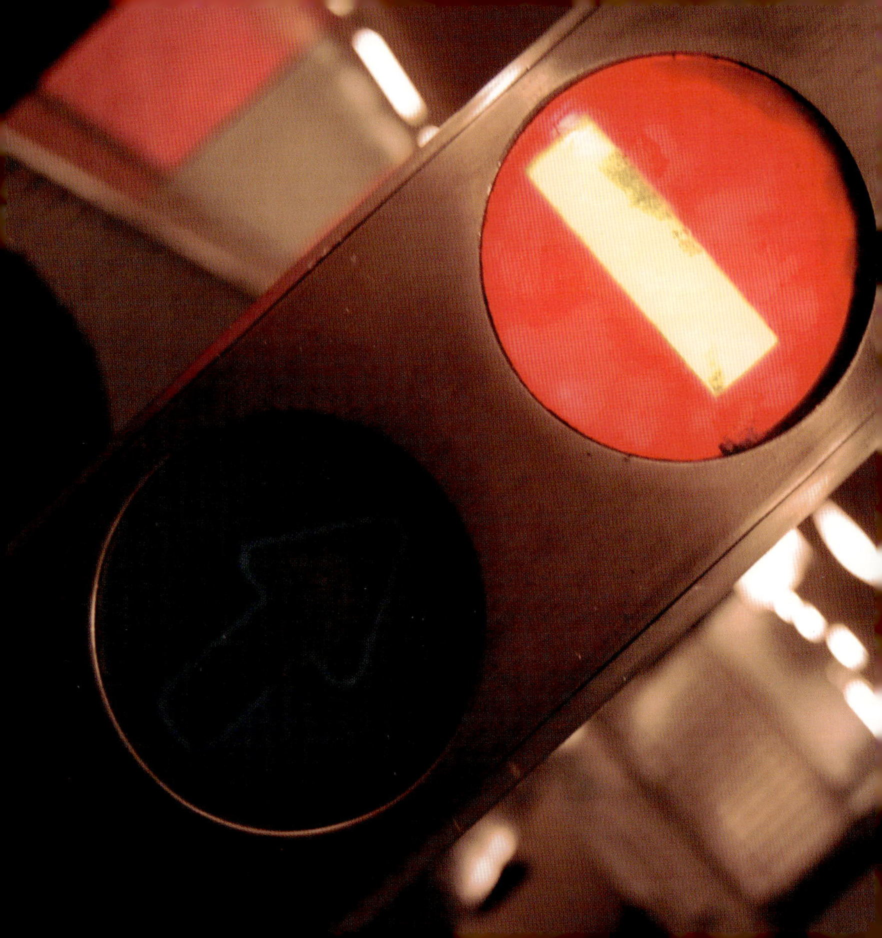

Florian Kettner (GER) www.rv20.com

Ausstellung
OHNE
Gewähr
44FLAVOURS
IN DER
BAGGE
&
BÖLLE
Artists
UNLIMITED
Galerie
EROFFNUNG
19.00 UHR
BIELEFELD
14.
NOV.
2008

Julio Rölle [GER] www.44flavours.de

Julio Rölle [GER] www.44flavours.de

342

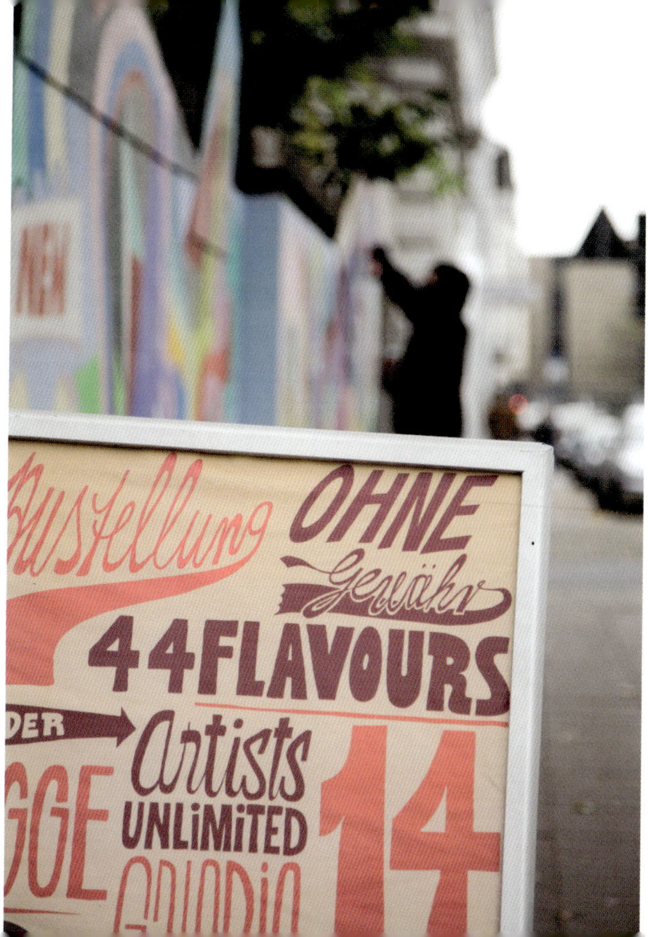
OHNE
Gewähr
44FLAVOURS
DER
Artists
UNLIMITED
14

DONT BITE LET EVE HYPE

PARADISE
INN
YOUR CHANCE TO STAY IN THE SAME LODGE AS JIMI HENDRIX & ENJOY THE COMFORTS OF QUICK SERVICE
A HOUSE OF
SATISFICATION IS OUR MOTTO
HYGENIC SUITABLE Breakfast
AVAILABLE HERE
come as a CUSTOMER go as our FRIEND.
HOT Shower
WE HAVE SOME facilities
LUXURY TAX ≈10%
FAST FOOD & Chat
Boiled filter WATER
BATHROOM
CLEAN ROOMS
COMFORTABLE
DINNING ROOM
HEATER
FRESH and DELICIOUS FOOD
GOOD MUSIC
WHAT MORE DO YOU NEED
PROVIDE
TRUE
FRIENDLY PEOPLE SMILING FACES

Anders Malmströmer [SWE] www.malmstromer.se

Luis Felipe Salas [CHI]

Luis Felipe Salas   [CHI]

VIA DE ESCAPE

- NARANJA con PLÁTANO **600** EL ½ LITRO
- JUGO FRUTILLA SOLO **700** EL ½ LITRO
- JUGO de PERA **500** EL ½ LITRO
- PURO JUGO de NARANJA EXTRACTO **1000** EL ½ LITRO
- JUGO PAPAYA **700** EL ½ LITRO
- TUTI... **8**...
- JUGO de MANGO **1100** EL ½ LITRO
- JUGO de UVA **500** EL ½ LITRO
- JUGO de POMELO EXTRACTO **1000** EL ½ LITRO
- JUGO de COCO LECHE + PLÁTANO **1000** EL ½ LITRO
- EXQUISITO CHIRIMOYA con LECHE **1000** EL ½ LITRO

NO ES PURA

JUGO de PIÑA **500**

Luis Felipe Salas [CHI]

ALMACEN-VARIOS
"EL BOLICHE"
PAN $600.00 1 Kilo
OFRECE
PAN $600.00 1 Kilo
VERDURAS CONGELADAS
HELADOS
HAMBURGUESAS
CROQUETAS
CHURRASCOS

353

W. Canin

CANISETTE

DECORATION

SANITAIRE

ANTIQUITES

TEL-43-22-63

SUECIA
SVERIGE
SWEDEN

Anders Malmströmer [SWE] www.malmströmer.se

356

357

Luis Felipe Salas   [CHI]

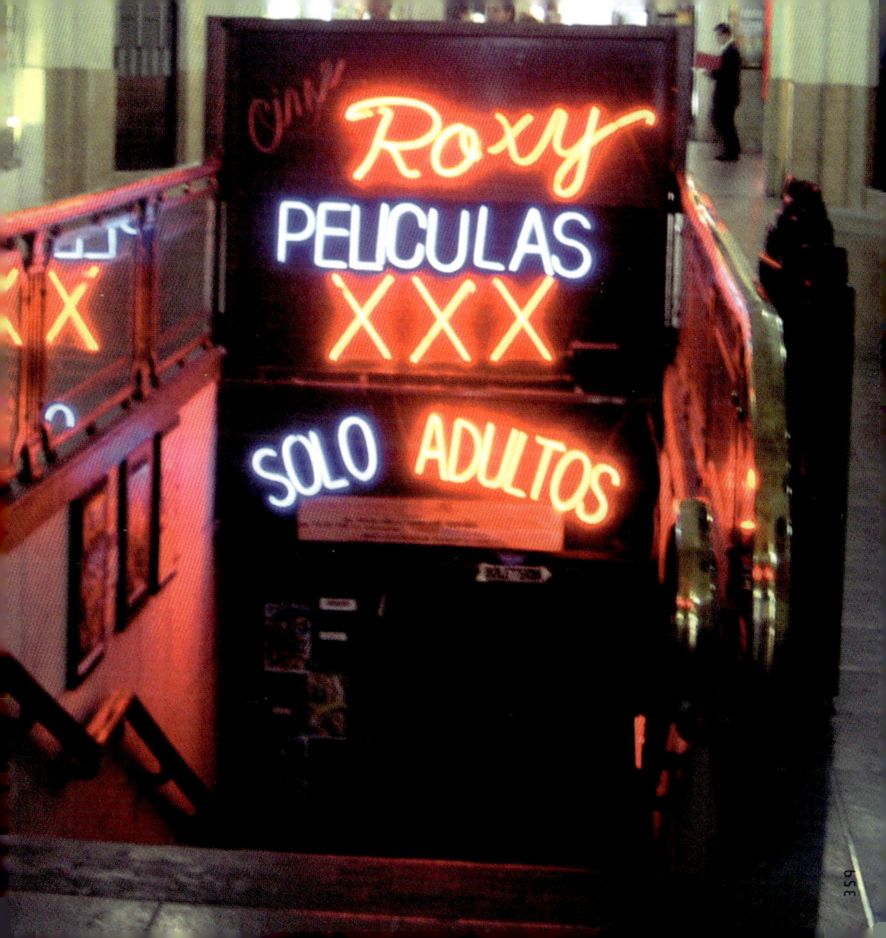
Roxy
PELICULAS
XXX
SOLO ADULTOS

www.studiotwentysix2.com

Tom Davie [USA]

361

Wladimiro Bendandi   [ITA]   www.d-plus.it

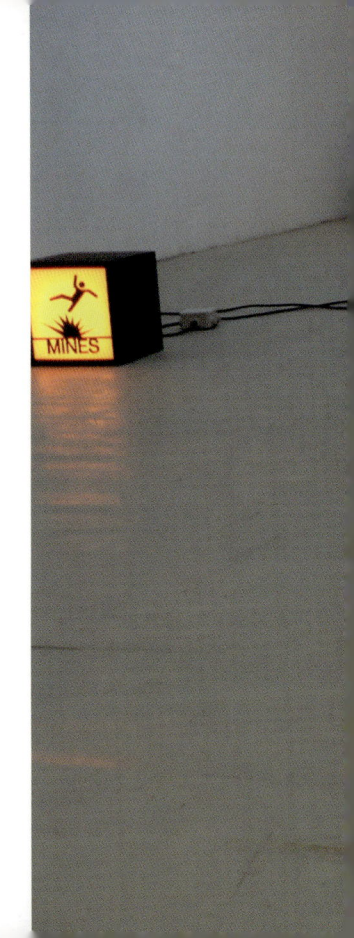

363

Wladimiro Bendandi   [ITA]   www.d-plus.it

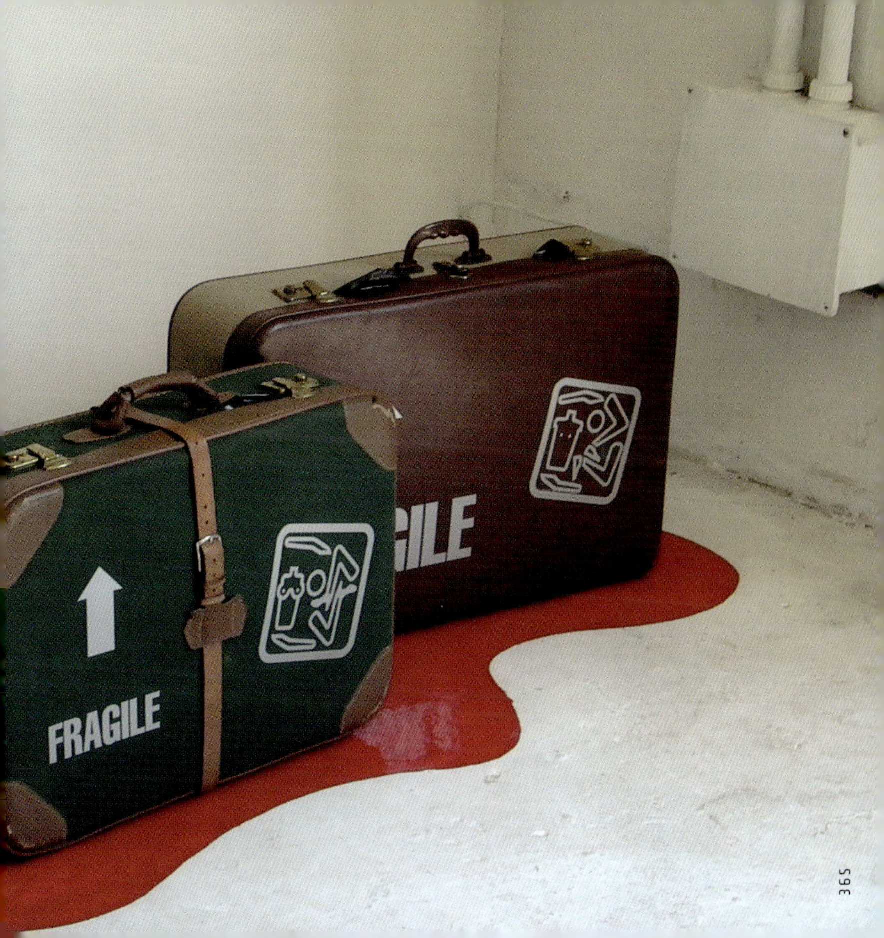
FRAGILE
GILE

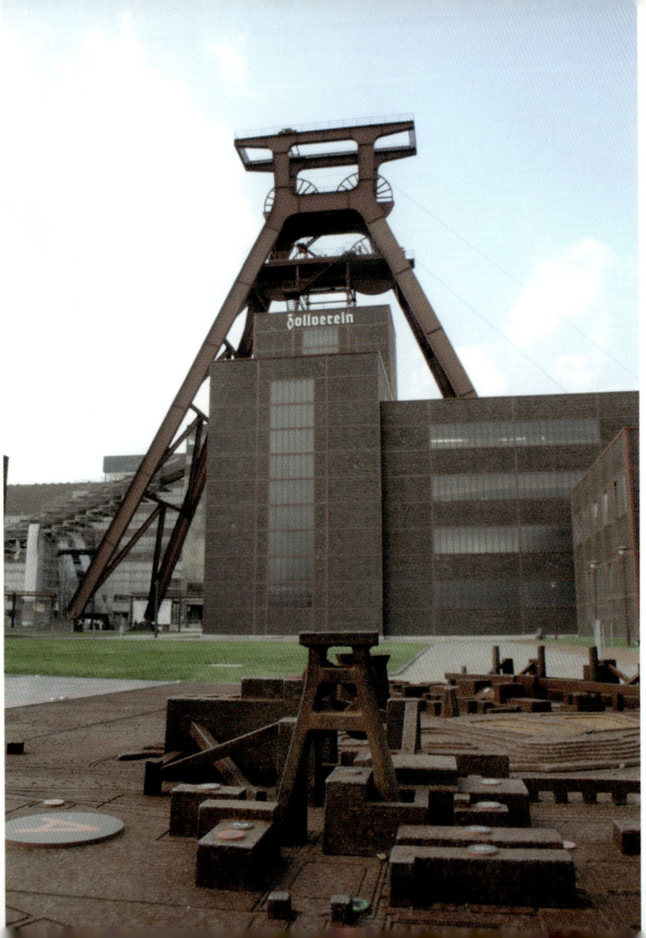

Christopher Ledwig (GER) www.f1rstdesign.com

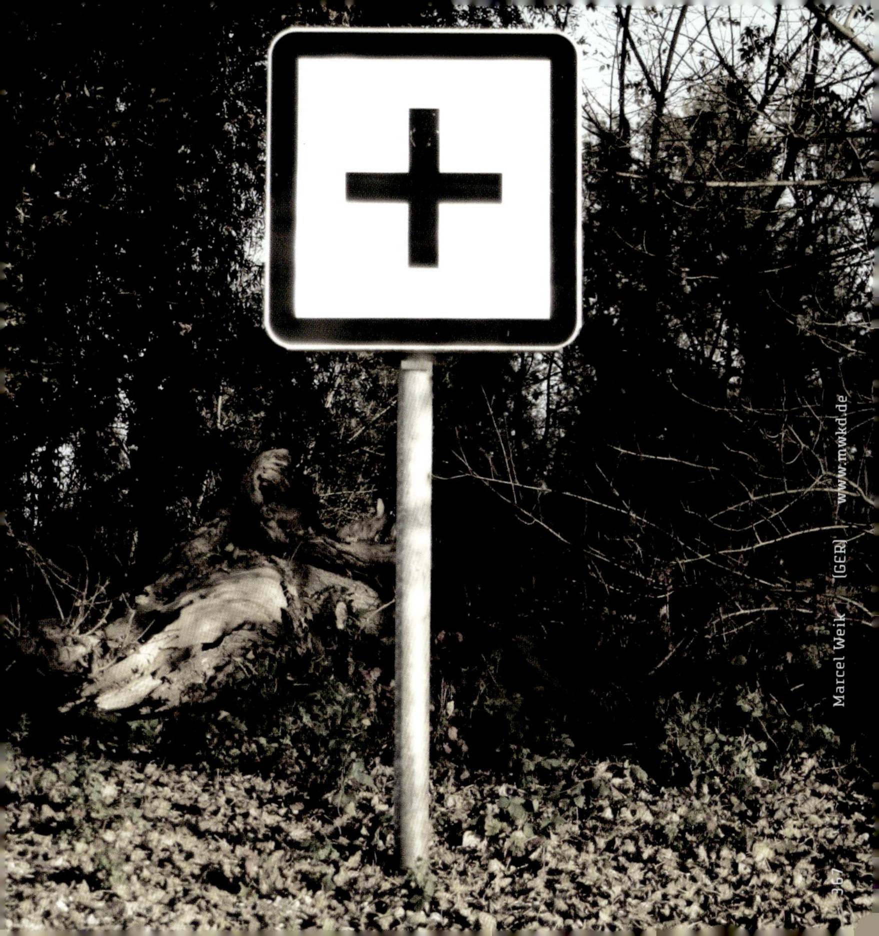

Marcel Weik [GER] www.mwkd.de

GIB' ACHT
SCHEIN

Julio Rölle [GER] www.44flavours.de

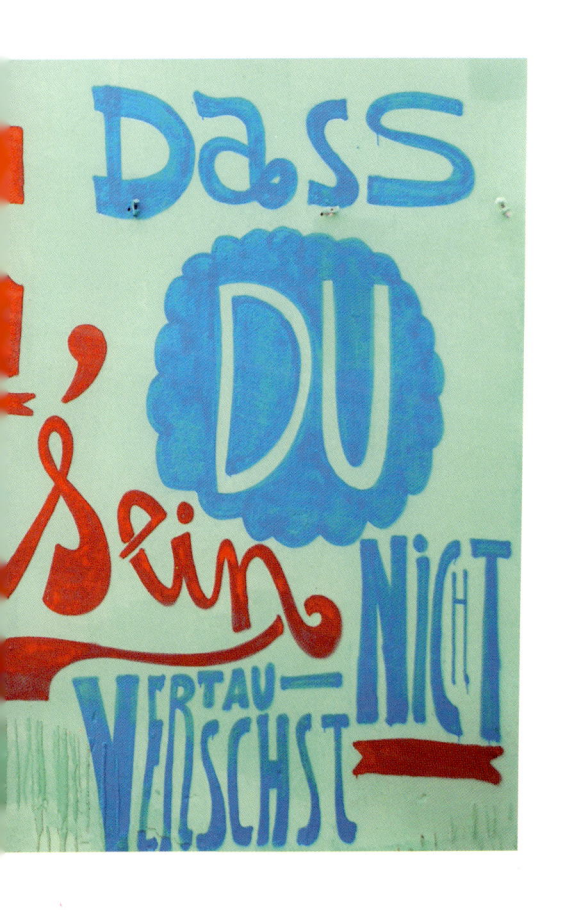

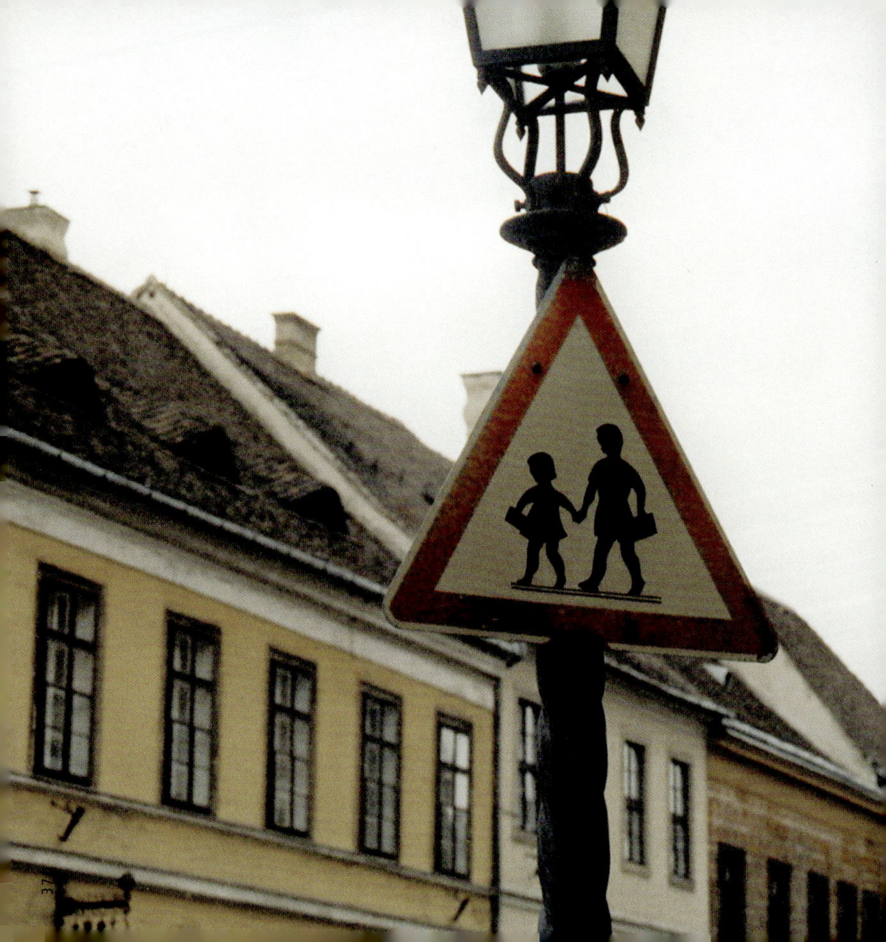

Ann Katrin Siedenburg [GER] www.katigraphie.de

TABAC

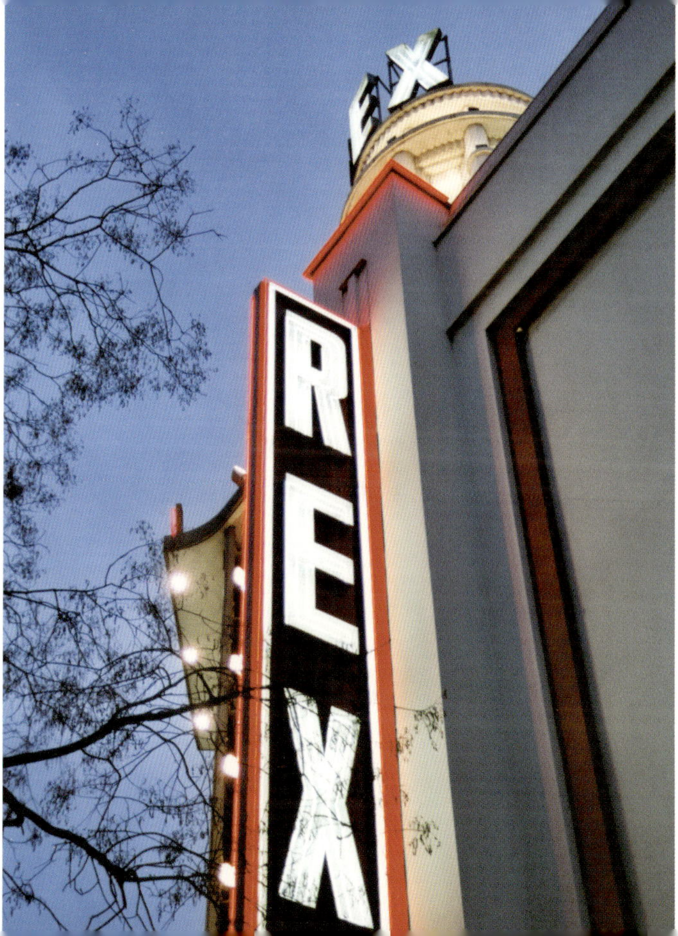
EX
REX

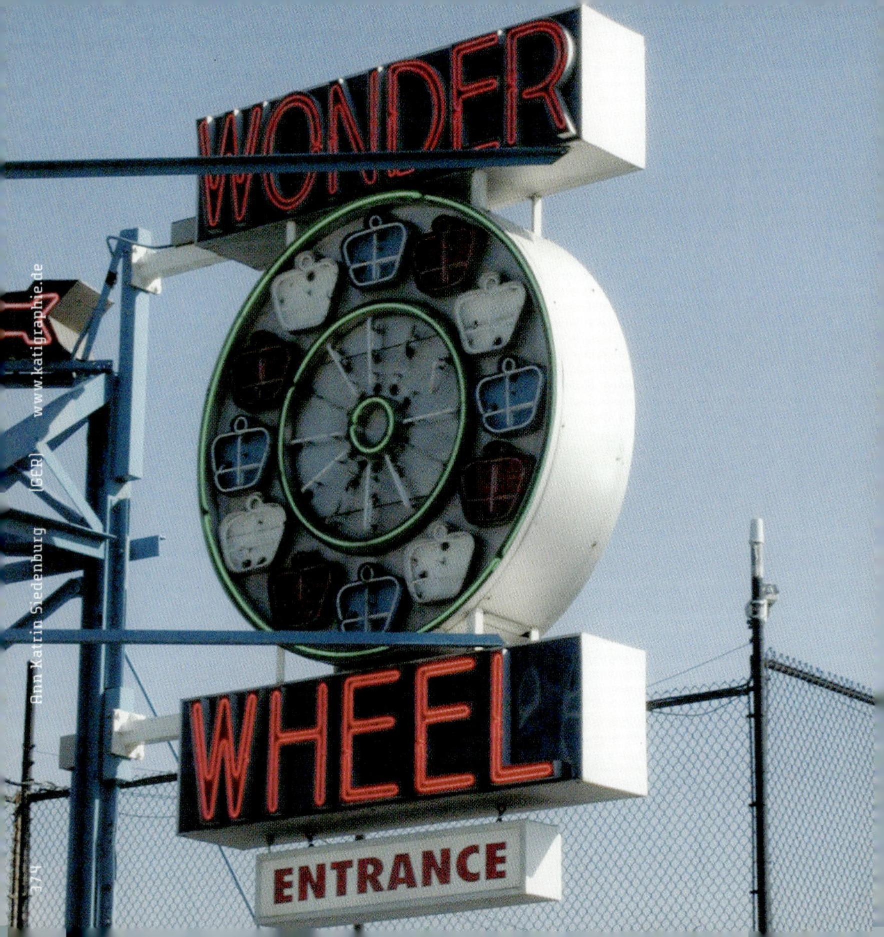

Ann Katrin Siedenburg (GER) www.katigraphie.de

375

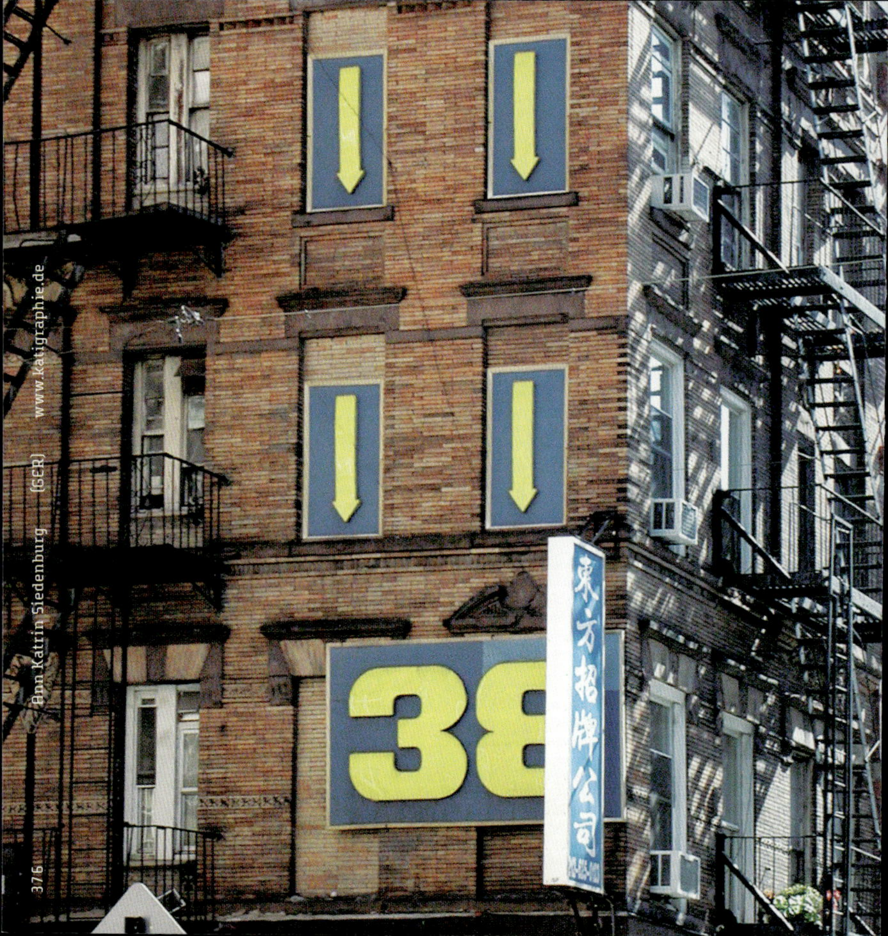

Ann Katrin Siedenburg [GER] www.katigraphie.de

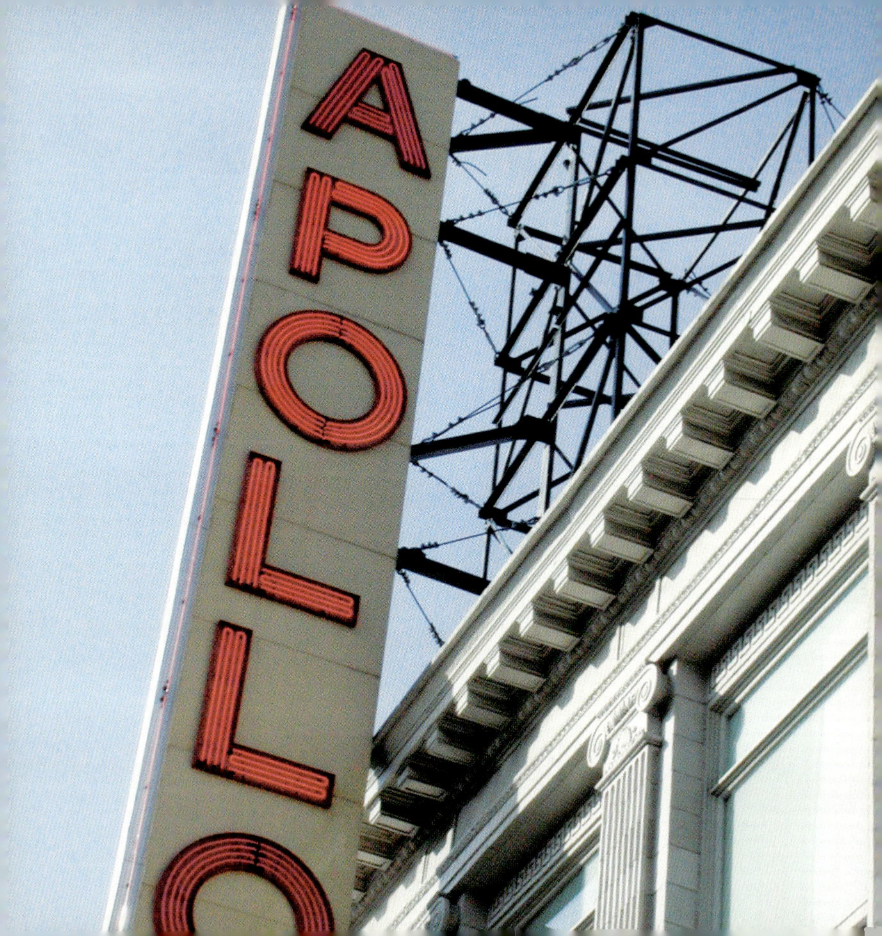
APOLLO

Sandra Hofacker [SUI] www.apfel-z.de

かづら清　稲葉英子　玉半

平成二十年二月初午建之
平成二十年十月吉日建之
平成二十一年六月吉日建之
平成二十年十月吉日建之
平成二十年二月吉日建之
平成二十年六月吉日建之
平成十九年十月吉日建之
平成十九年六月吉日建之
平成十九年八月吉日建之
平成十八年二月初午建之
平成二十一年二月初午建之
平成二十年四月吉日建之

平成十八年三月吉日建之

Alejandro Ovalles [VEN]

382

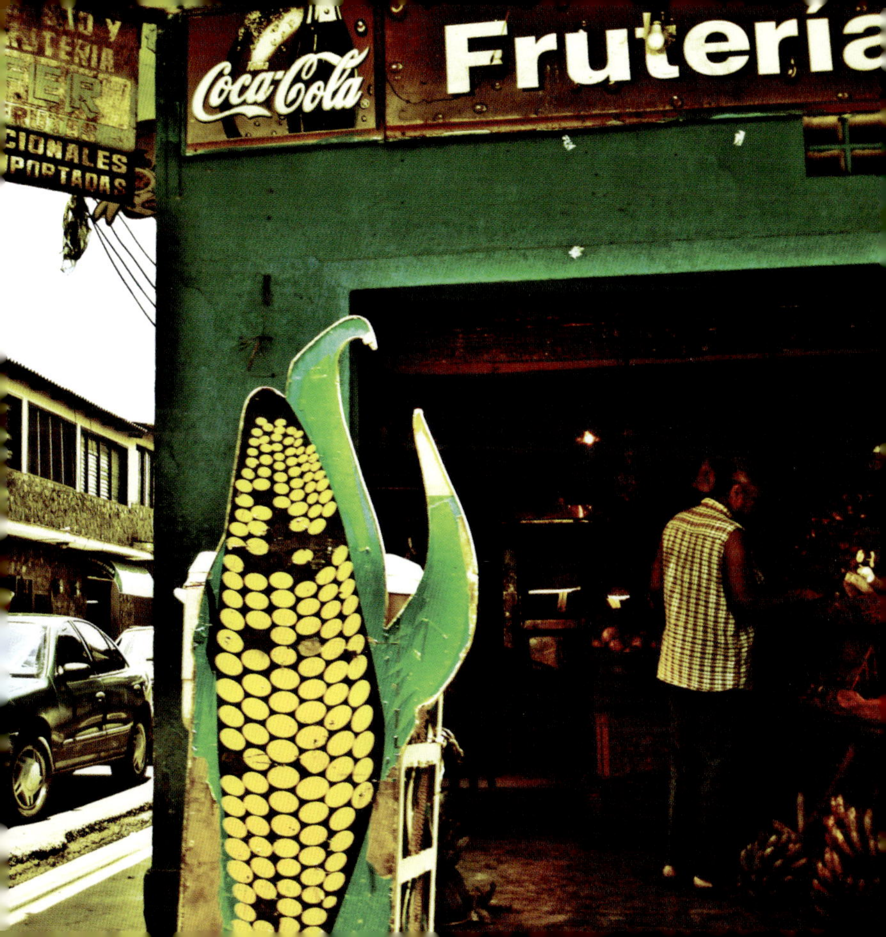
Coca-Cola
Frutería
CIONALES
PORTADAS

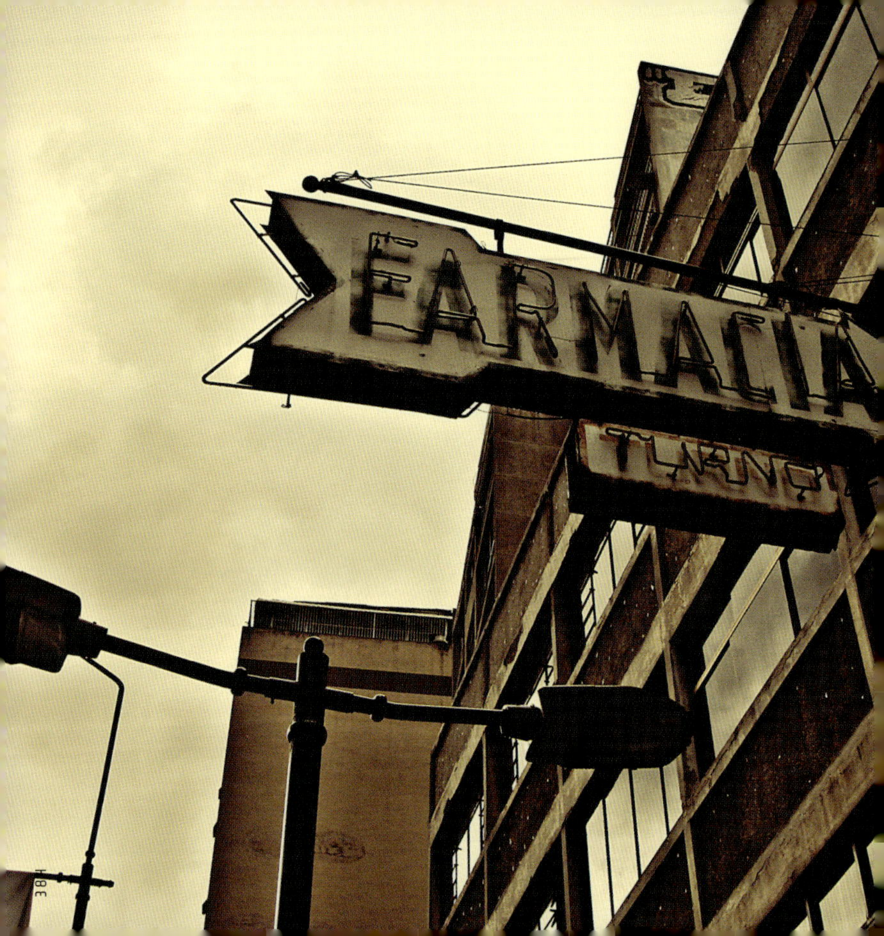
FARMACIA
TURNO

Alejandro Ovalles [VEN]

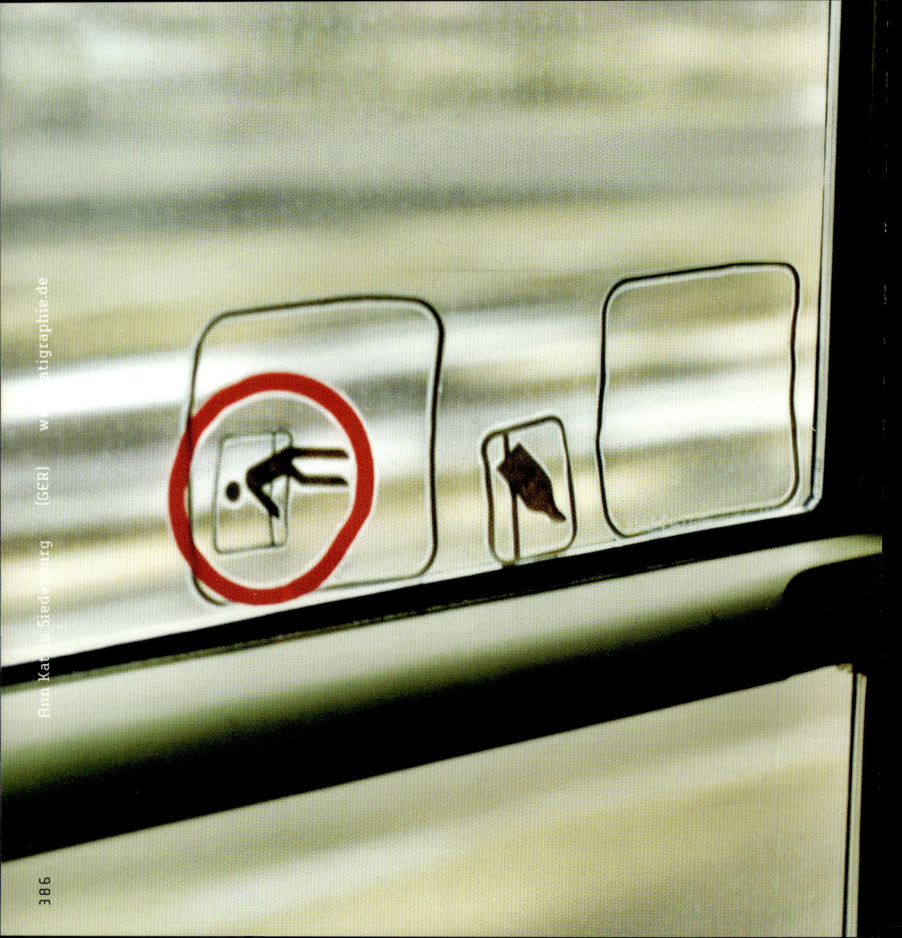

Ann Katrin Siedenburg (GER) w[illegible]atigraphie.de

TOILETTER

Bo Vinkelyst Jensen [DEN] www.addsoul.com

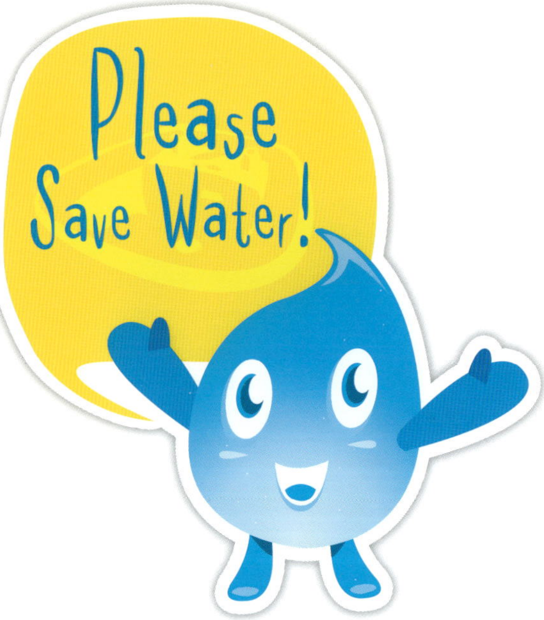

JayLim (MAS) www.tsubakistudio.net

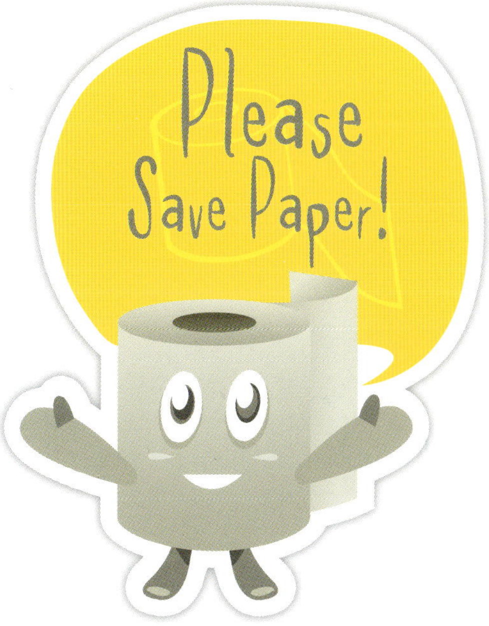
Please
Save Paper!

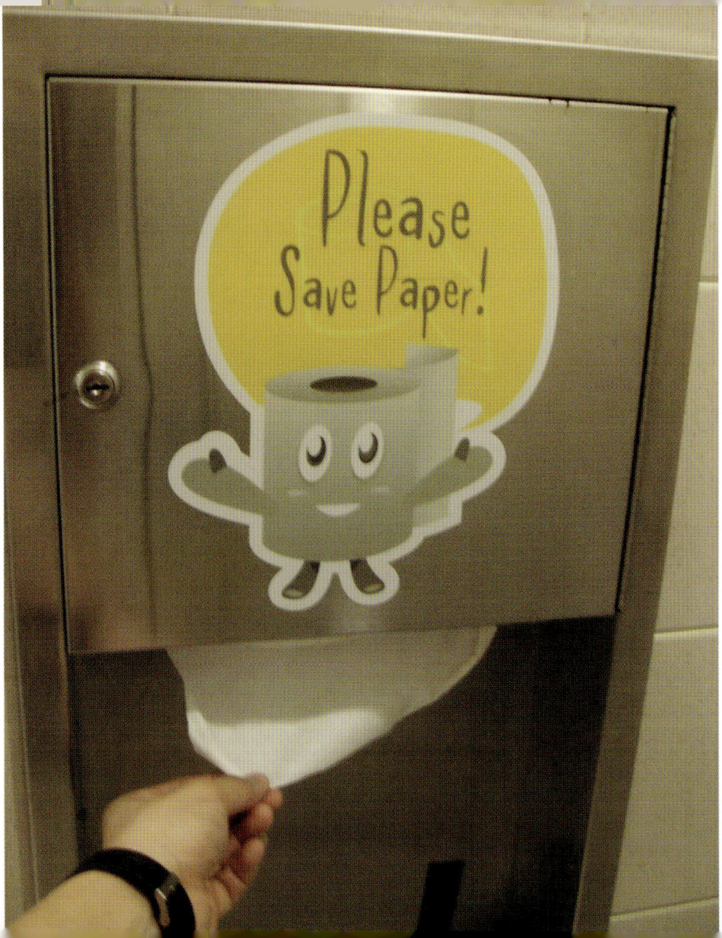

JayLim [MAS] www.tsubakistudio.net

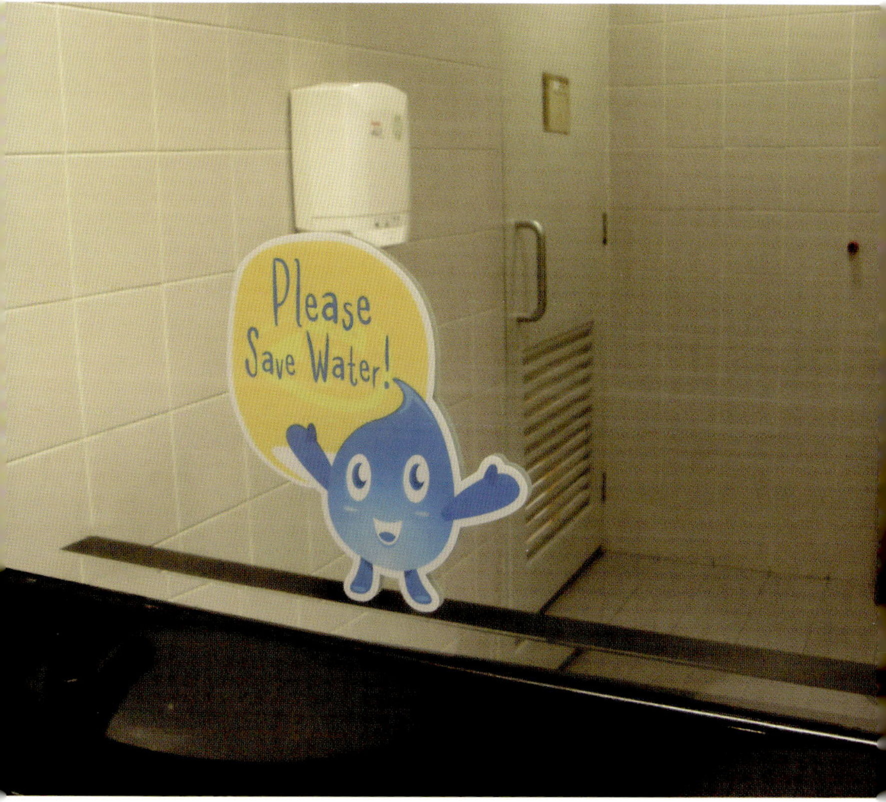
Please
Save Water!

Marc Prien   [GER]   www.aurorise.com

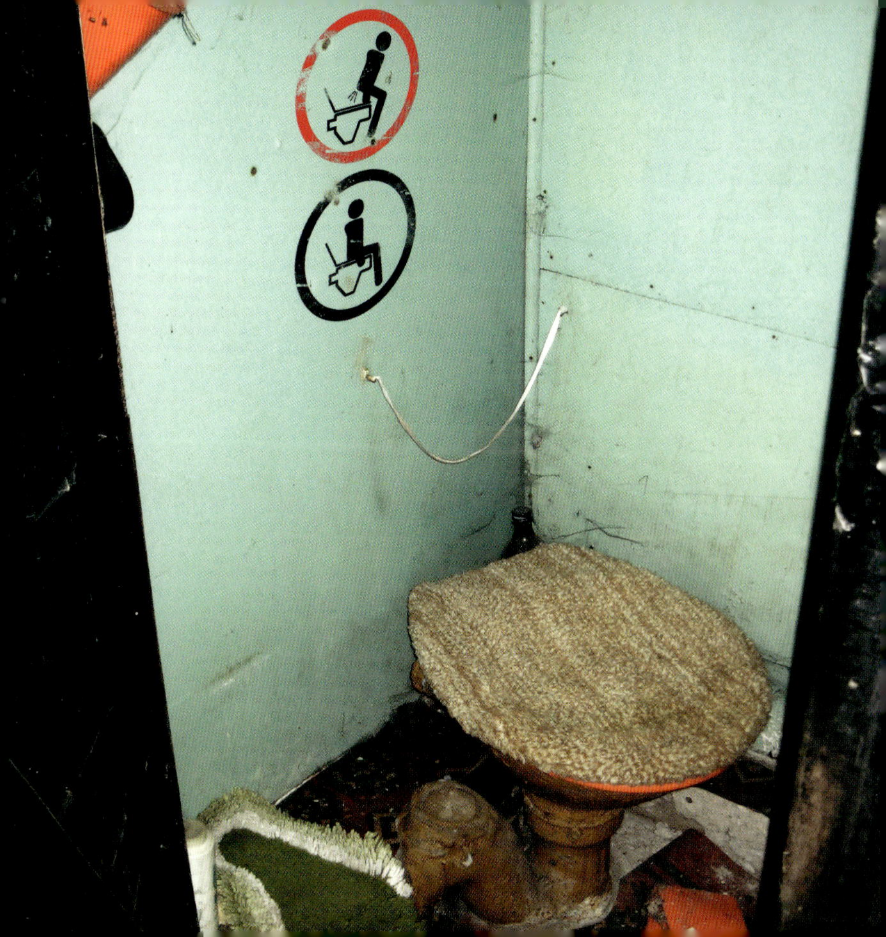

BERLIN 2405,5 KM
BOLHORN 2888,3 KM
KÖLN 2636,2 KM
BOLTIGEN 2518,8 KM
AMSTERDAM 2864,6 KM
HORLEY 3136,9

Lars Harmsen   [GER]   www.magmabranddesign.de

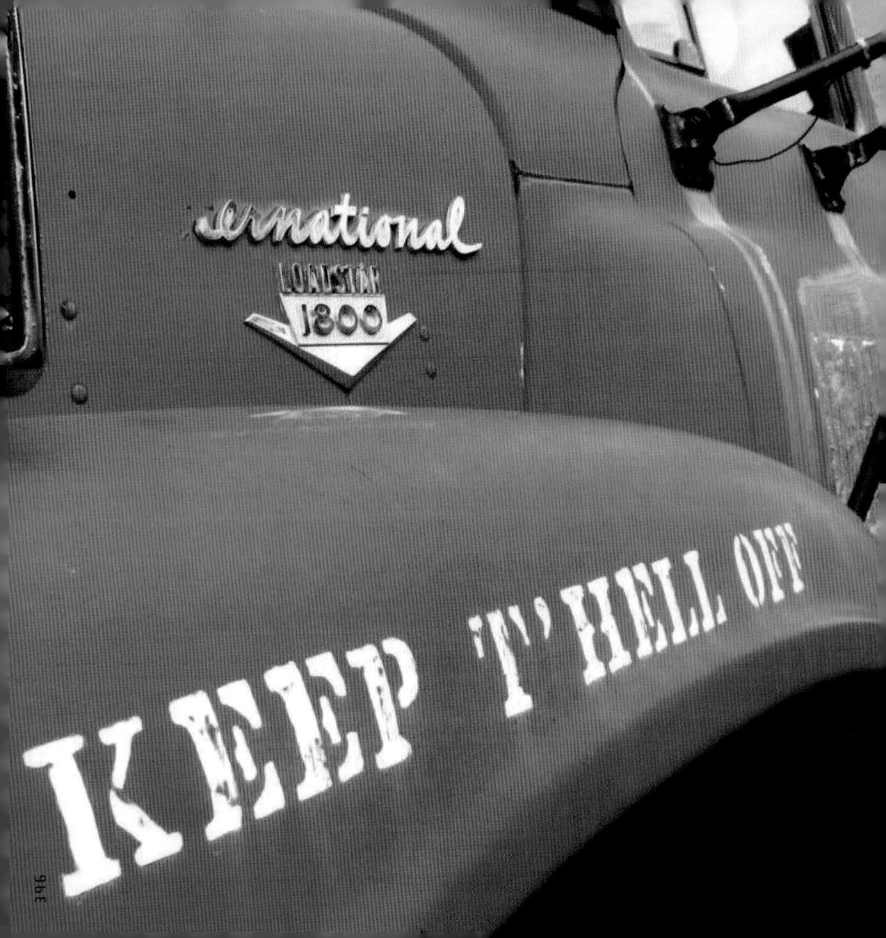
LOADSTAR
1800
KEEP 'T' HELL OFF

Judith Reiser [GER] www.judithreiser.com

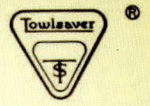

Judith Reiser (GER) www.judithreiser.com

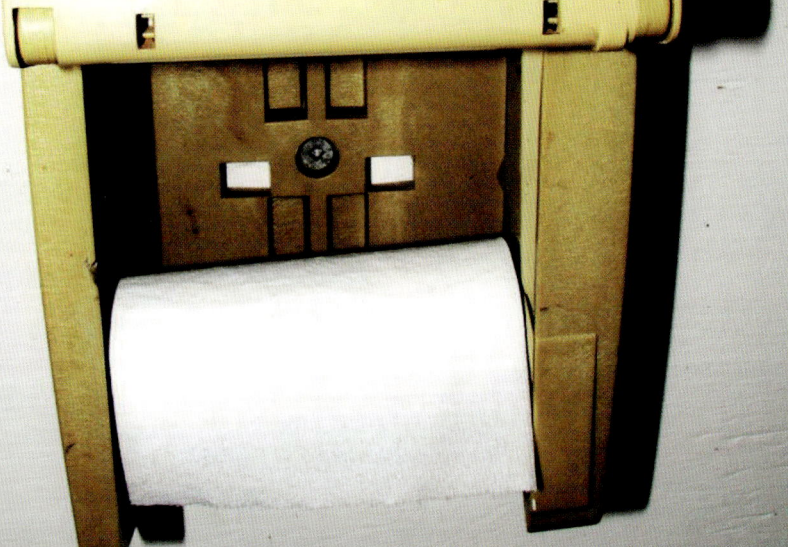

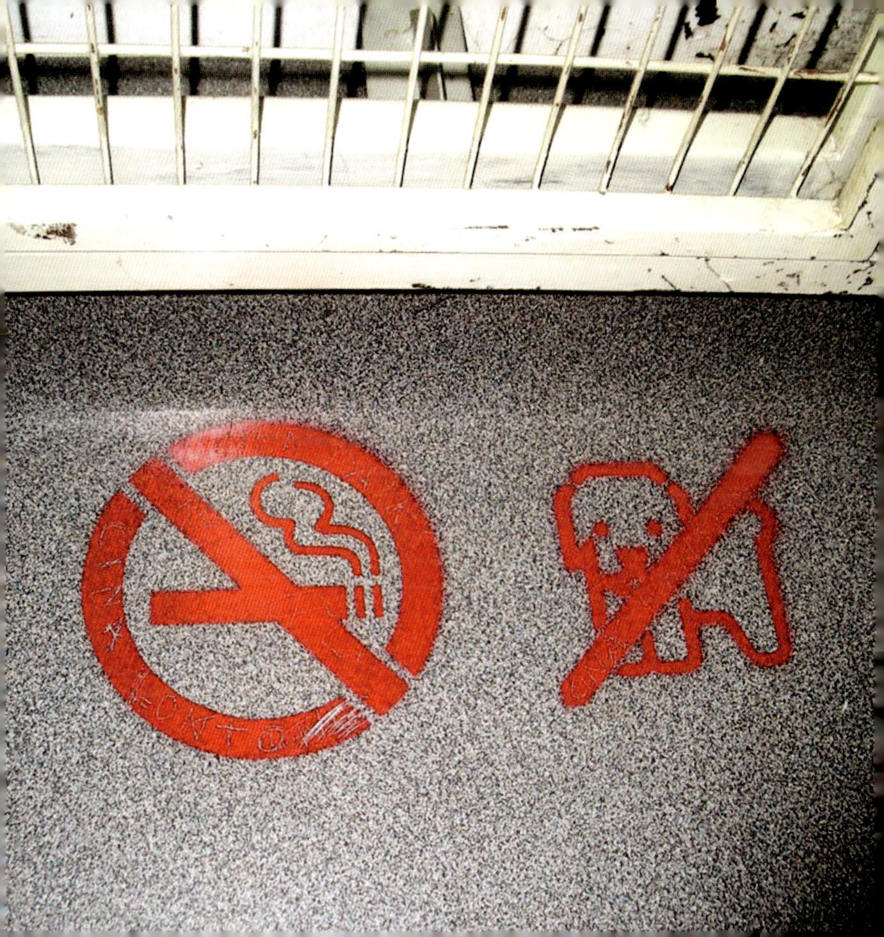

Judith Reiser [GER] www.judithreiser.com

400

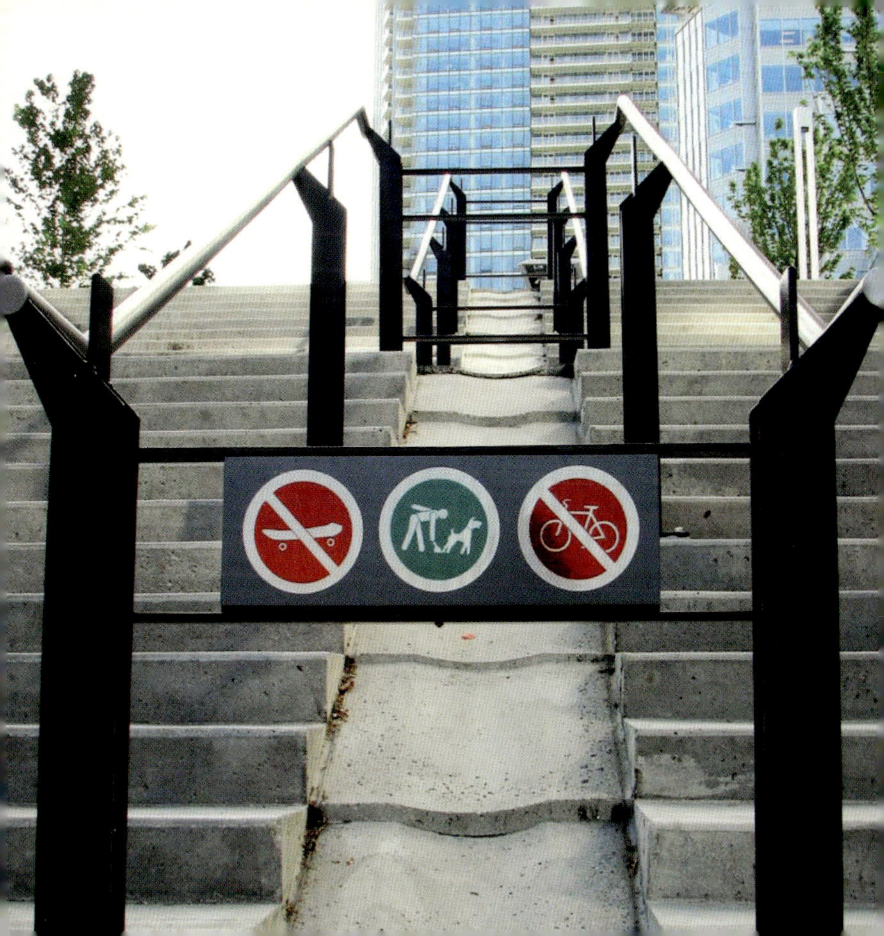

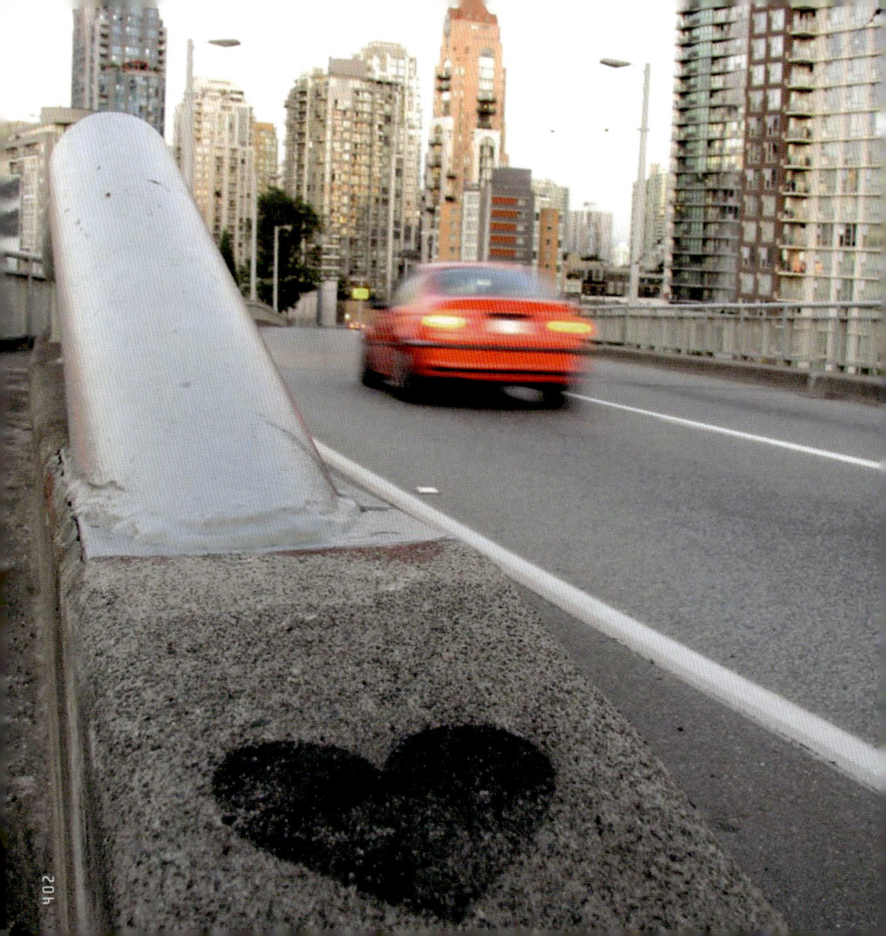

Judith Reiser [GER] www.judithreiser.com

Water is the only subst
matter - solid, liquid an
that sustains life. Huma
in just a matter of a few

It is with this understan
is quite literally, from *H
the chemical represen
the substance. This se
concept's visual outco

Illustration | The Water Cycle
Rain and snow fall as precipitation,
melting and/or flowing overland
into rivers and finally into oceans.
Water is evaporated along the way
and the cycle repeats itself.

Concept

Earth that occurs naturally in all three states of
ater is also the single most important substance
ve without food for weeks, but will die of thirst

t my concept for this project, *A Day With Water,*
'2)O is thus a conceptual development on both
water, as well as the all-encompassing nature of
ols are meant to aid in the interpretation of said

314 raindrops on my side of the car window

24 km of travelling by car

222 wine glasses

53 times washing my hands

17 mins **3** secs of Sea footage (Cape No. 7)

121 times using the water faucet

21 blobs of Almond Handwash

10 km of travelling by bus

98 ice cubes for Sugar Cane

22 blobs of Dishwashing Liquid

A Day With Water

H(2)O Iconography
Record of events for 7th February 2009

314 raindrops on my side of the car window

24 km of travelling by car

222 wine glasses

53 times washing my hands

17 mins **3** secs of Sea footage

121 times using the water faucet

21 blobs of Almond Handwash

10 km of travelling by bus

98 ice cubes for Sugar Cane

22 blobs of Dishwashing Liquid

LOVE'n PEACE

Tom Davie [USA] www.studiotwentysix2.com

Tom Davie (USA) www.studiotwentysix2.com

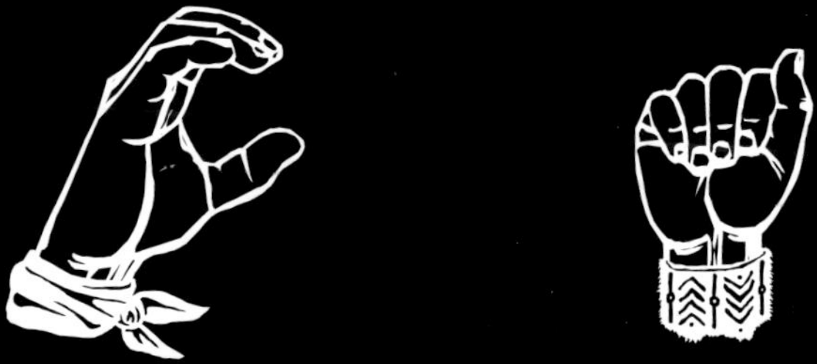

Lucas Rampazzo [BRA]

412

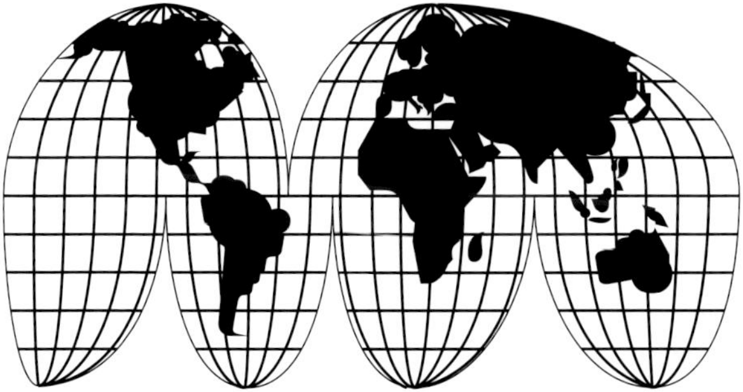

Lucas Rampazzo [BRA]

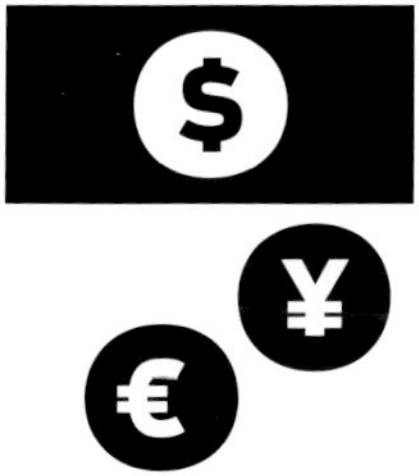

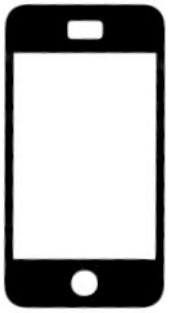

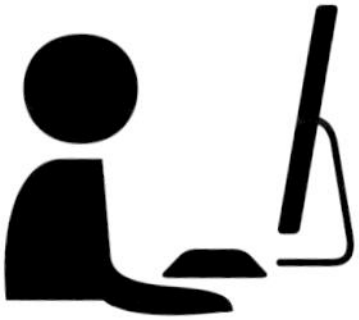

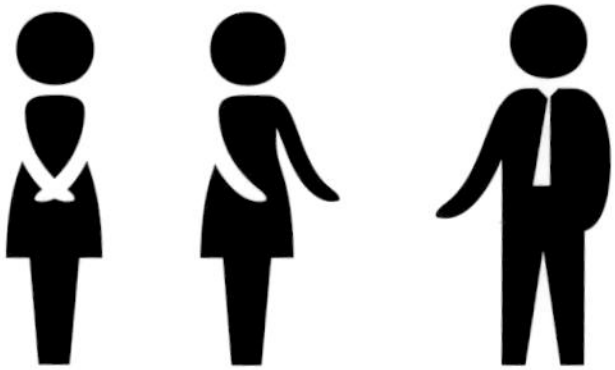

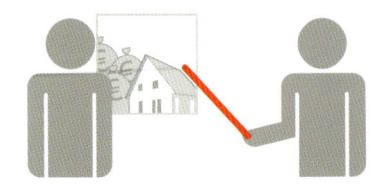

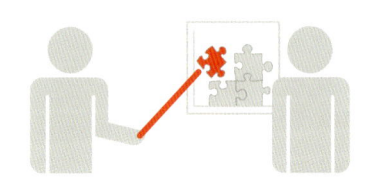

Christian Rothenhagen [GER] www.christianrothenhagen.com

416

417

Christian Rothenhagen (GER) www.christianrothenhagen.com

418

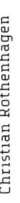

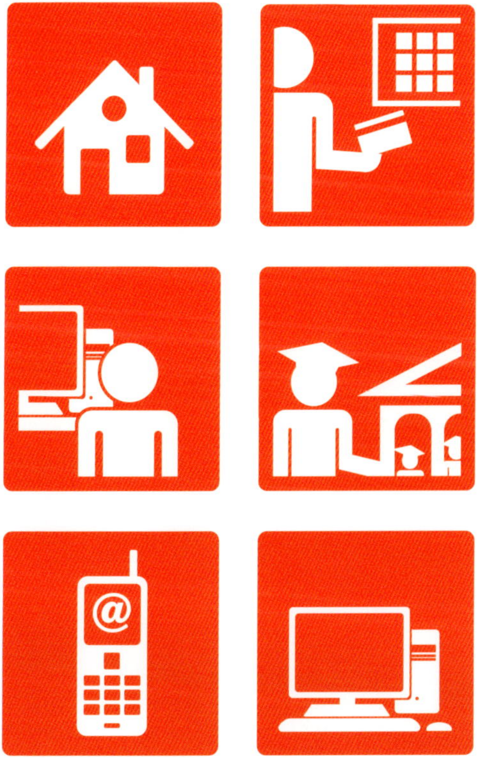

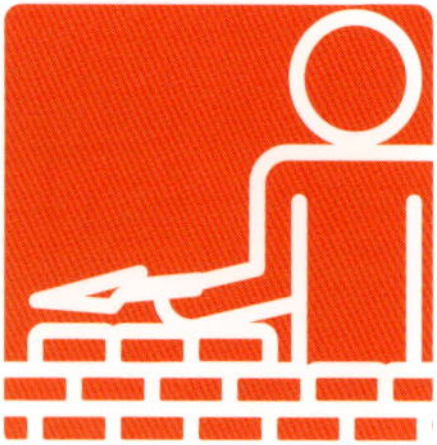

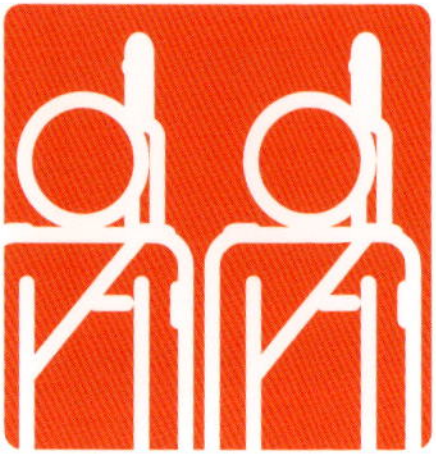

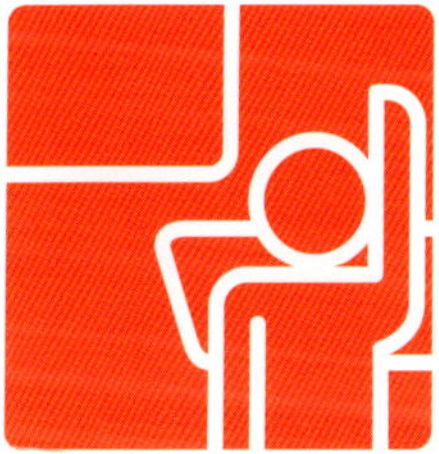

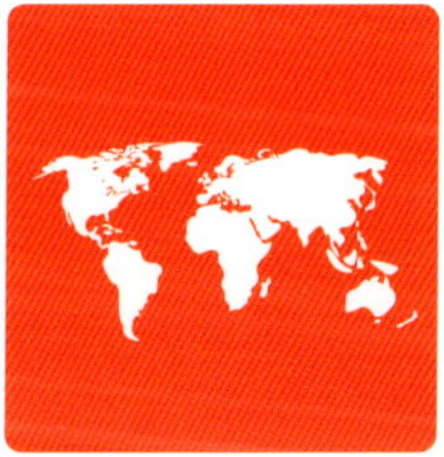

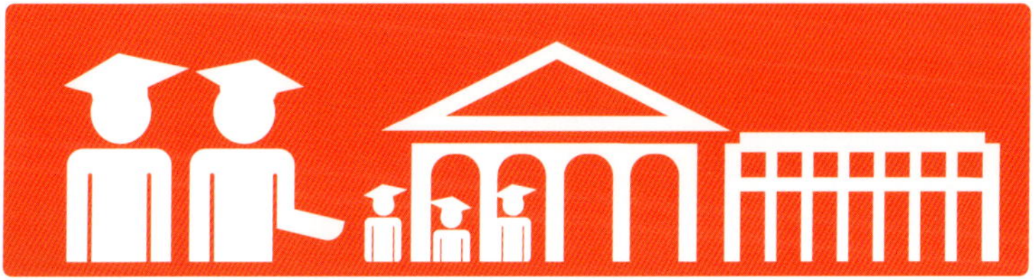

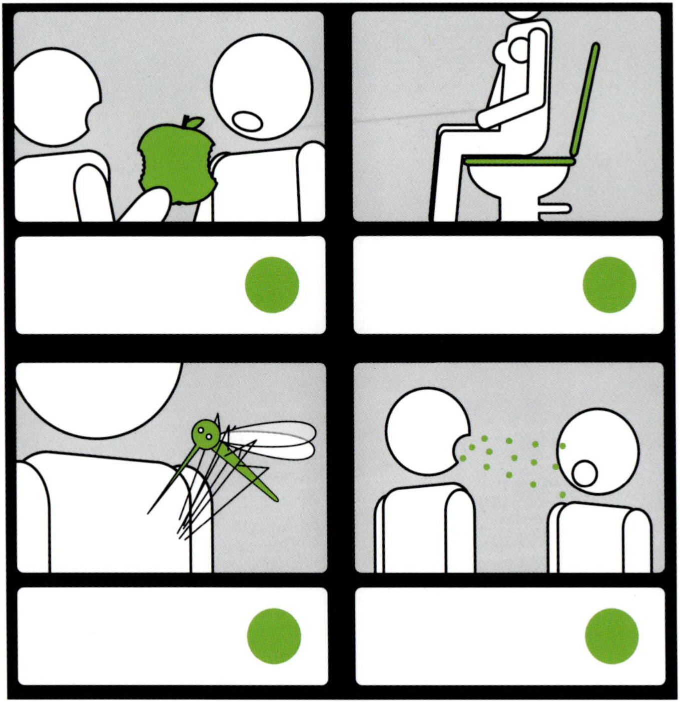

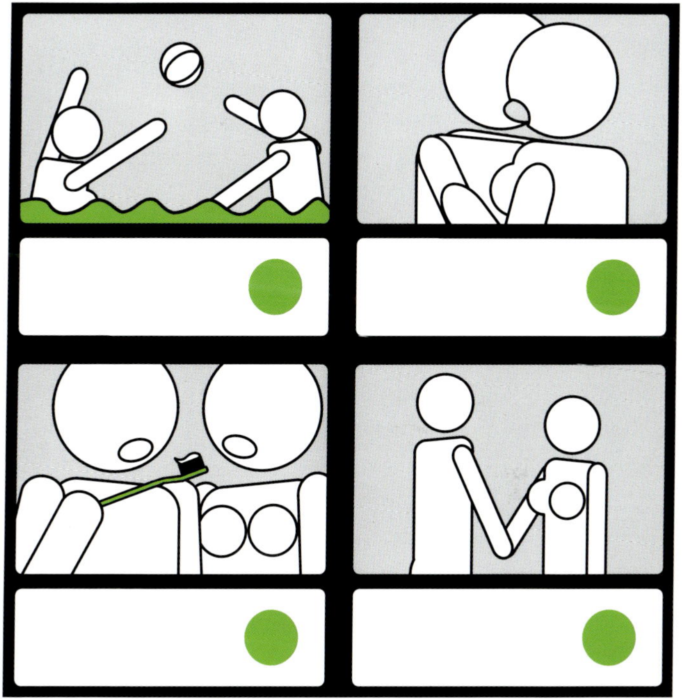

Harmonia Pastelis Icon Set

Teekatas Suwannakrua [THA] www.raindropmemory.deviantart.com/

426

MODEEEERN Icon Set

Summer, Love & Cicadas Icon Set

Fungiiiiiii Icon Set

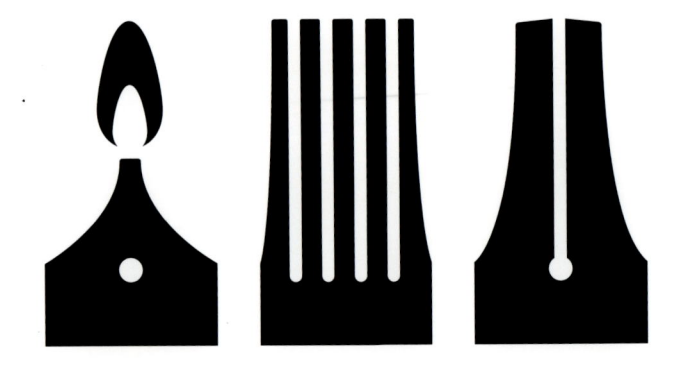

Chill. Cook. Create.

Retreats

marmalade
ski school

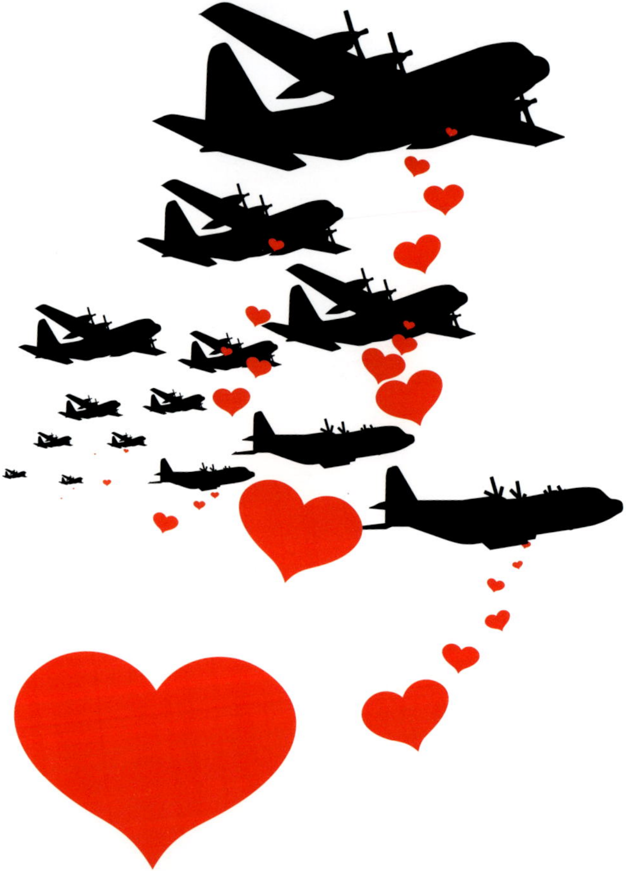

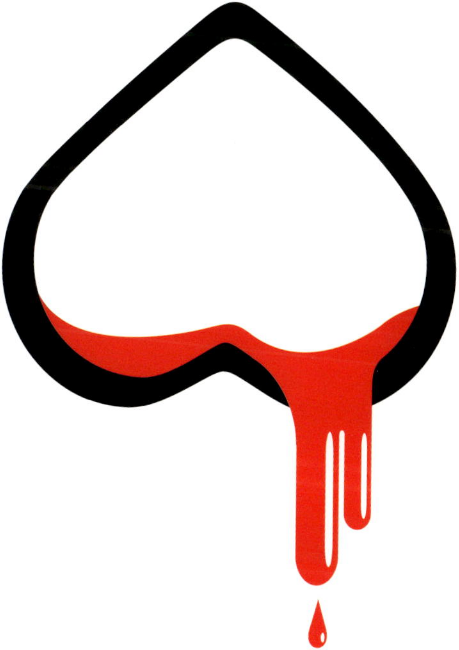

URST
DURST

Andreas Eck (GER) www.apfelgernhaber.de

434

Fabrizio Paccagnella   (ITA)   www.spritzer.it

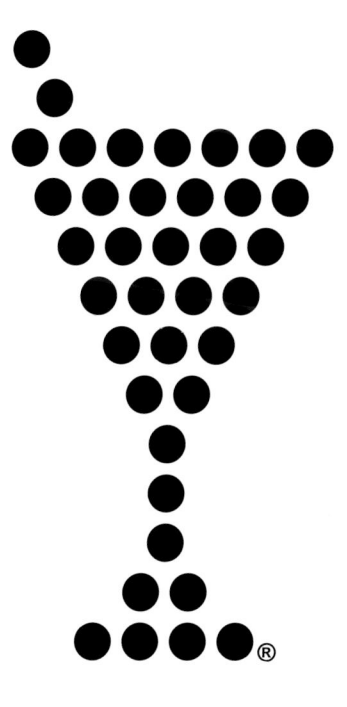

Fabrizio Paccagnella [ITA] www.spritzer.it

437

Fabrizio Paccagnella [ITA] www.spritzer.it

438

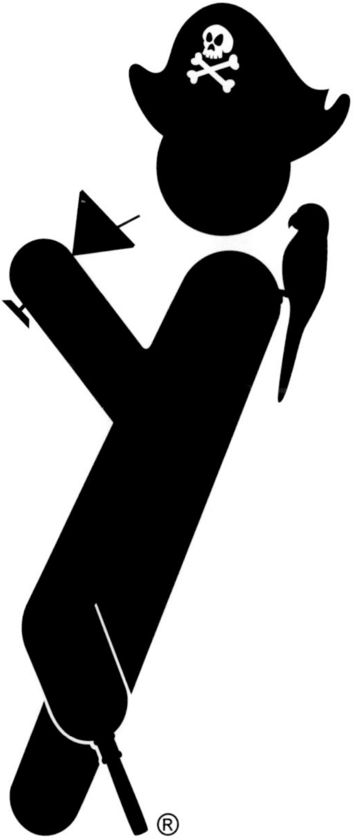

Andreas Eck (GER) www.apfelgernhaber.de

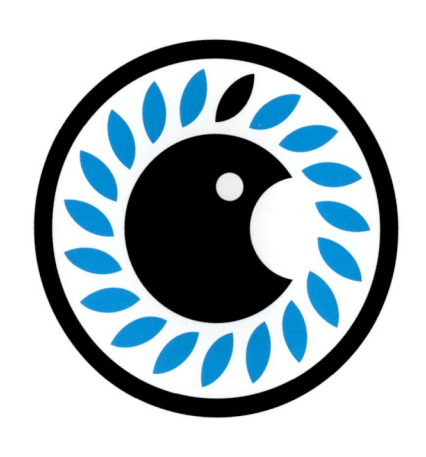

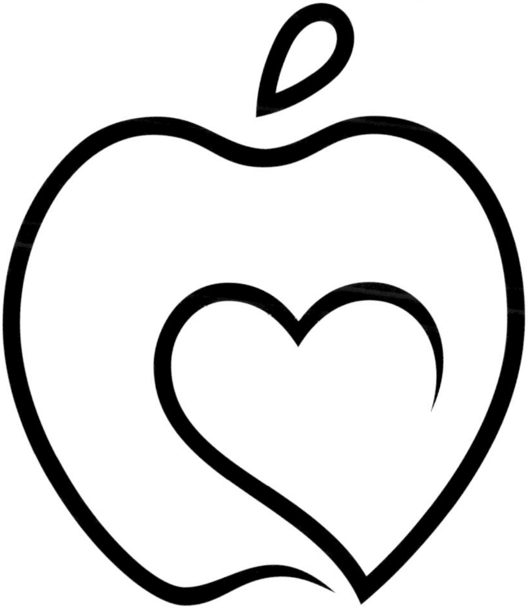

Davide Giulio Aquini (ITA) www.ad-g.it

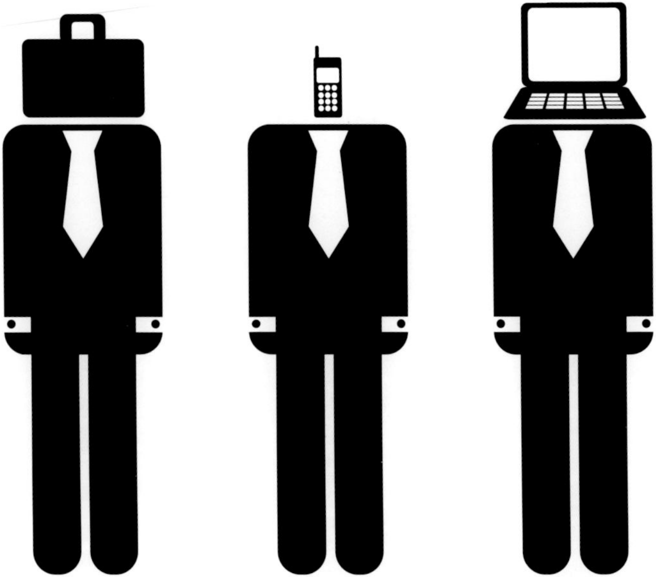

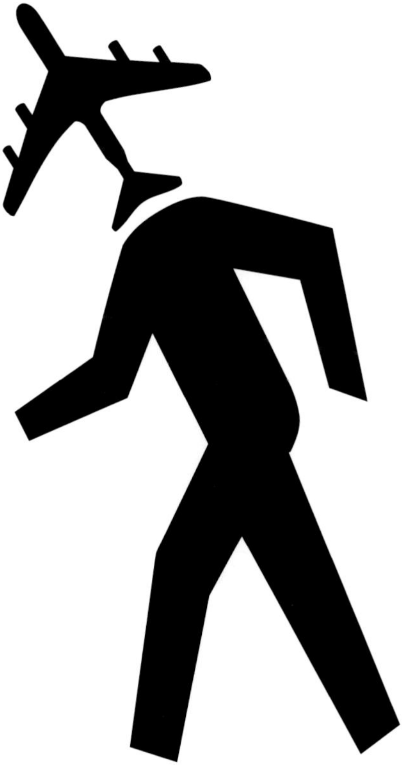

www.natindesign.com

Andre Weier [GER]

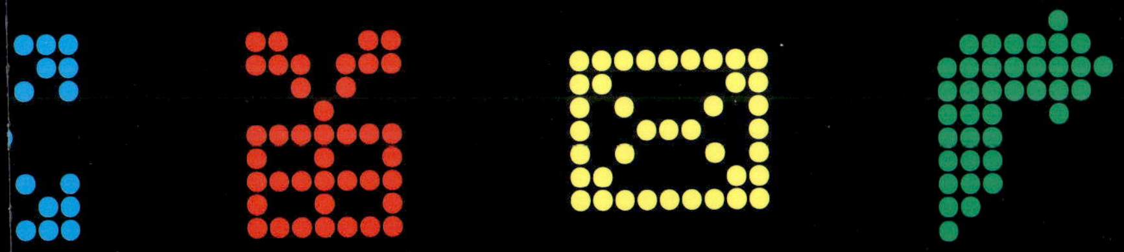

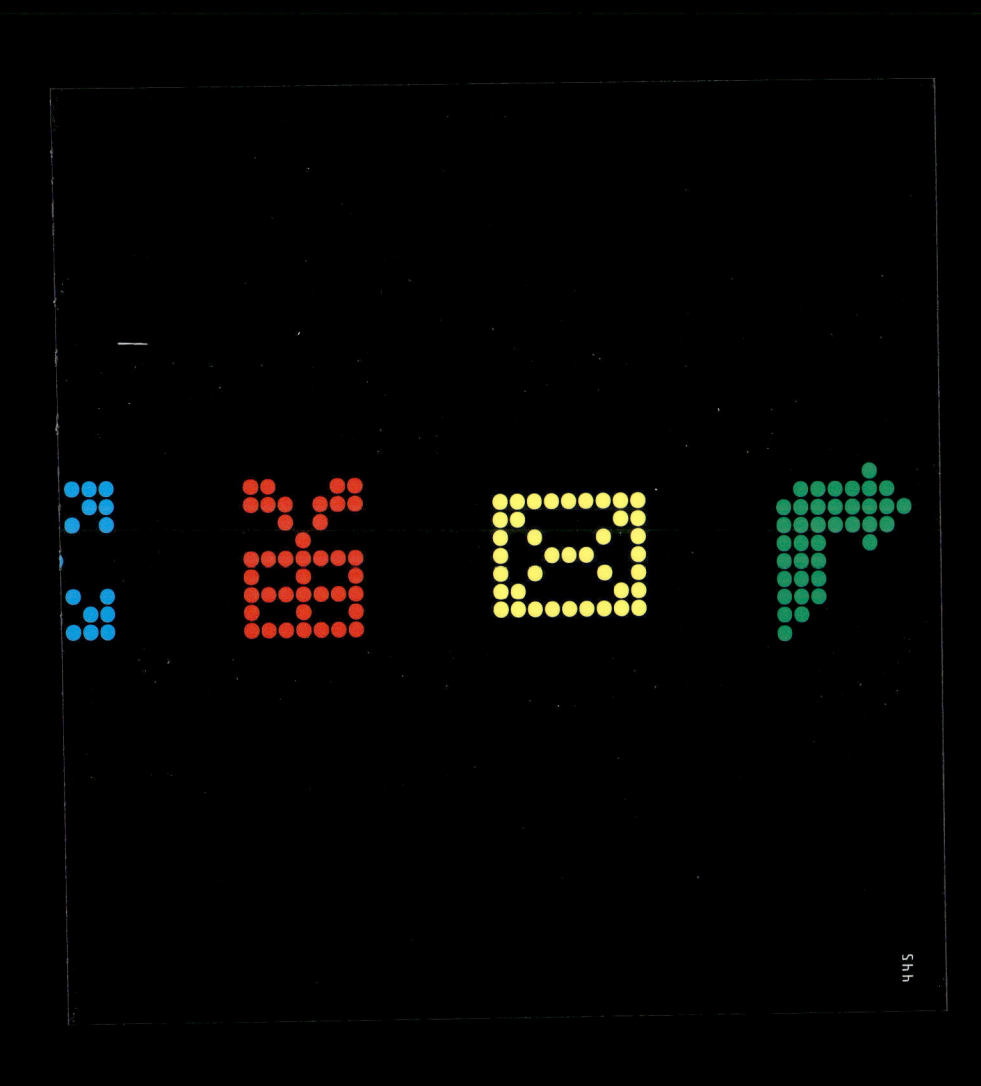

Andre Weier (GER) www.nalindesign.com

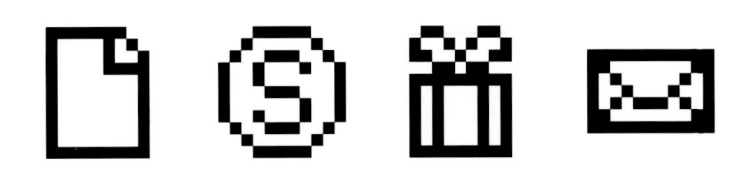

446

Andreas Eck (GER) www.apfelgernhaber.de

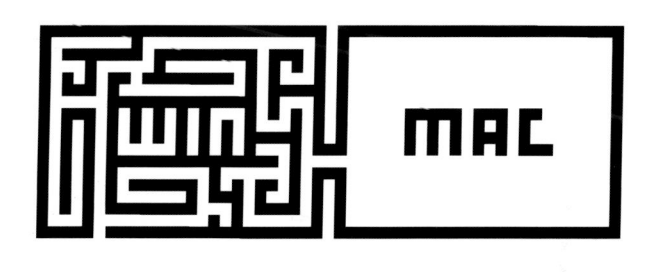

Davide Giulio Aquini [ITA] www.ad-g.it

448

Andrea Mühlbauer [GER] www.purpleblackdesign.com

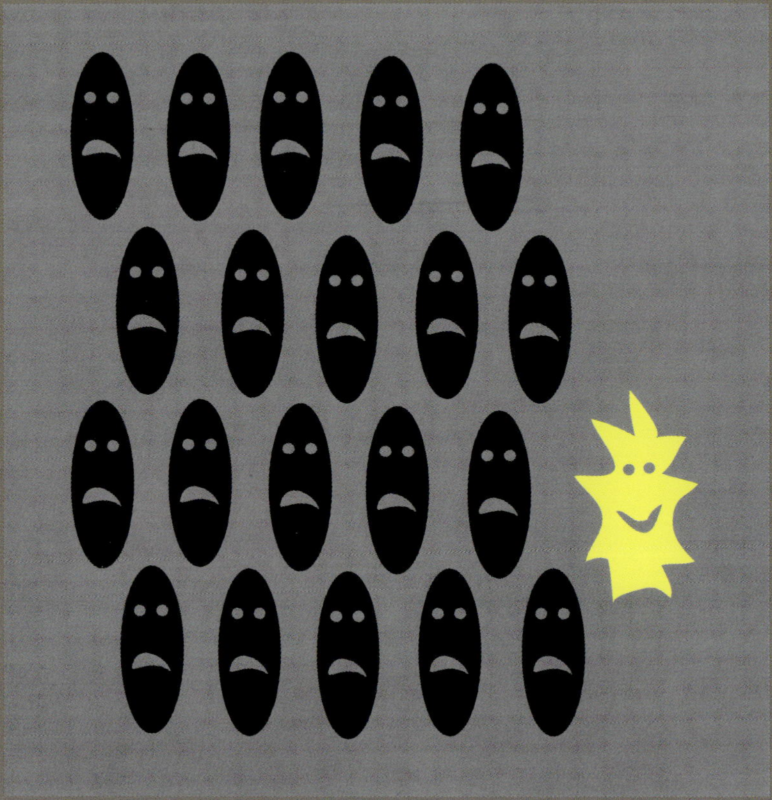

Andrea Mühlbauer (GER) www.purpleblackdesign.com

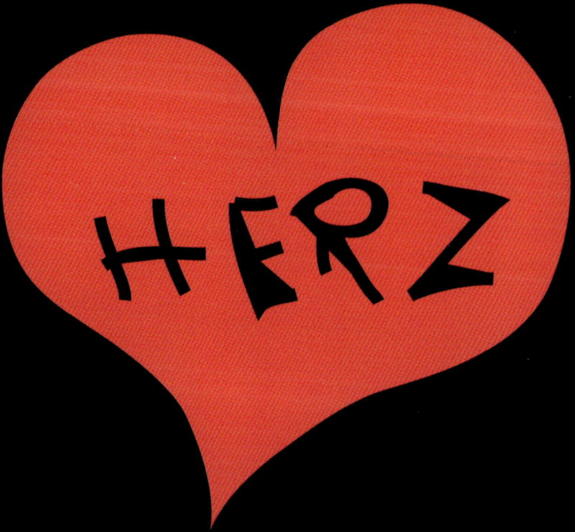
HERZ

Randy Hosang, (CAN)

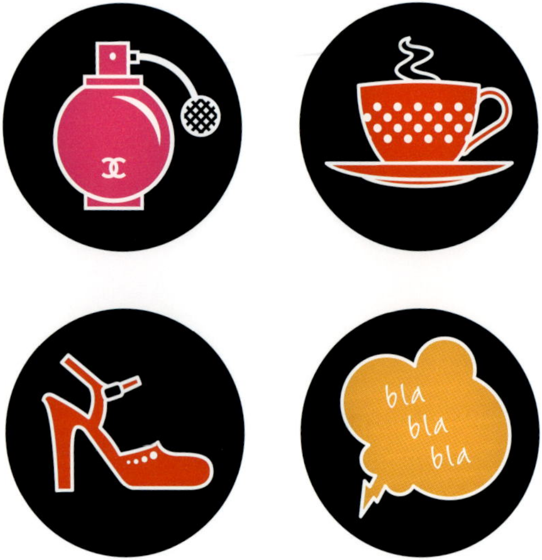
bla
bla
bla

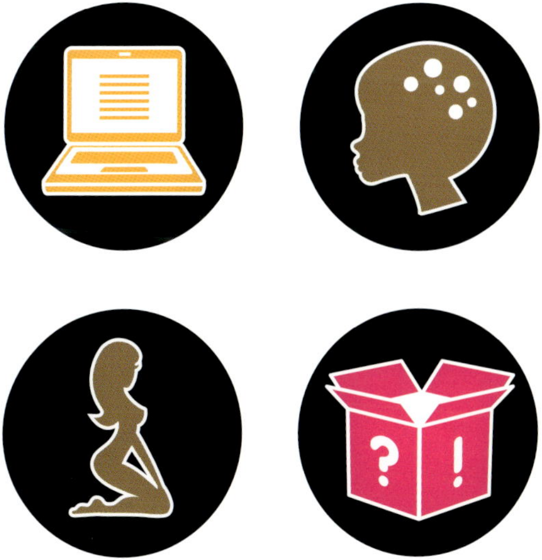

Puk Fenneman [NED] www.coolpuk.com

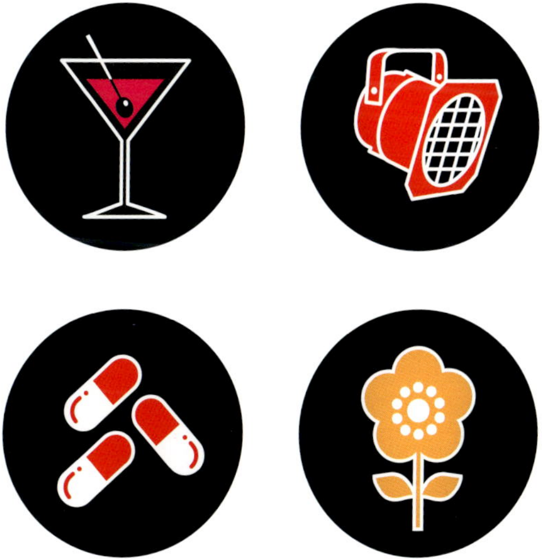

Bernd Wiesenauer [GER] www.uid.com

458

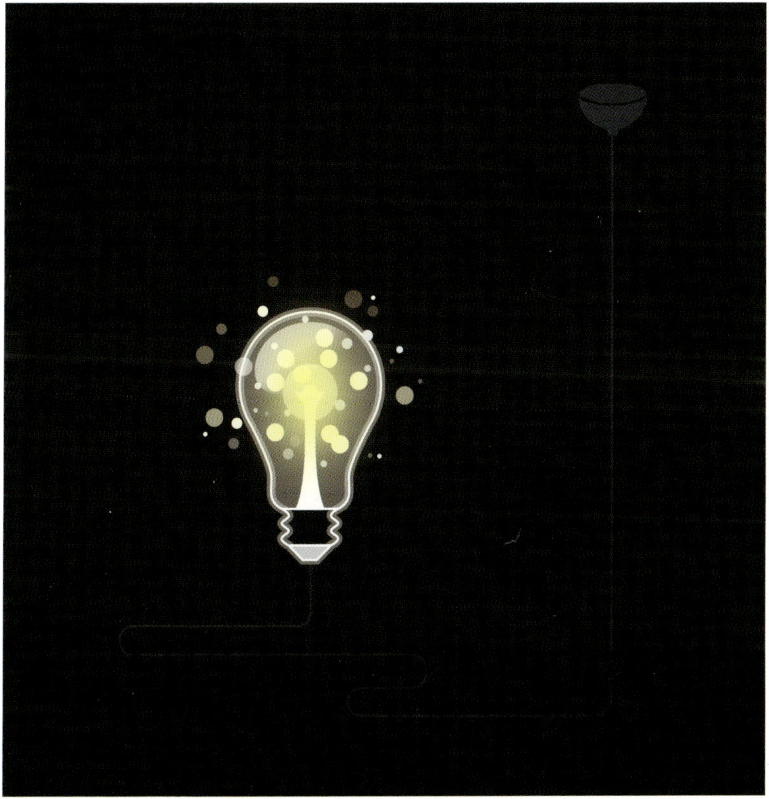

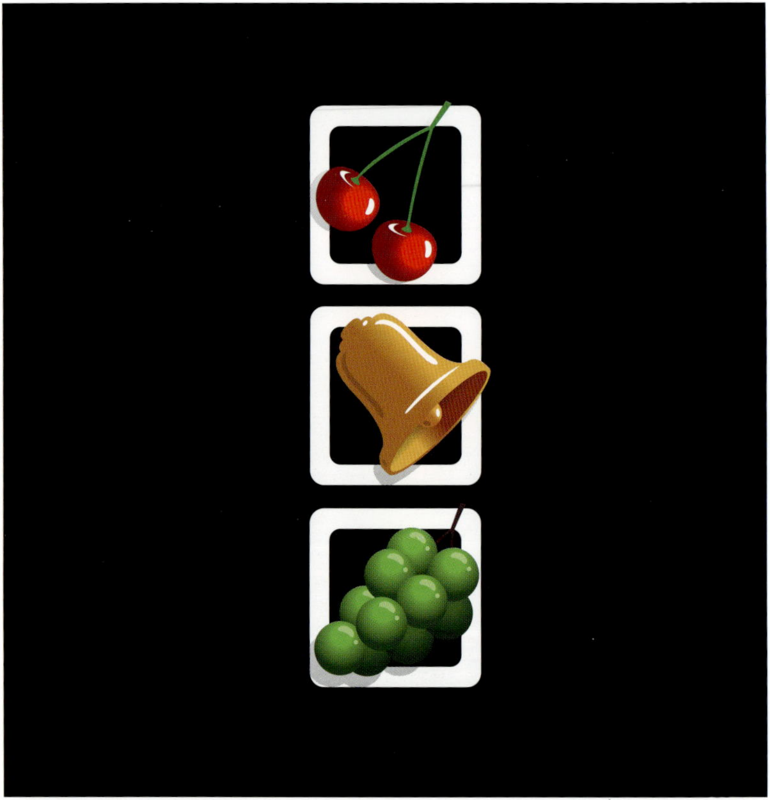

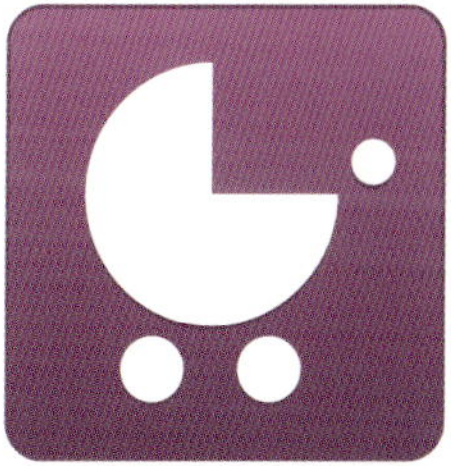

Bo Virkelyst Jensen [DEN] www.addsoul.com

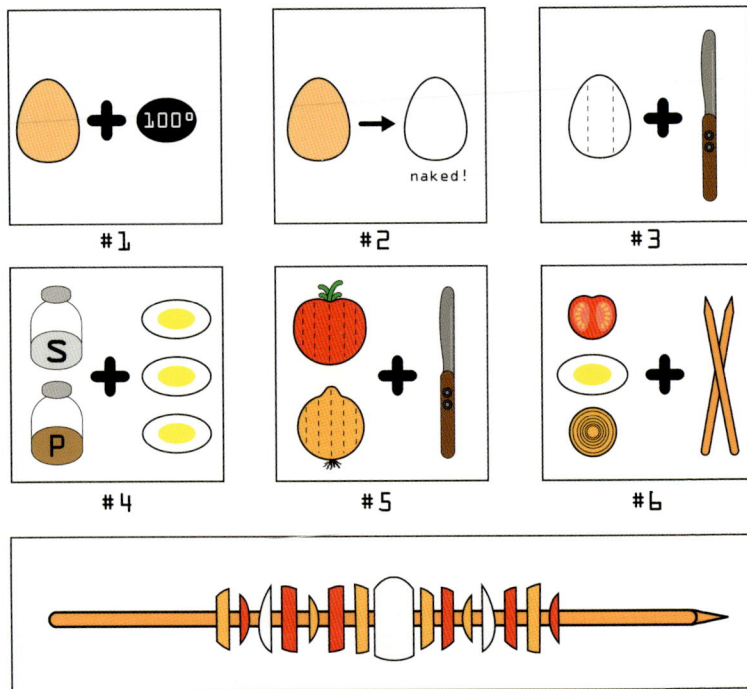

EI AM STIEL

ORTOVOX

Marcel Weik [GER] www.mwkd.de

Linosso   [GER]   www.linosso.com   464

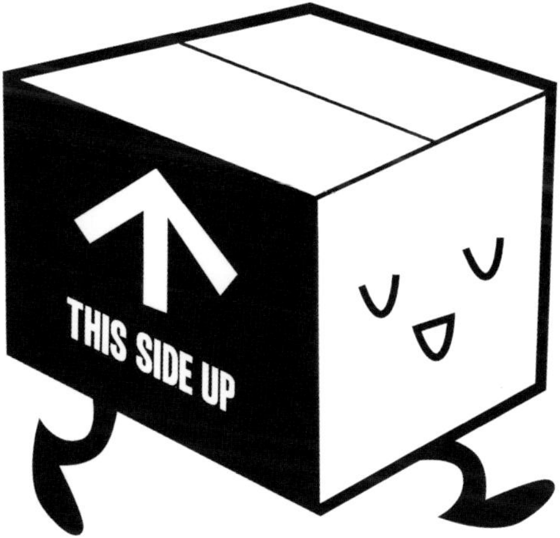

Alejandro Ovalles (VEN) www.jaoc.net

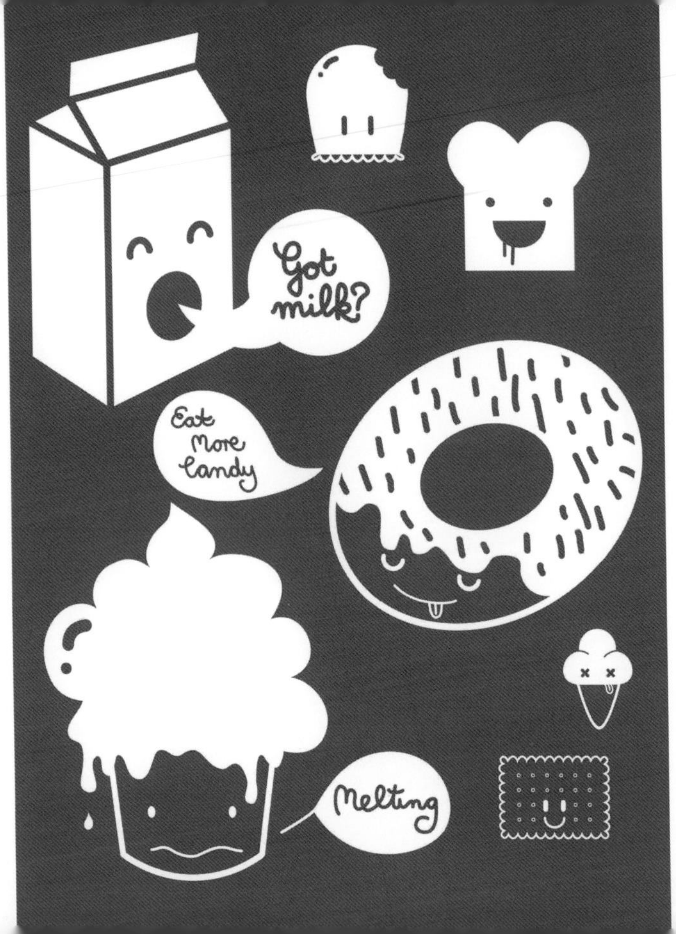

Sandra Hofacker (SUI) www.apfel-z.de

nature

سِرْنَهْ

Vasilis Magoulas [GRE] www.vamadesign.com

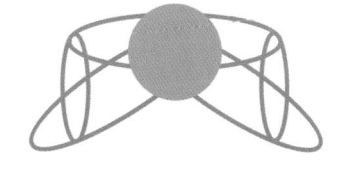

471

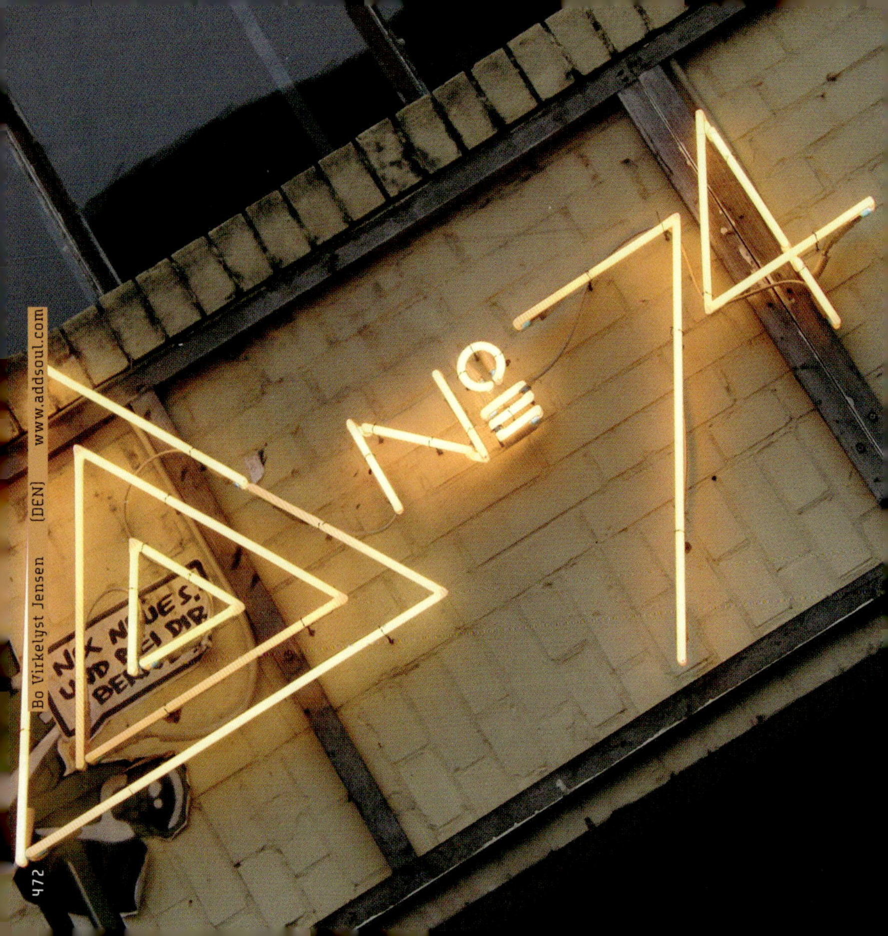

Bo Virkelyst Jensen [DEN] www.addsoul.com

2,800

飛騨の旅

VIA
DE'GUICCIARDINI

MAD

Ann Katrin Siedenburg   (GER)   www.katigraphie.de

手水のつかいかた

◎柄杓に口をつけないこと。

④柄杓をたてて、柄に水を流し、柄杓を伏せて元の位置に戻す。

③左手に水を受け、口をすすぐもう一度左手を、清める。

②右手を清める。

①左手を清める。

歩きたばこは、やめよう
Please do not smoke while walking

ポイ捨て防止条例制定区
台東区

HAND CAR WASH

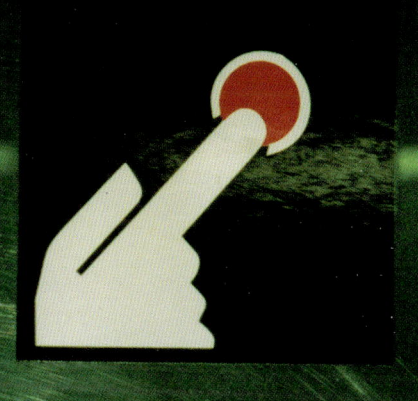

Ann Katrin Siedenburg   (GER)   www.katigraphie.de

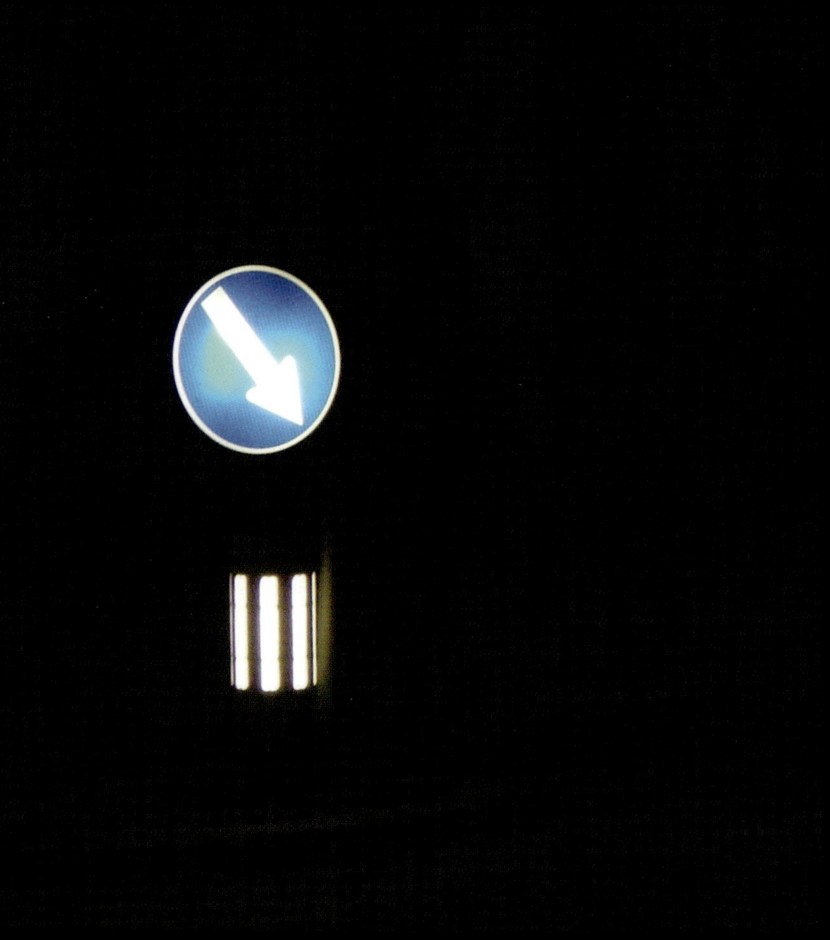

Daniel Bretzmann (GER) www.eyegix.com

181

www.magmabranddesign.de

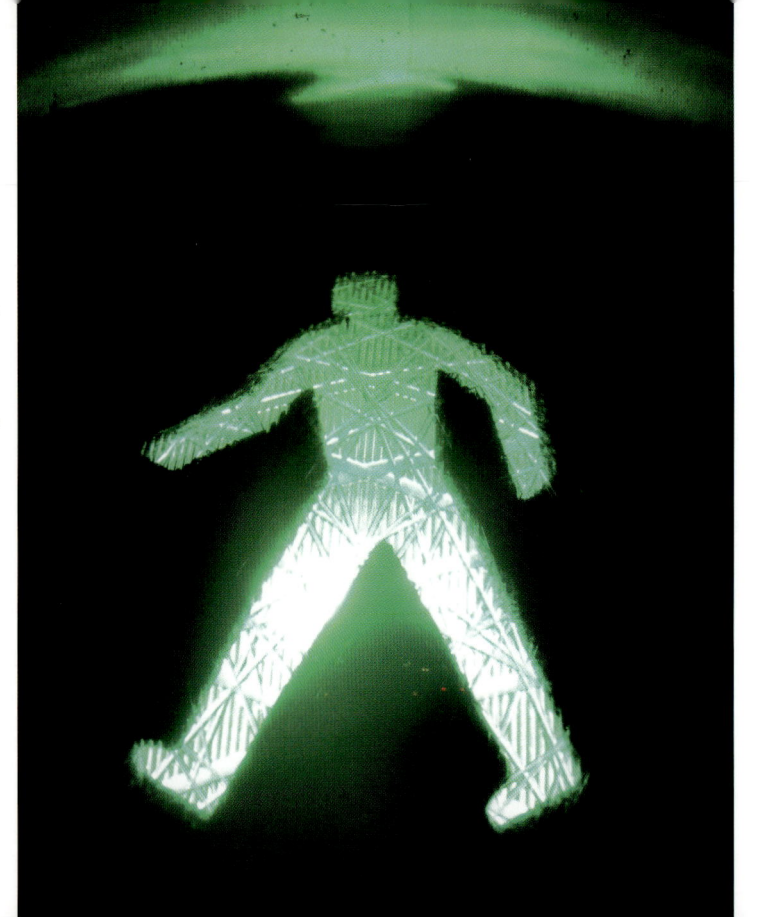

Lars Harmsen [GER]

482

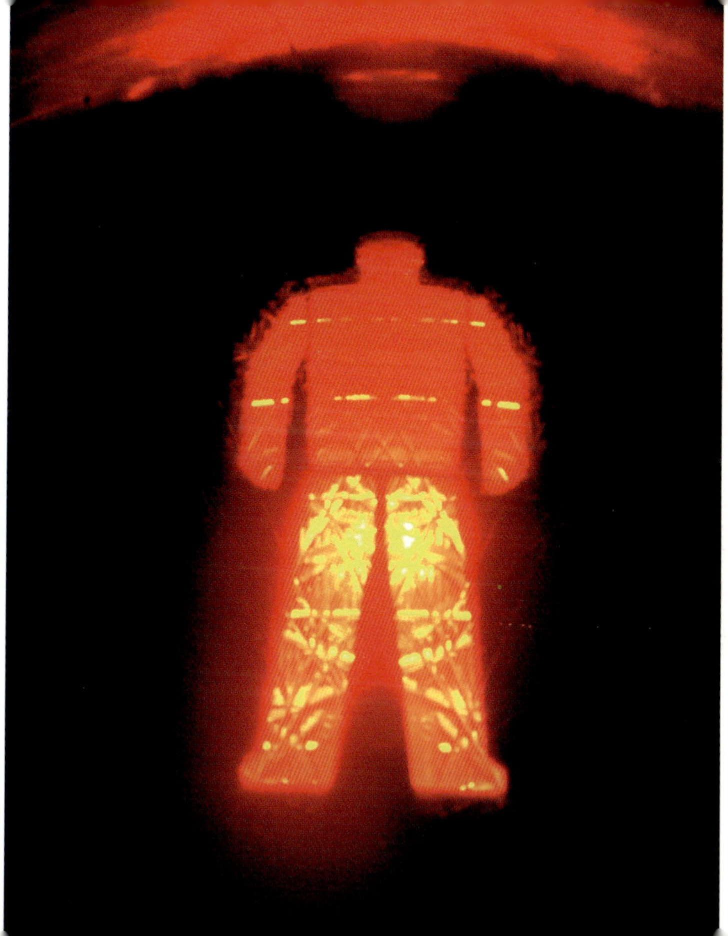

Lars Harmsen   [GER]   www.magmabranddesign.de

484

terrain
de sport

Kätlin Kaljuvee (EST)

486

487

Peter Wölfel [GER]

STOP
Sachsenhausen
DER SICHERHEIT WEGEN!
DER SICHERHEIT WEGEN!
PRIJAVITE ORUŽJE
DECLARE WEAPONS
moking
ea
besam
besam

Eduard Cehovin & Tanja Devetak   (SLO)   www.cehovin.com

Anna Morena [GER] www.annamorena.de

Transportation

Quality of Life

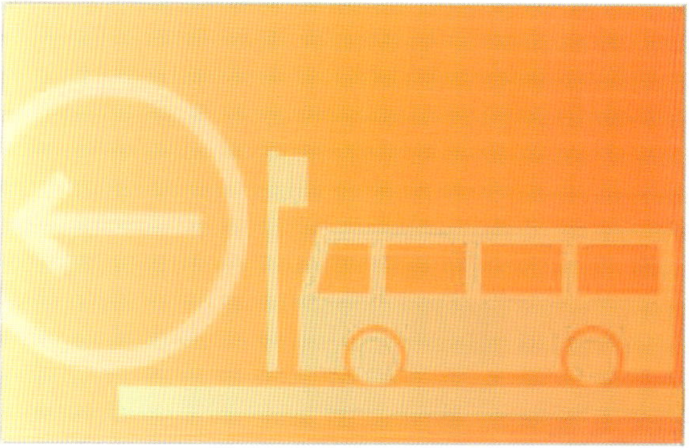

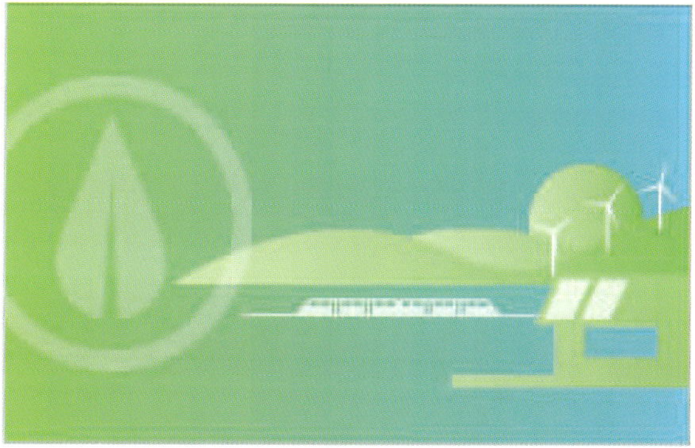

Water

Water is a study for the University of Davis, it is in the most evident as seen as [illegible] in the world. The fact that certain [illegible] the amount of [illegible] in the establishment of modern [illegible] passage and [illegible] in all fields of water technology.

World's Leading Exporter

Over two thirds of Israel's water is exported. Moreover, the country plans to make near no.

Major Fresh water

Lake of several and water is also highest in Israel, which has famously [illegible] and fish technology [illegible] the Dead Sea Scrolls.

Novel Advanced Irrigation

The drip irrigation method is developed by Israel. Its technical grade line was being practiced under throughout the developing and industrialized world.

The fact that Israel is already a major exporter of water technology can contribute to Israel's growth as a hub in its demonstration to the past is that Israel already paid of the way to a great pace that it can cover and through the current vision of the early development of Israel land.

Land

Israel's population density is in the same range as India but Japan's among the densest on the planet, and is expected to [illegible] the world's heavily populated territory by 2030. That said, however, some 75% of Israel land is open space or "Park".

Free the Architects

Israel has undergone a decade to be a water conservative architecture and urban planning, which architects and act on a high level of [illegible] and urban regulation requirements and [illegible] planning within the confines of a small footprint on your footprint Israel is should be created to all but the past [illegible] of landscape in Israel lost.

Rebuild/or Waste

Any development's sale is the option for "recycling" waste, instead of beginning to develop on a brownfield and construction and routes treatment. There effort should be considered and intensified.

Develop Smartly

For most Israelis a strong connection to the land, its geography and its nature identified in an early age and not be reinforced in the military. Experienced consumers of the land public to them of open spaces out, actual and not be just content all but can help ensure that Israel can continue to develop its economic and economic side. Any [illegible] a operation while maintaining the integrity of the [illegible] enjoy. Smart and sustainable development is the key for the future of the land.

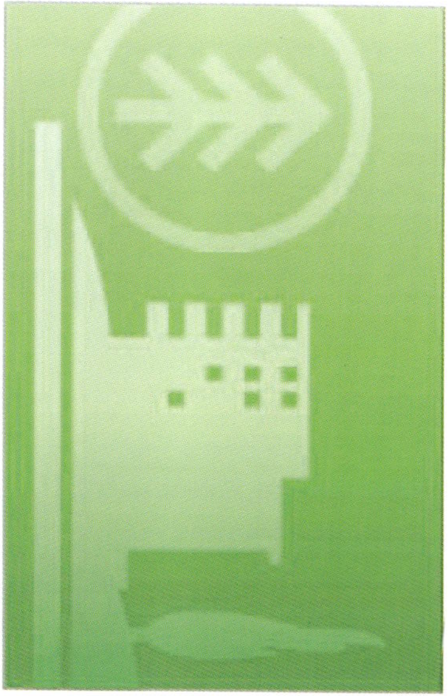

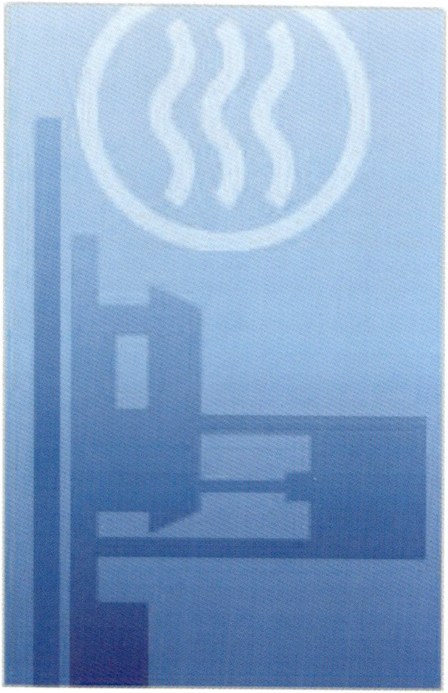

Background

Our Mandate

Following a series of meetings with the Panel and in April of 2014, Brown has articulated a conceptual framework together with talking points that our presenter to the President and below and the title "Clean Energy" in June. The core content of the framework is we feel a much sound cautionary element for environment using the hybrid tag tag of the text of the "green mark" that would be most been the tasks to be set to be security, cleanness, courage, but to maintain a vivid sense of its appeal, and a connection to Hamilton 2 winter vision. Subsequently the Panel set requested that Brown prepare a plan of introduction, which the Senate of the President's activity to act, in order to implement the program if we are.

Step a has given several months expanding to say out the United States including commence worth one fifth project we environments, economic policy education and other related areas. We are confident not to present the resulting report to the President.

The Vision

Response to the fact that the angles Fast met country 1974. It is the type to promote, transferring our economy to a clean one, energy feeling our area and incentivate transit to become the leader of a Clean Economy by 2025.

Ideal has some small price to build this. We have the world's largest history in the solar business. We have the most economic level of technology and building desalination on the planet. We are here the largest and most clear to experience in shear energy research and explication. These and more on our environment and government have unequalled amount for the people of our country and are committed to building a new a base together of inspiration reaching our prized.

Tomorrow forces have taken on a distinct proper adhesion around project by have formed as wise and with the trait you are correctly anticipating a net five and climatic people on to take an economic value as secondary. These people are inspired to carry us across our research and in the an exciting growth of the Common sector in the broad sense of.

Our research has yielded to our enlightening chapter out inspiring discussion of our country's best practices to a Clean Economy. We have present three under the headings Energy, Water, Land and Transportation, also future back to Quality of Life.

Energy

Since it has been global forecast 1974 has, it almost government realize that world bids and have to push over to this course foot in stand to exist and channel bridges. But last count on of international activity in this program. Forest based is an expert as a critical base specific classes in which exist can take action.

How Energy Technologies

Invest in an energy based, relying on imported coal and oil for most of it energy needs with it base for example of sense exits an existing of secondly source, would head to increase energy independence, and has to kind of other relatives, exist has a heart, we can grant that use. It is united one on fewer back and the ideal build up not only for research and development, but also for the heart line present use of the existing more factors and. While on a global scale international to no more action cases not cannot be of use, ideal technology since at alleviating of our means of energy we are more environmental and make me of heavier state making latest more proper and bridges make while are off of existing technologies.

Investment in Conservation

First, this is a concept that can applies to beings on it having it is which we can conserve in any other various short that apply energy consumption leaks sharper the times's is at an order additional significant cut aside in some innovation is required.

Existing energy efficiency solutions, if implemented on a wide scale can arise head up to 30% of its energy consumption, which can be the practice, and without any considerable production or growth. Energy efficiency conditioned based have be arrives to incentivise more reliable set of existing seas on sense impress net only temsis' Quality Of Life, but feel the needle of large overall.

Identification and Nurturing a Class Energy Business

Used forecast we act the form feeling year and the solar tech component. We Nation, which should become the greatest name on third a Lassative, biologist and garthemal center of research and present for should use contacts offer a sense components and the world to solar forecast and geothermal electricity generation, and least short particular, it what more believes in a Nasking set grand and pay, Questions content feeling for energy projects most coaches to be sequestered at Heba, in order to feed head heart's decision technology in the face. The Qualification of such center certainly to arrives at the entire project.

Background

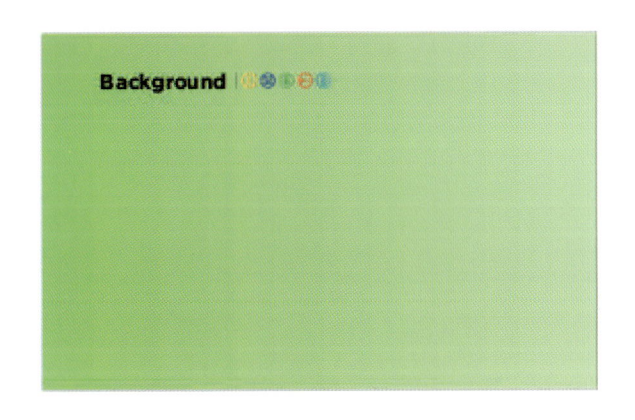

Marcus Wolf   Kocht!

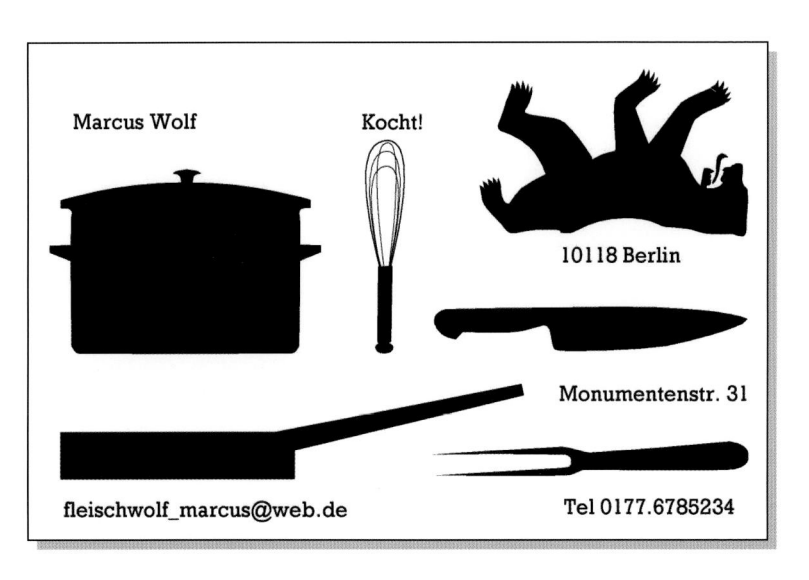

10118 Berlin

Monumentenstr. 31

fleischwolf_marcus@web.de   Tel 0177.6785234

Sandra Mahn   [GER]   www.zweinullsieben.com

[BN Km ZERO]
per un' ecovicinanza* a persone e a merci

Aurora Lobina [ITA] www.aurorise.com

Institut für Geographie Gießen

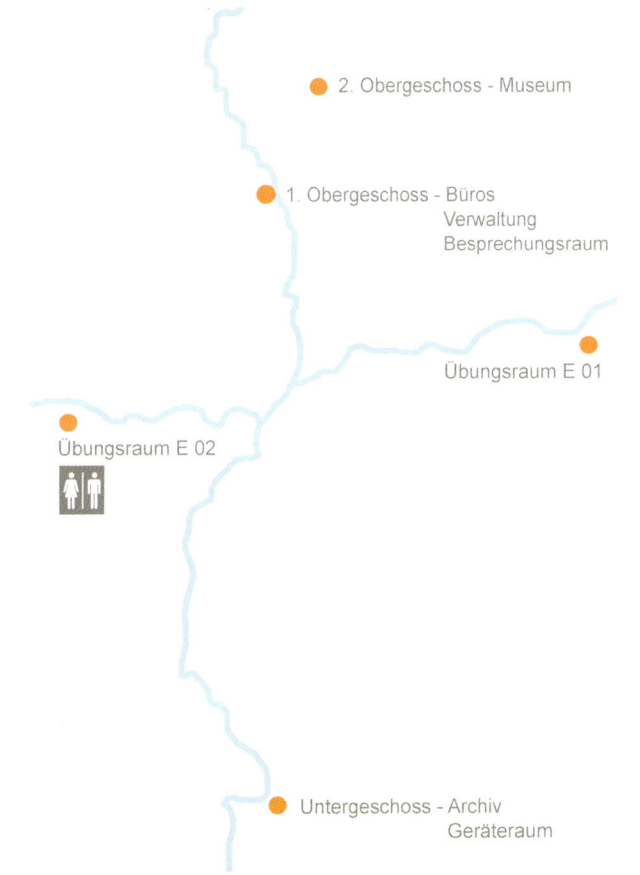

- 2. Obergeschoss - Museum
- 1. Obergeschoss - Büros
  Verwaltung
  Besprechungsraum
- Übungsraum E 01
- Übungsraum E 02
- Untergeschoss - Archiv
  Geräteraum

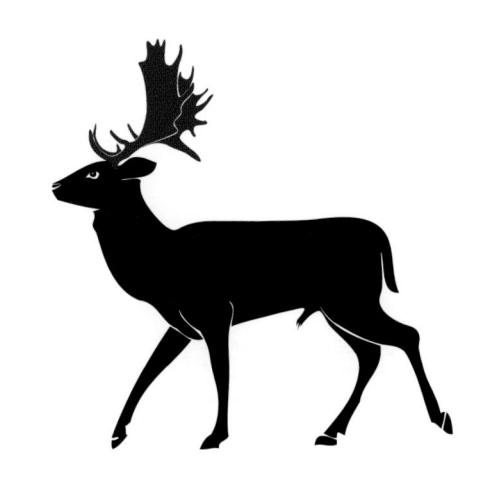

Anna Morena [GER] www.annamorena.de

502

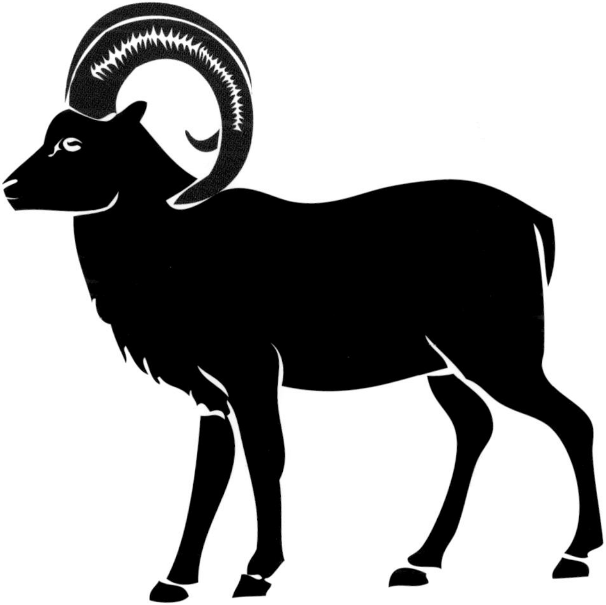

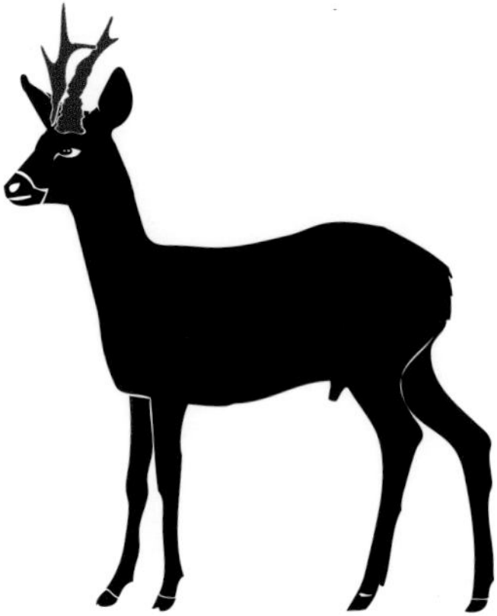

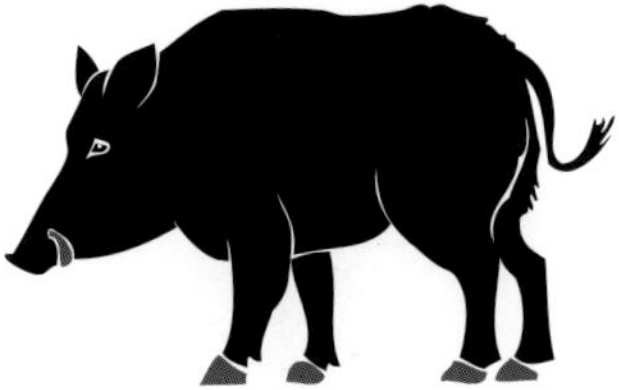

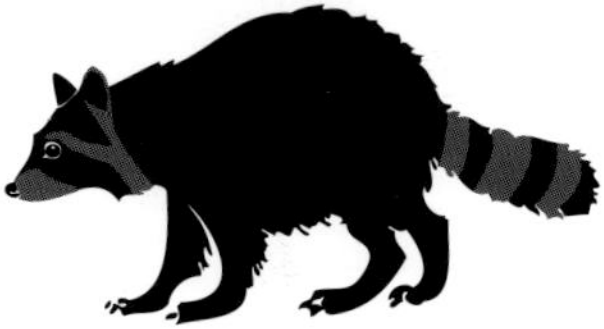

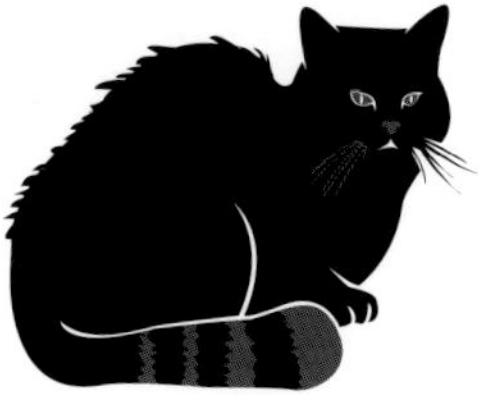

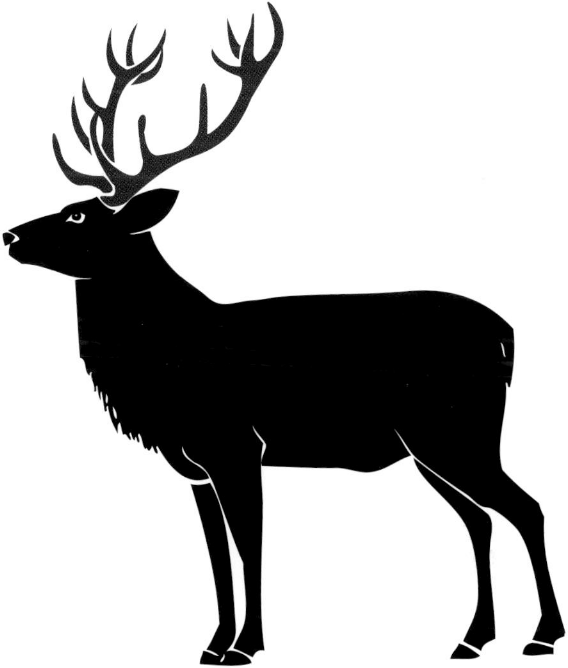

Anna Morena [GER] www.annamorena.de

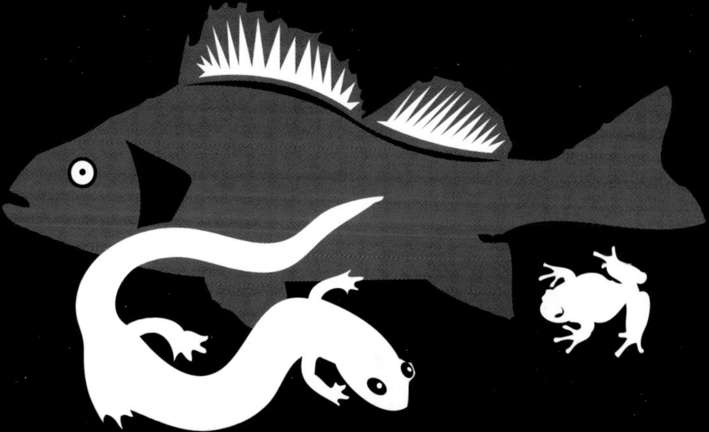

Anna Morena (GER) www.annamorena.de

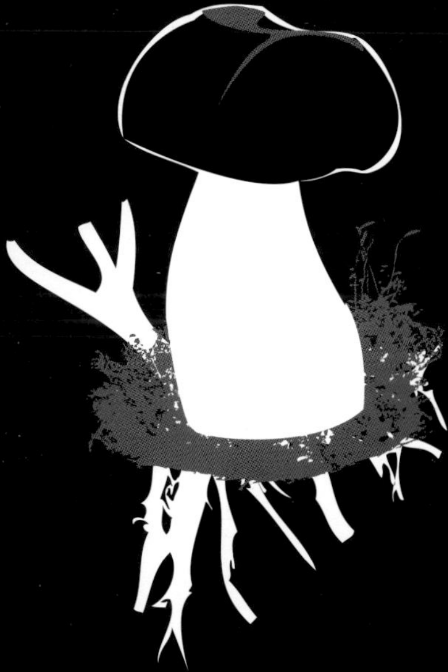

Orangen-Geschmack

Pfefferminz-Geschmack

Johannisbeer-Geschmack

Pfirsich-Geschmack

- Aprikosen-Geschmack
- Zitronen-Geschmack
- Himbeer-Geschmack
- Karamell-Geschmack
- Erdbeer-Geschmack
- Bananen-Geschmack

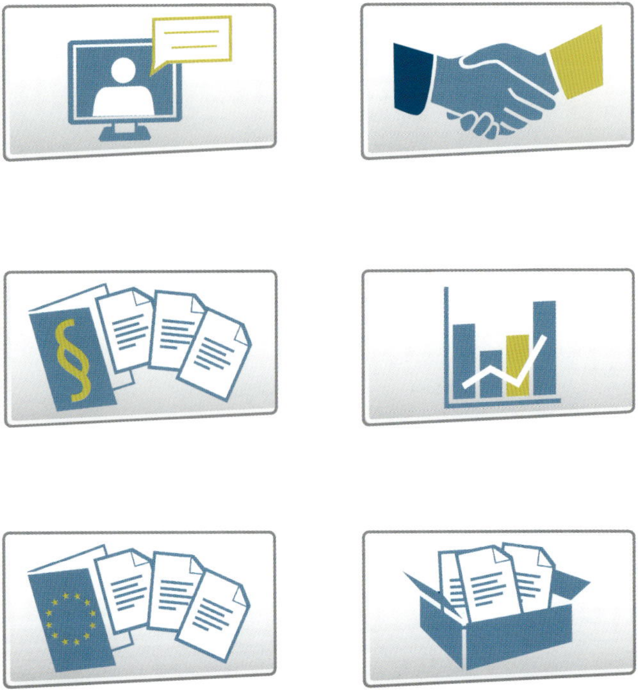

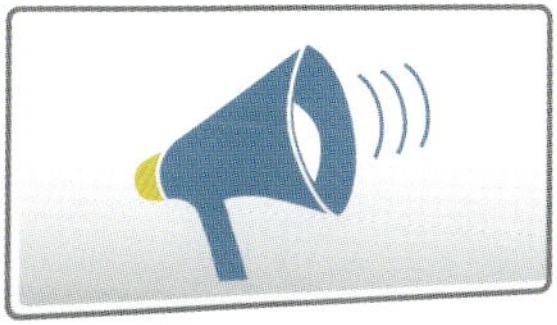

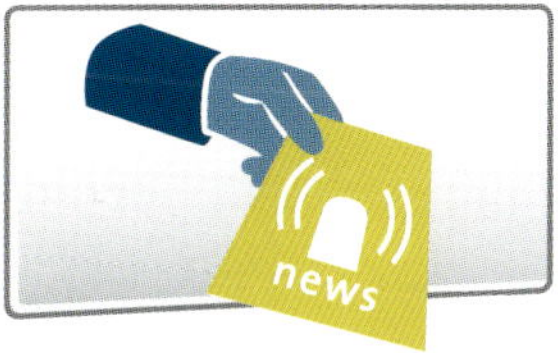
news

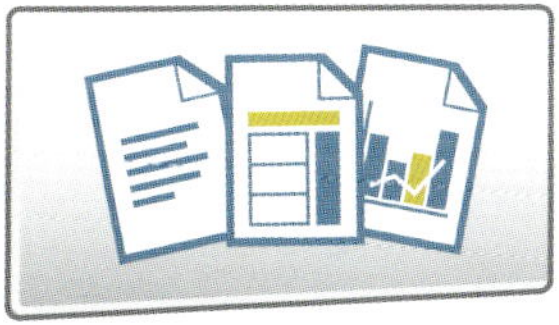

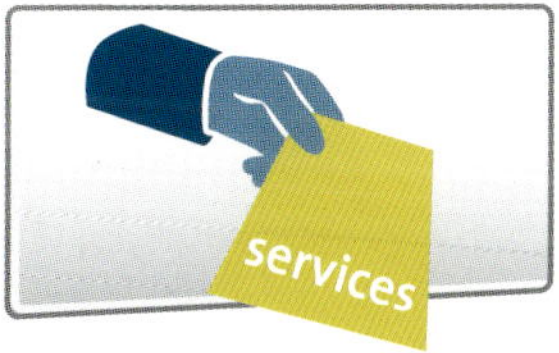
services

Klaus Pelzer   (GER)   www.b7UE.com

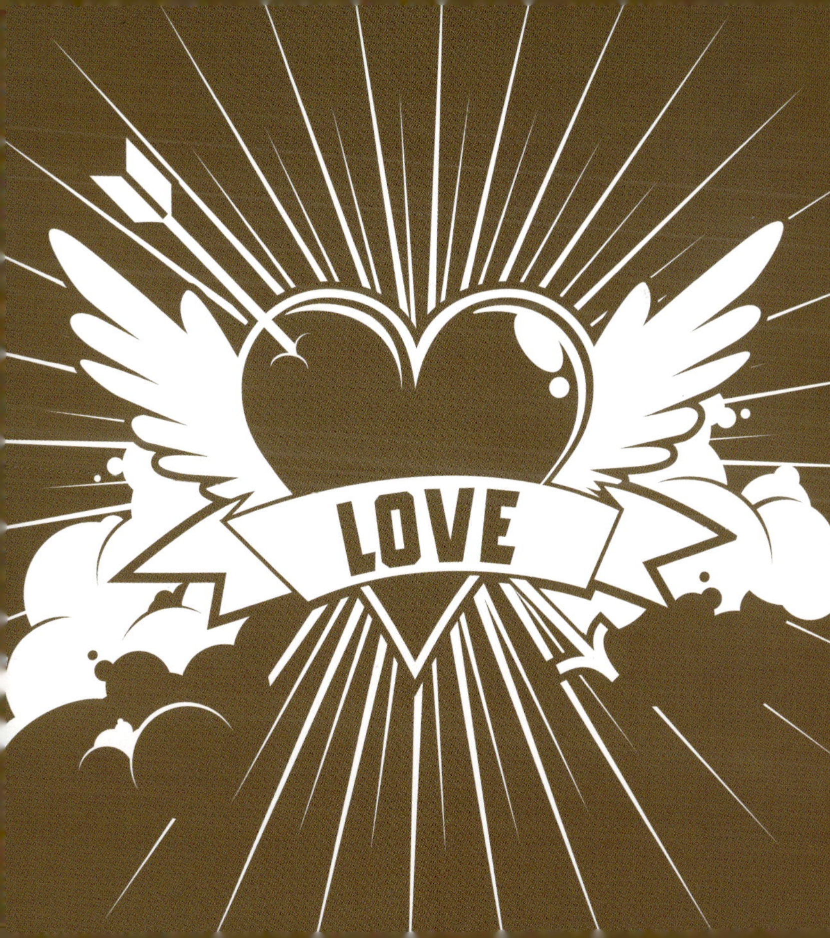

Linus von Moos (GER) www.rips1.ch

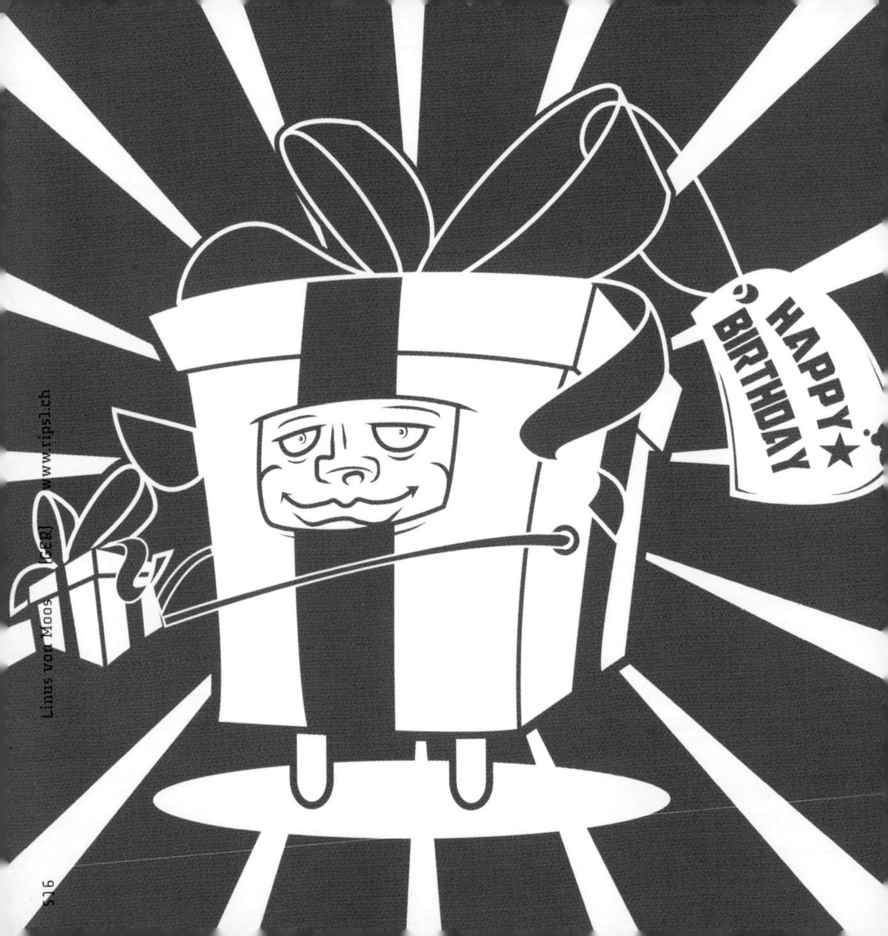

Linus von Moos (GER) www.ripsl.ch

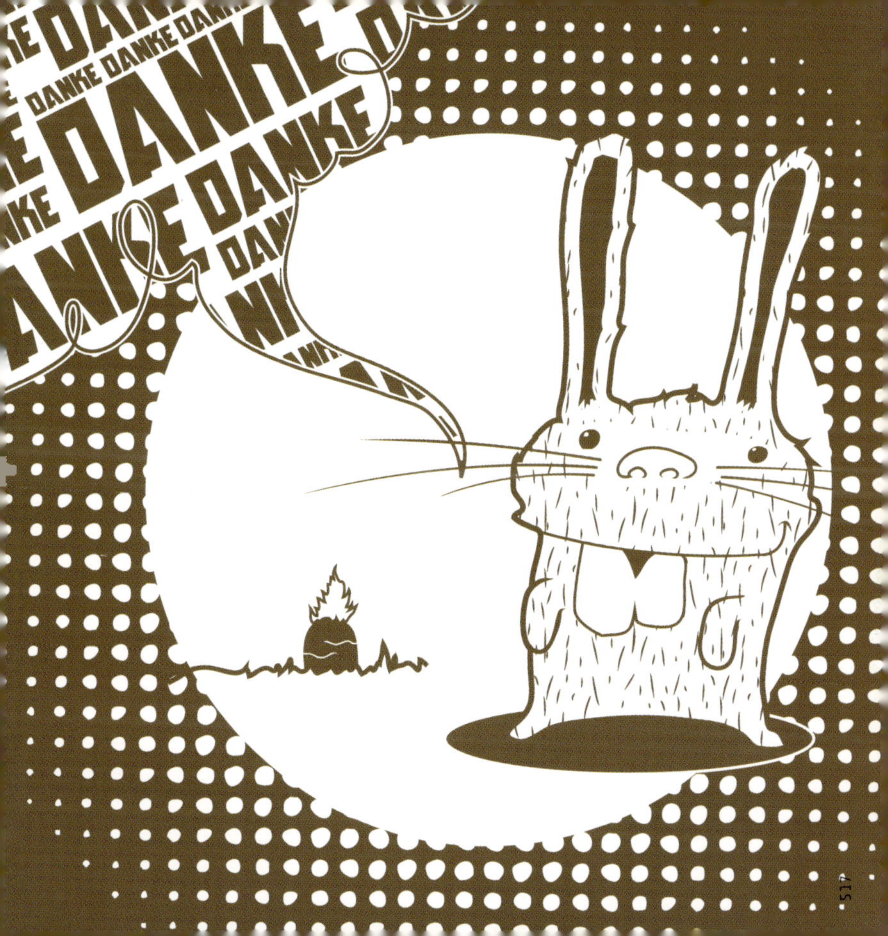
DANKE DANKE
DANKE
DANKE

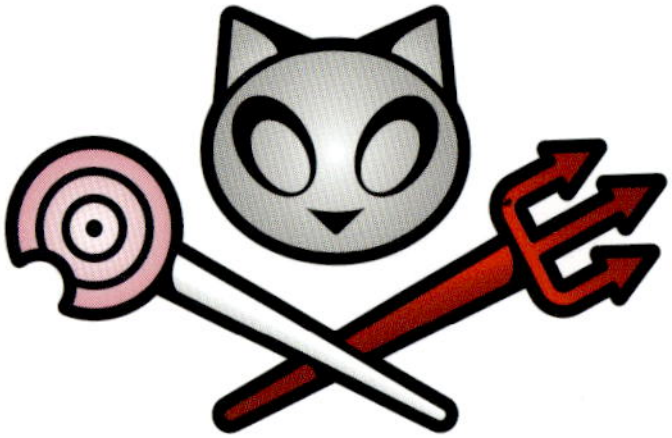

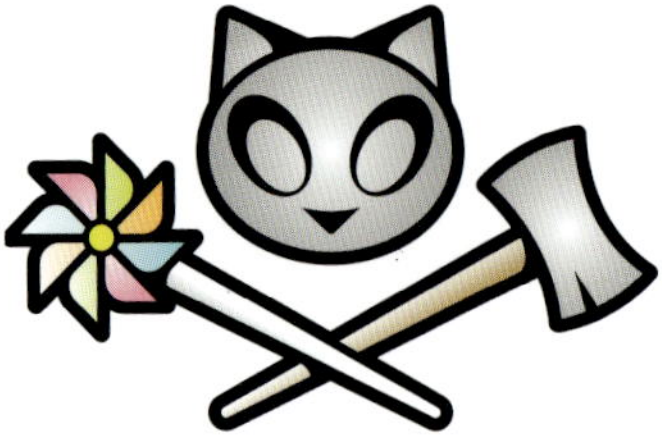

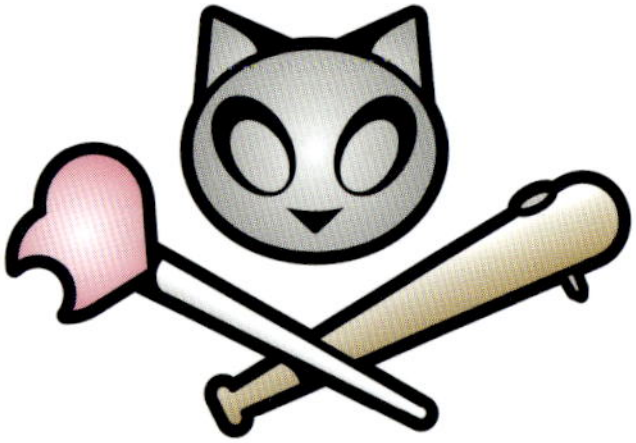

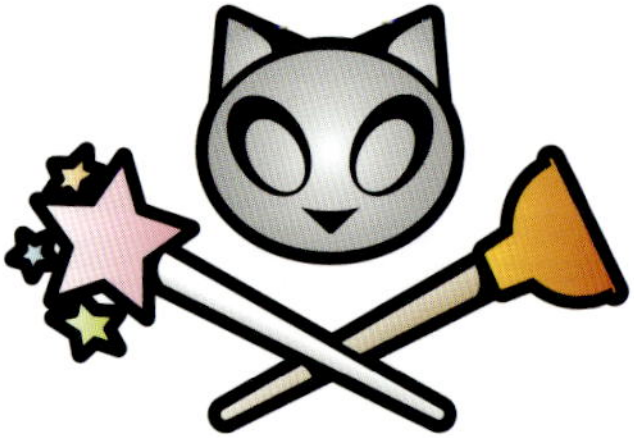

I'm
not
a
groupie::

I'm
not
a
groupie::

Peter Wölfel (GER)

520

Peter Wölfel (GER)

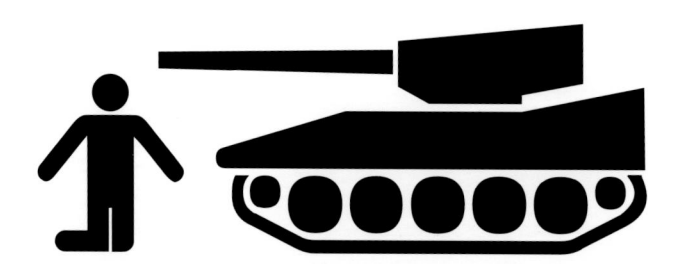

522

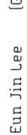

1 Look outside world / 2 Look inside world(=home) / 3 The groom / 4 The bride

ANSICHT OST M 1_200

Kristina Markovic (GER) www.kristinamarkovic.com

Tono
BUNGAY

a novel by
H.G. Wells

George Ponderevo, a student of science, is enlisted to help with the promotion of Tono Bungay. Tono Bungay is a harmful stimulant disguised as a miraculous cure-all, the creation of his ambitious uncle Edward. As the tonic prospers, George experiences a swift rise in social status, elevating him to riches and opportunities that he had never imagined, nor indeed desired. Meanwhile, George ricochets romantically between his unsuccessful marriage to Marion, his affair with the liberated Effie and his doomed relationship with the Hon. Beatrice Normandy, a childhood friend. But the Tono Bungay empire eventually over-extends itself and George must try to prop up his uncle's finances by stealing the radioactive compound 'quap' from an island near Africa.

Books in the series:
The History of Mr Polly
Kipps
Ann Veronica
Tono Bungay
Love and Mr Lewisham

Part of a brand new series of books by H.G. Wells, this edition comes with a specially commissioned introduction by XYZ.

---

his aunt and
ers to a draper,
on reading a
the grandson of
er of his fortune.
classes, he
quette and rules
overs, becoming
y nor as desirable

Part of a brand new series of books by H.G. Wells, this edition comes with a specially commissioned introduction by XYZ.

Books in the series:
The History of Mr Polly

Love and Mr Lewisham

---

is read
you the review
with the
tracting his
buring his
r his unexpected
ncle's life
of heroism

Part of a brand new series of books by H.G. Wells, this edition comes with a specially commissioned introduction by XYZ.

Tono
BUNGAY

a novel by
H.G. Wells

KIPPS:
The Story of a Simple Soul

a novel by
H.G. Wells

The History of
MR POLLY

a novel by
H.G. Wells

don tango

Claudia Müller [GER] www.studio-kniften.de

17x17

32x32

Claudia Müller [GER] www.studio-kniften.de

532

S 33

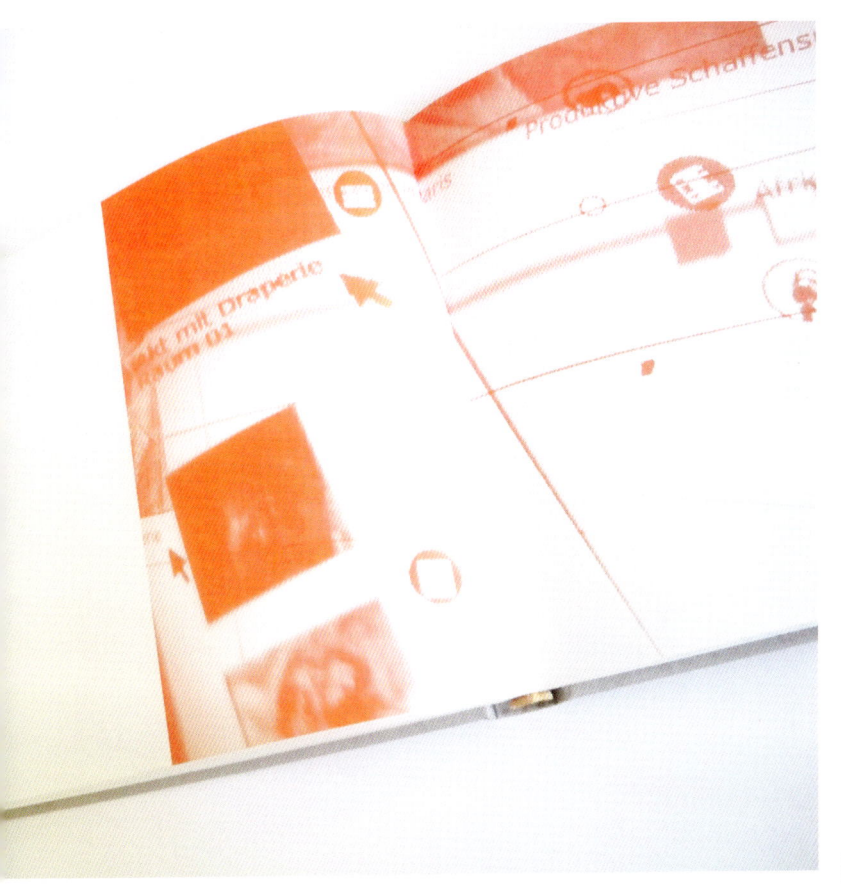

LKW und Gabelstapler beim Beladen

Lagerhalle

Logistik

Michael Hartmann [GER] www.finalart.de

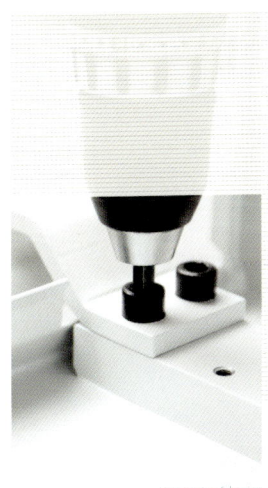

Montage eines Scharniers

Montage

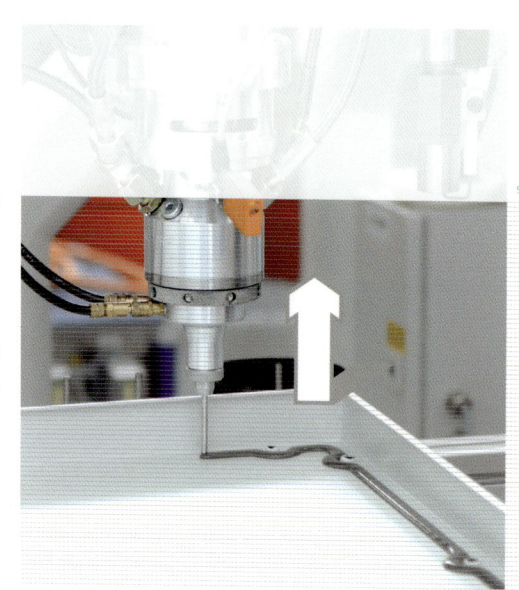

Schaumdichtungsroboter im Prozess

Schaumdichtung

Michael Hartmann (GER) www.finalart.de

536

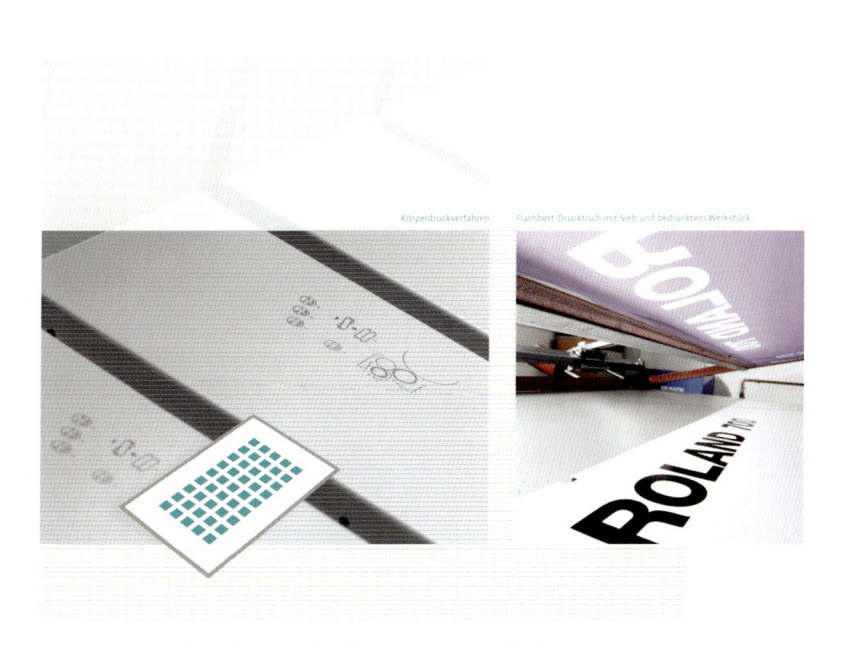

Körperdruckverfahren Flachbett-Drucktisch mit Sieb und bedrucktem Werkstück

Siebdruck | Digitaldruck

Nasslackierung

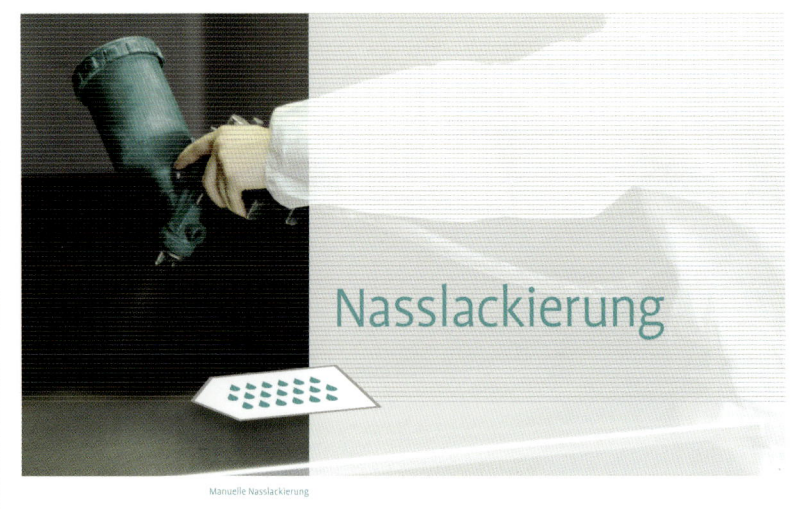

Manuelle Nasslackierung

Michael Hartmann (GER) www.finalart.de

Automatische Pulverlackierung

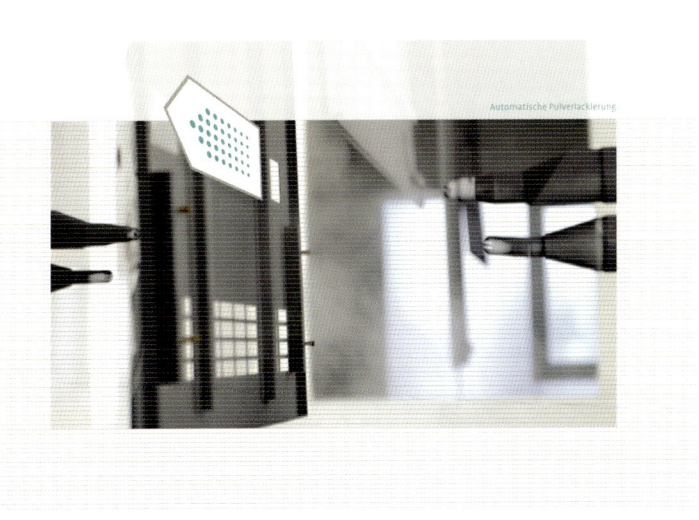

Pulverlackierung

SONNENENERGIE BELEBT

Jede Blume nutzt die saubere, unbegrenzte Energie der Sonne.

Nutzen auch Sie die Sonne in Form von Solarstrom* und Ihr Dach als Sparbuch!

PHOTO SYNTHESE

PHOTO VOLTAIK®

Powersolar
Die Sonnenseite der Energie

Powersolar
Die Sonnenseite der Energie

Powersolar GmbH

Wilhelmstraße 47
63071 Offenbach
Tel 069. 247 52 19-0
Fax 069. 247 52 19-99
info@powersolar.de
www.powersolar.de

Solarstromanlagen

Blockheizkraftwerke

Regenerative Heizsysteme

Energieberatung

Michael Hartmann [GER] www.finalart.de

Sonnenenergie * Gleichstrom

Regenerative Brennstoffe * Kraft-Wärme-Kopplung

Regenerative Energiequellen * Wärme

Anliegen * Beratung

Sebastian Kühnert
Geschäftsführer

Elf Morgen 1 | 64589 Stockstadt
Tel 0 61 58. 99 08-15 | Fax 0 61 58. 99 08-10
s.kuehnert@**kpl-gmbh.de**

Kühnert
Pulverlackierungen

kpl

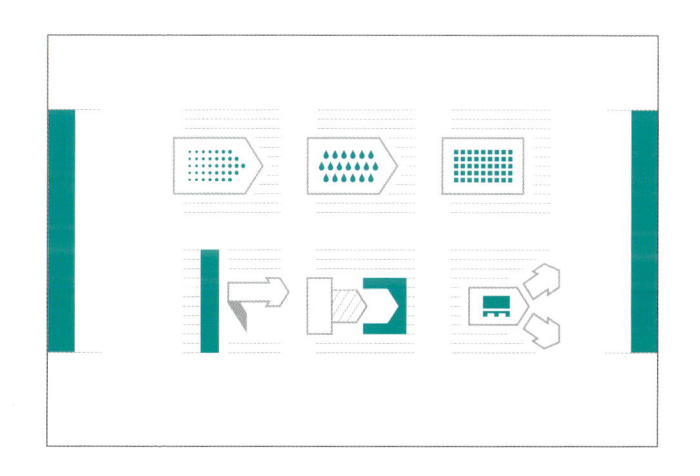

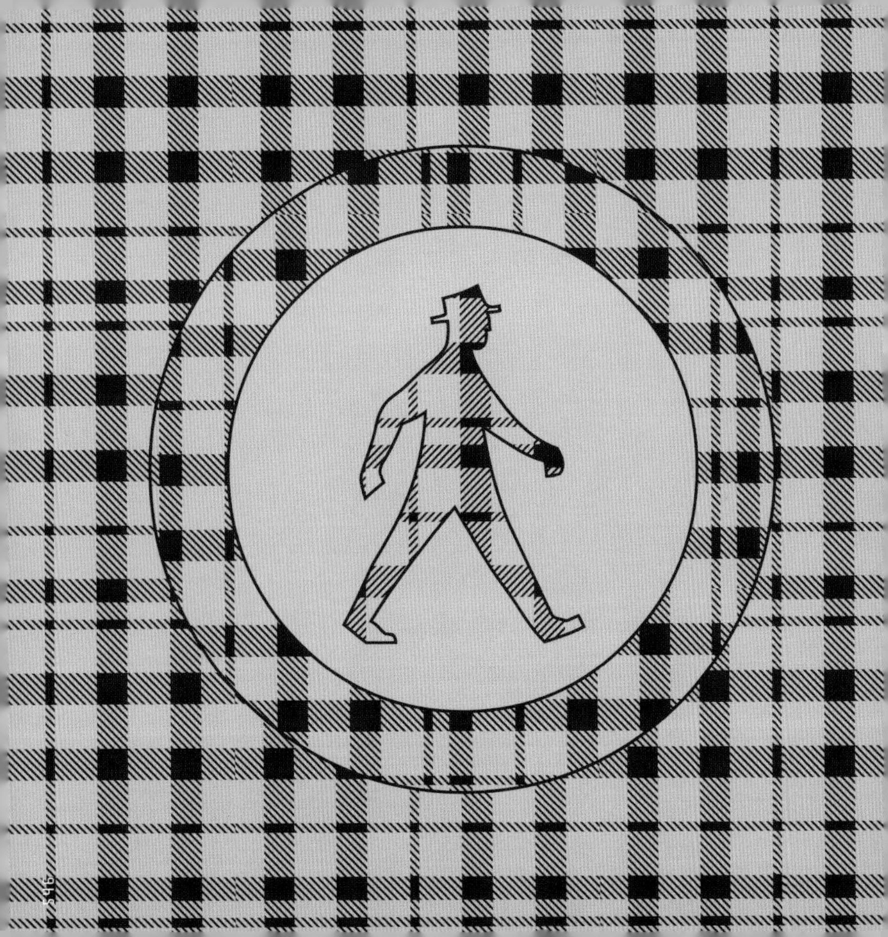

Peter Wölfel (GER)

547

Stadt **Viersen**

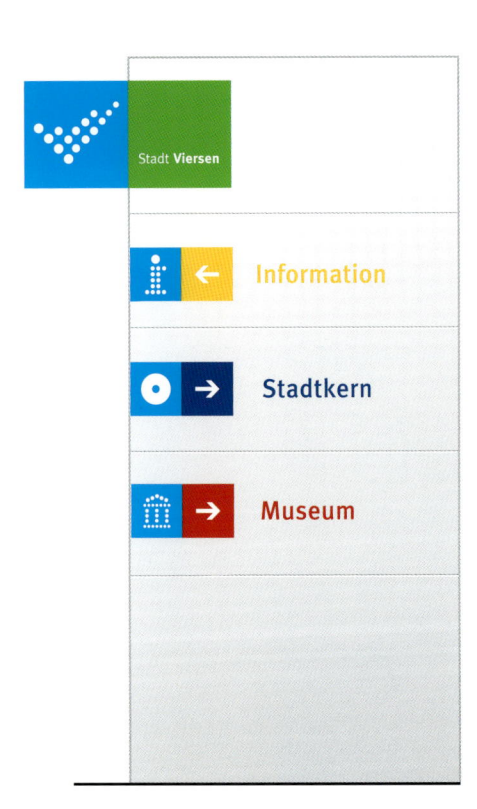

Information

Stadtkern

Museum

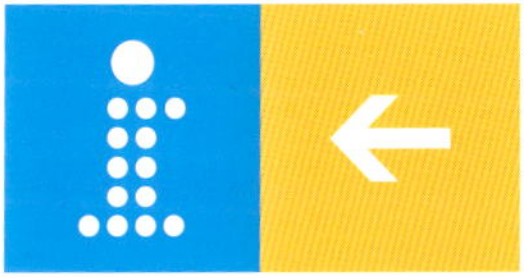

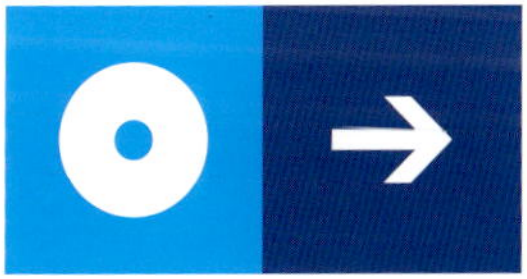

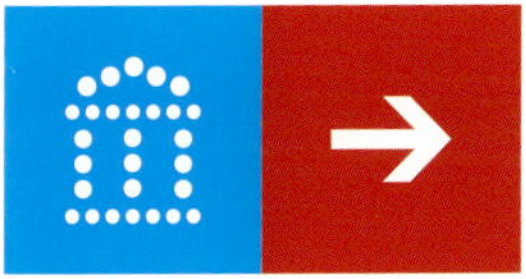

Mirco Kurth (GER) www.no28.de

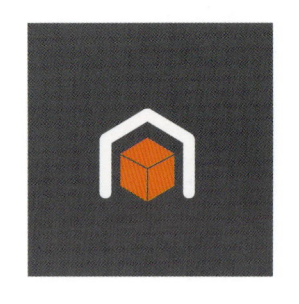

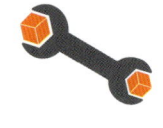

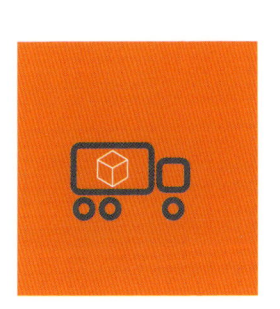

Corporate Design

Kommunikationskonzepte

Printmedien

Digitale Medien

Abbildungskonzepte

Beratung und Betreuung

Michael Hartmann [GER] www.finalart.de

| Kraftwerk | → 62% → | Stromproduktion |

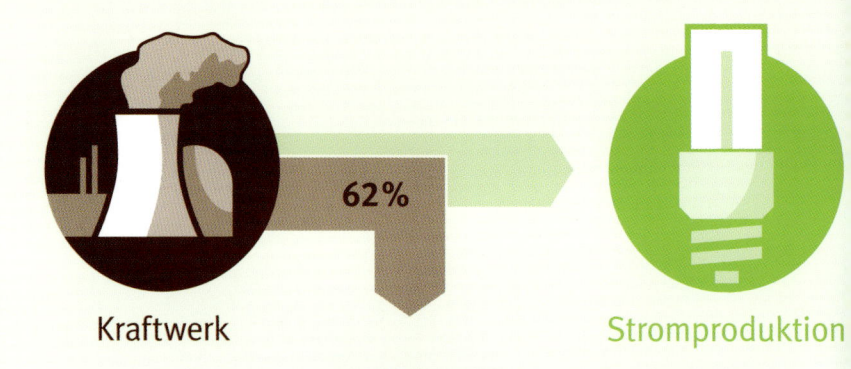

Verlust

| NT-Heizkessel | → 10% → | Heizwärme und Warmwasser |

Verlust

4%

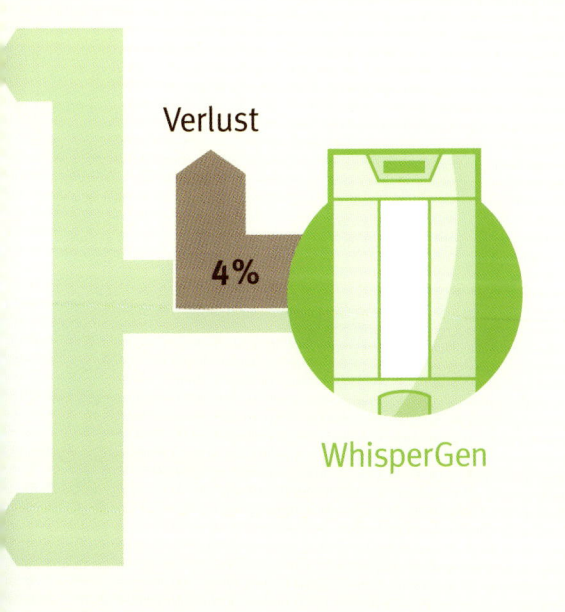

WhisperGen

VG++ IS REALLY GOOD!

www.whatiswrongwithgrooving.com

[GER]

Martin Kühnel

554

WHAT IS WRONG WITH GROOVING
世界的なレコード交換

WORLDWIDE RECORD EXCHANGE BY MARTIN KÜHNEL
ENJOY THIS SELECTION OF RARE AND EXTRAORDINARY VINYL

▶ WWW.WHATISWRONGWITHGROOVING.COM

WHAT IS WRONG WITH GROOVING

世界的なレコード交換

取り扱い注意 RARE AND FRAGILE RECORDS

▶ WWW.WHATISWRONGWITHGROOVING.COM

März–Mai
25 cm
Sept.–Okt.
10 cm
10 cm

STANDORT

AUSSAAT

KEIMUNG

BLÜTE

SAATBAND

SAATPLATTE

SAATSCHEIBE

PILLENSAAT

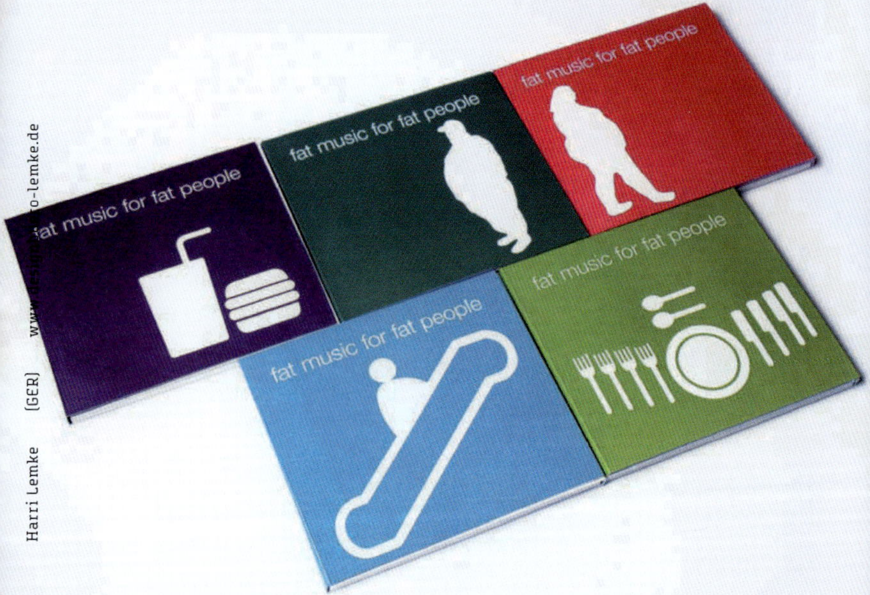

Harri Lemke (GER) www.design[illegible]o-lemke.de

music for fat people

Dänische Delikatessen

Harri Lemke · (GER) · www.designbuero-lemke.de

Dänische Delikatessen

Harri Lemke (GER) www.designbuero-lemke.de

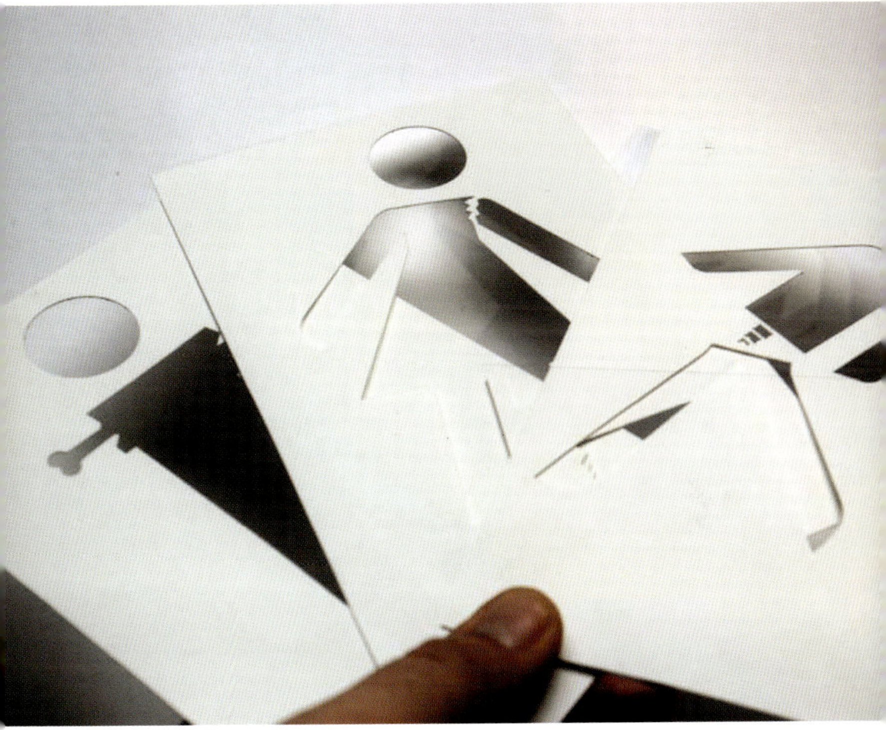

Andrey Nagorny [USA] www.unit-y.com

566

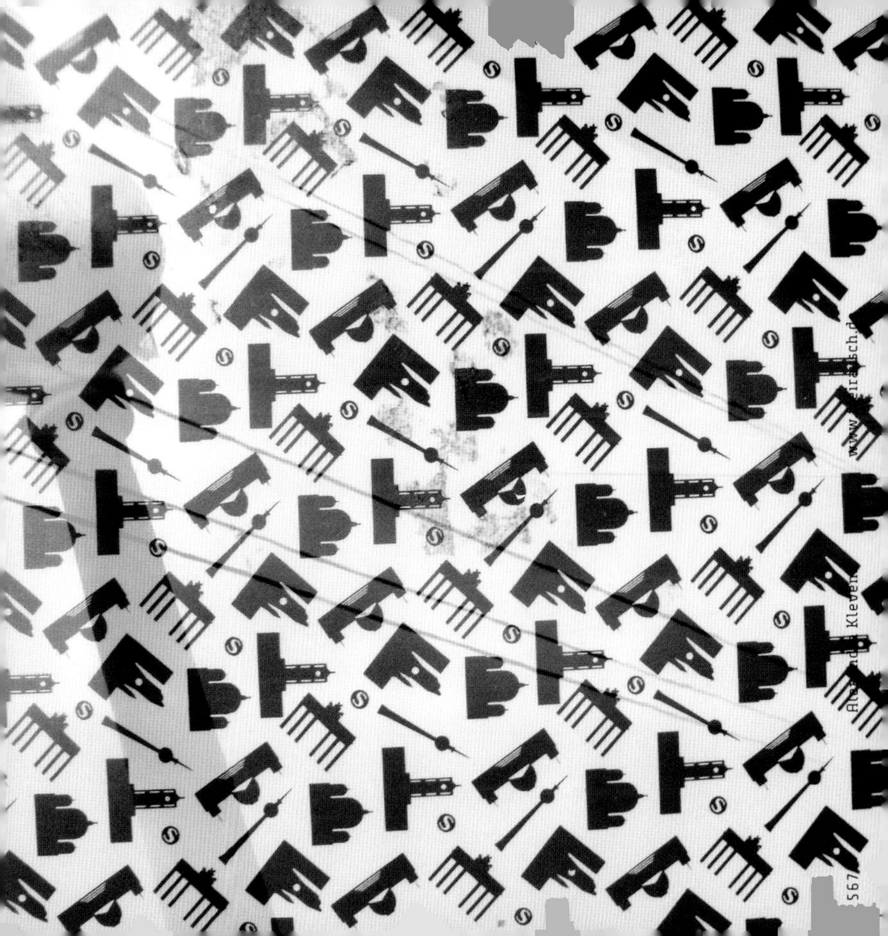

ESTADO D

VALLE DEL DELTA
(VALLE

RÍO N

E ORLAND

L RIO "NO IMPORTA"
ORLAND)

PORTA

Luis Miguel Cabanzo [ITA] www.2ngry.com

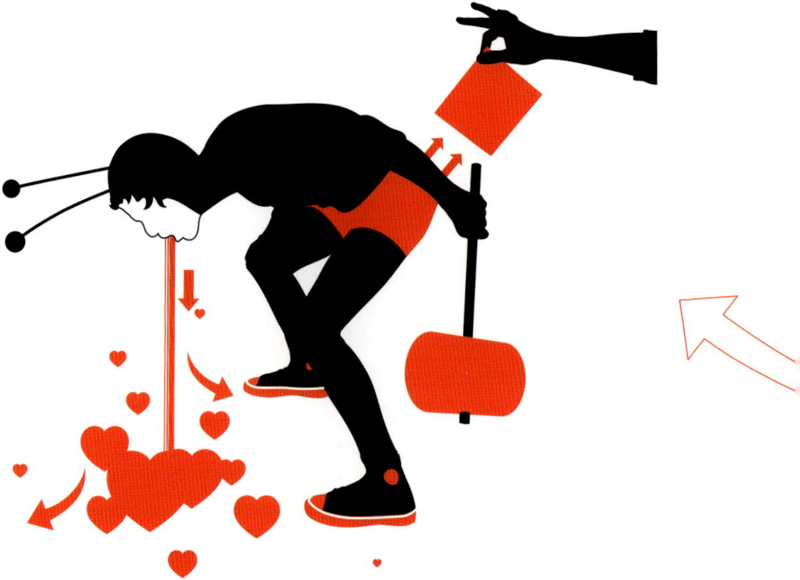

1

② ③ ④

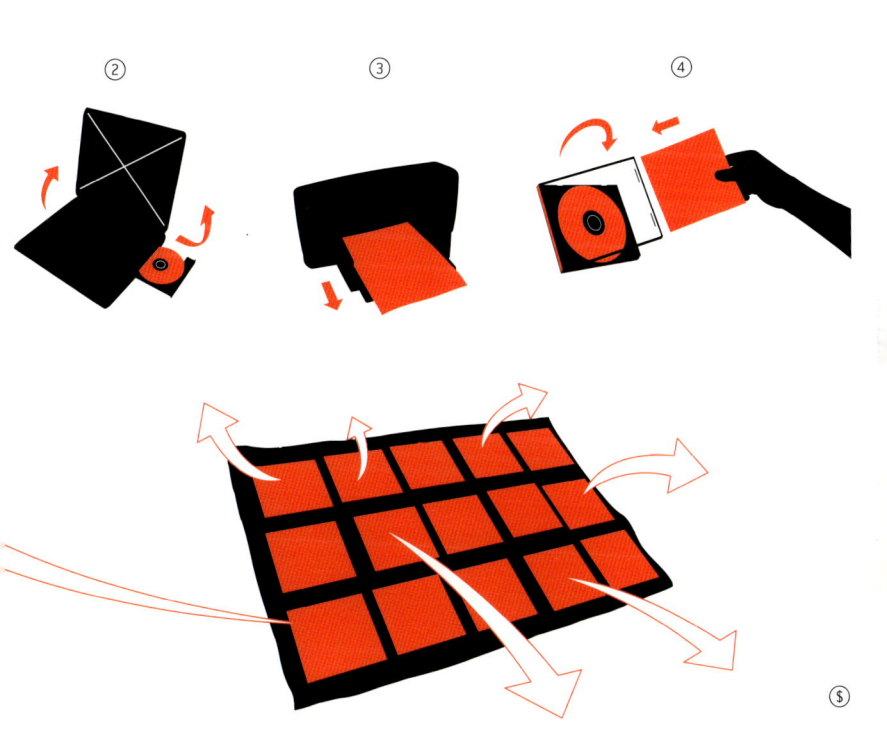

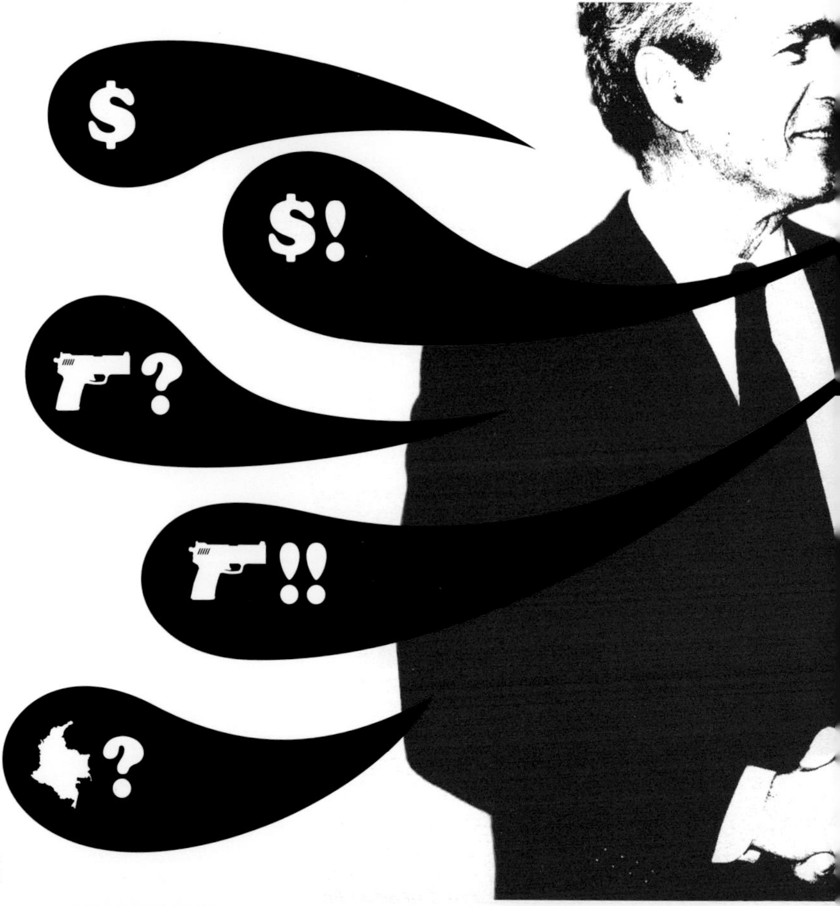

Luis Miguel Cabanzo [ITA] www.2ngry.com

Eyal Holtzman & Myrthe Stel [NED] www.2kilo.nl

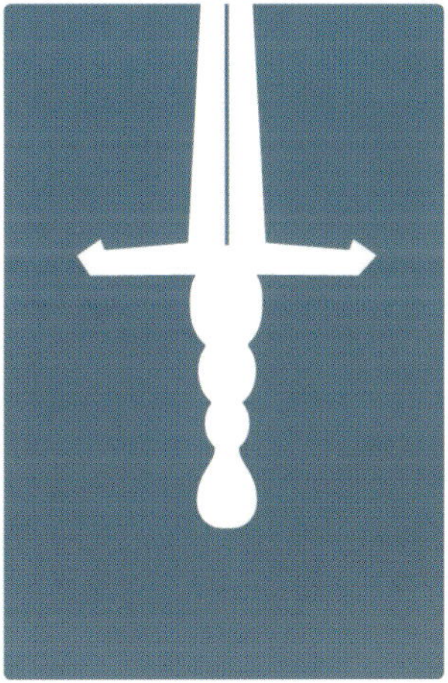

Andrey Nagorny [USA] unit-y.com

576

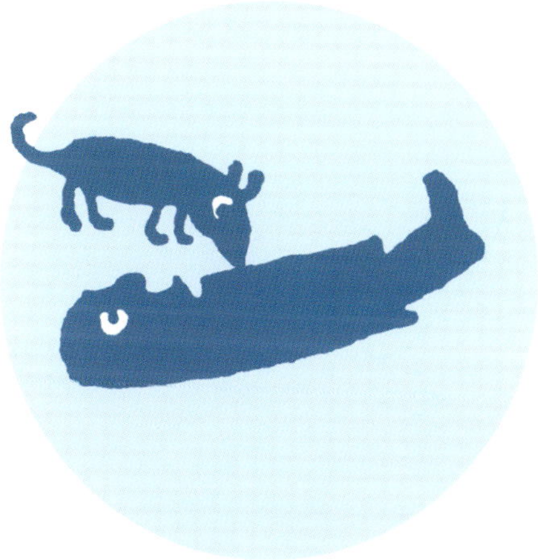

WHEAT
1300 litres per kg

BARLEY
1300 litres per kg

MAIZE
1300 litres per kg

BEEF
15500 litres per kg

PORK
4800 litres per kg

www.angelamorelli.com

Angela Morelli (GBR)

578

COTTON
11000 litres per kg

RICE
3400 litres per kg

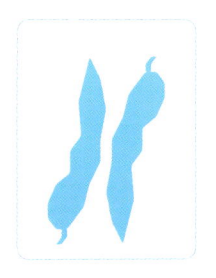

SOYBEANS
1800 litres per kg

GOAT
4000 litres per kg

CHICKEN
3900 litres per kg

HORSE
4100 litres per kg

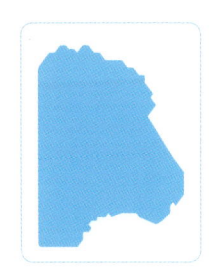

SHEEP
6100 litres per kg

CHEESE
5000 litres per kg

HAMBURGER
2400 litres

COFFEE
140 litres per 1 cup

BEER
75 litres per 1 glass

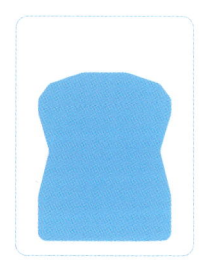

BREAD
40 litres per 1 slice

www.angelamorelli.com

Angela Morelli (GBR)

MILK
1000 litres per litre

APPLE
70 litres per 1 ap.

LEATHER
16600 litres per kg

TEA
30 litres per 1 cup

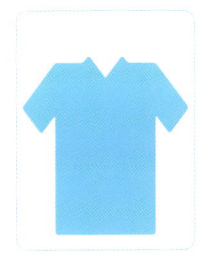

T-SHIRT
2700 litres per 1 t-shirt

A4 SHEET
10 litres

Angela Morelli   (GBR)   www.angelamorelli.com

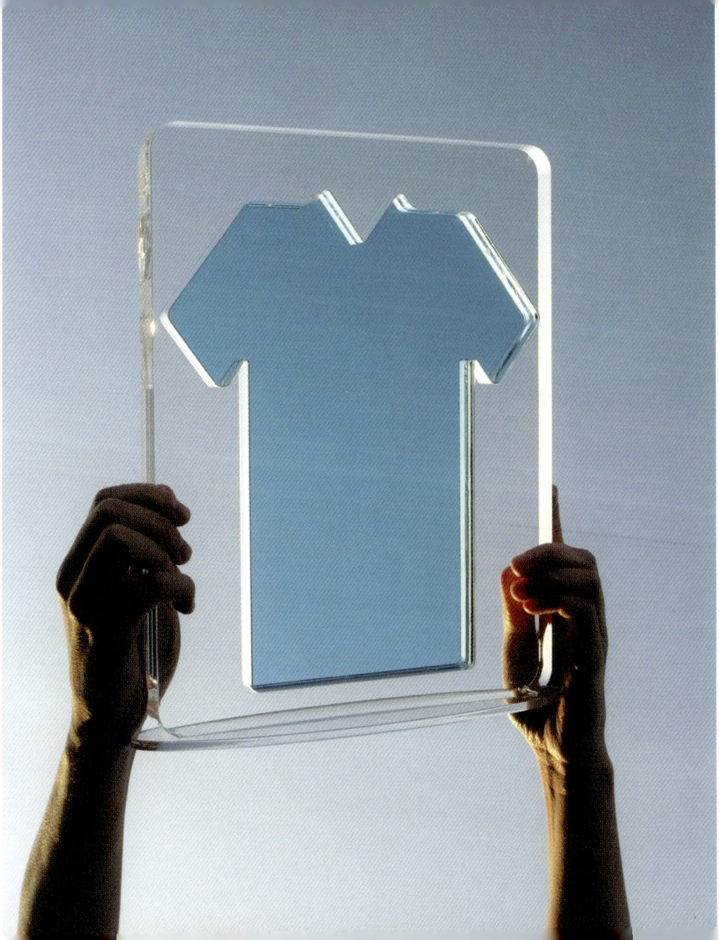

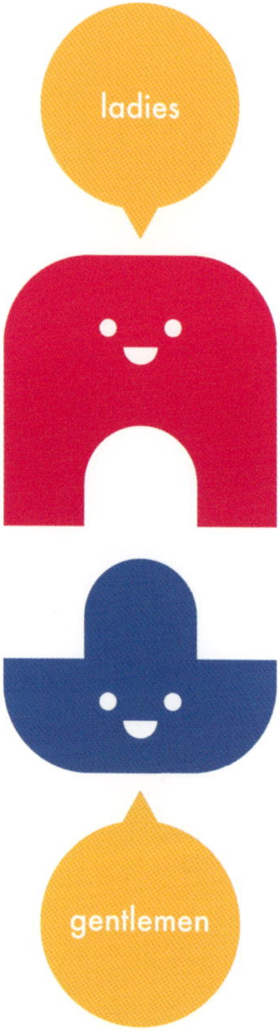

Alejandro Ovalles [VEN] www.jaoc.net

MEN ▬ **WOMEN** ▬

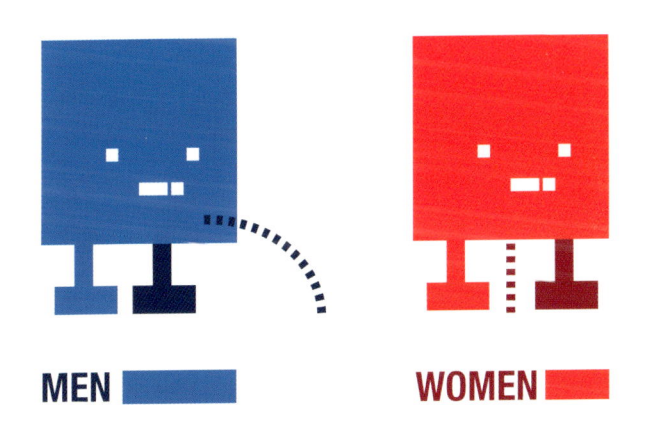

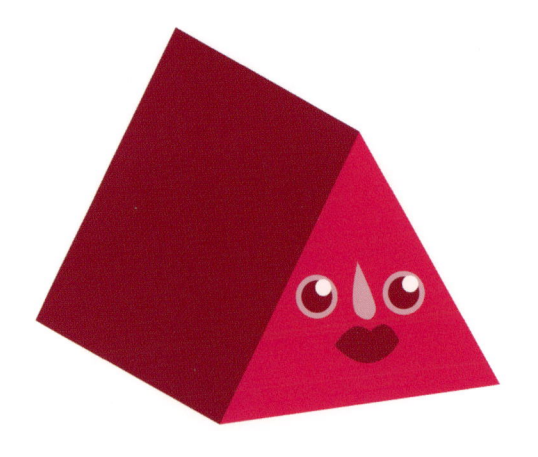

ladies

gentlemen

:: **MICO** MA

Der medizinische Assistent für Klinikpersonal

manage · inform · calculate · organize

LABORBERICHT
DRINGLICHKEIT 3
X

| Timer | Benutzerkonto | RFID-Scanner | Wissen | Rechner | Werk |
| Laborbericht | Blut / Plasma | Medikamente | Internet | Patienten-ID | Zurück |

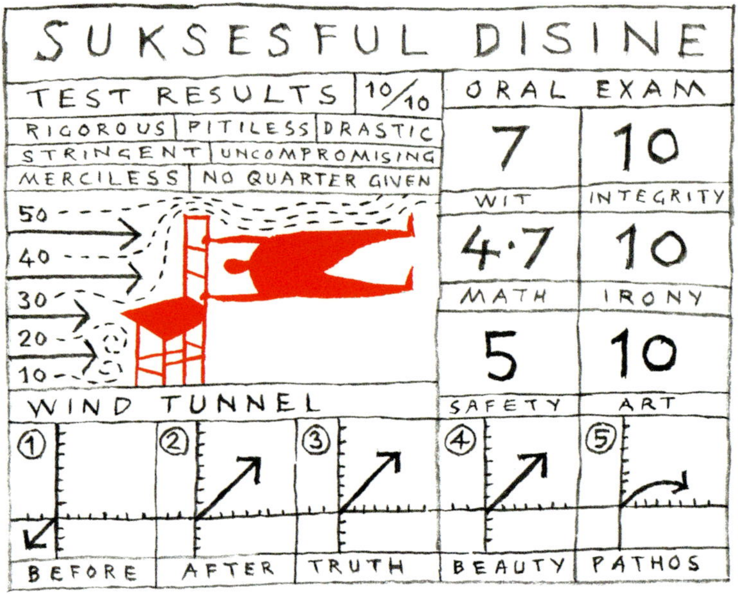

James Webb (GBR) www.webbandwebb.co.uk

THIS IS NOT A CHAIR

2½ dimensions. We are chair 🪑🪑🪑 Why the bottom is so important. Comfort leads to idleness. GOOD POSTURE leads 👑👑 to glory. Comfort 🚲 is an illusion. You never relax in a good chair. ⓑⒻ devote their lives to this. 🪑→🪑 Start from a drawing of a chair, extrapolate into a 3D object. The result is a sculpture of a drawing. (BF) look at the chair from 2½ directions, & impossibly, have reinvented the chair. The middle ground between 2D & 3D is a landscape (BF) will ultimately widen to encompass everything. Nicholas Von der Borch & Jeff Fisher are chair.

AUGUSTA
SPORTS COUNCIL

archery

tennis

softball

basketball

boxing

equestrian

cycling

golf

running

soccer

track

disc golf

adaptive

swimming

Travis Tom (USA)

rowing

Travis Tom [USA]

600

Chris Rooney [USA] www.looneyrooney.com

603

news	opinion	food
drink	coffee	payment
shopping	nationwide	city

Chris Rooney [USA] www.looneyrooney.com

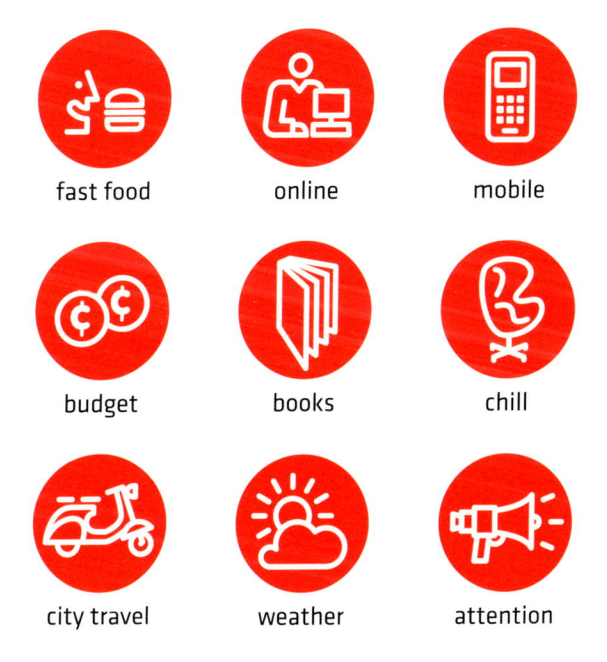

fast food	online	mobile
budget	books	chill
city travel	weather	attention

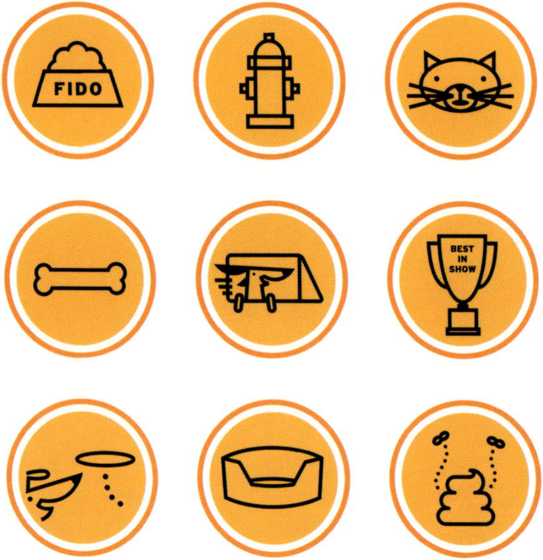
FIDO
BEST
IN
SHOW

Chris Rooney (USA) www.looneyrooney.com

THE LITTLE **RED WAGON** DAYCARE

learning

reading

eating

drinking

playing outside

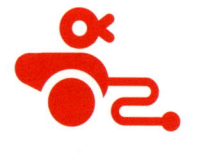

playing

music making

playing

www.looneyrooney.com

Chris Rooney [USA]

608

Mom
Said

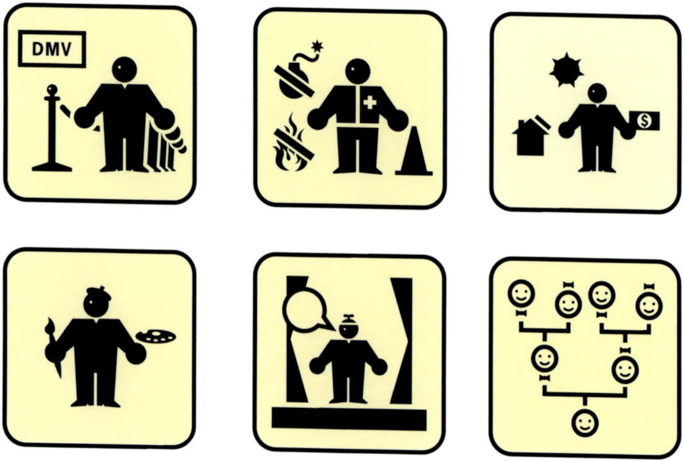
DMV
$

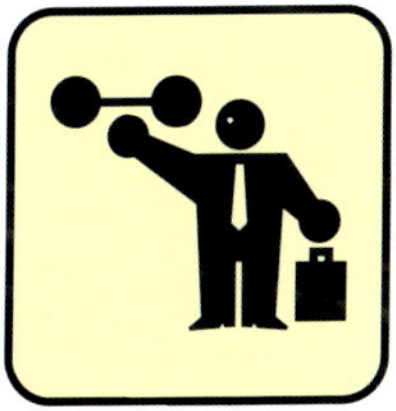
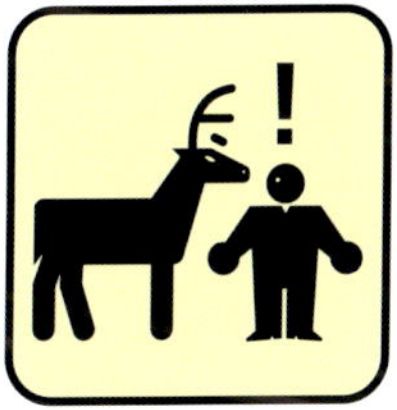
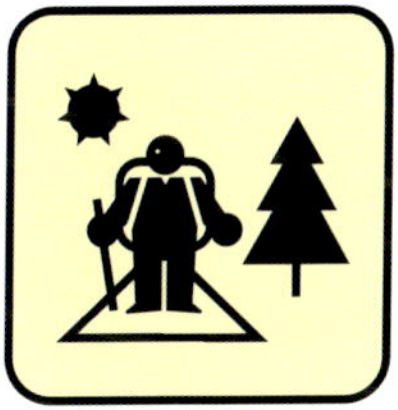
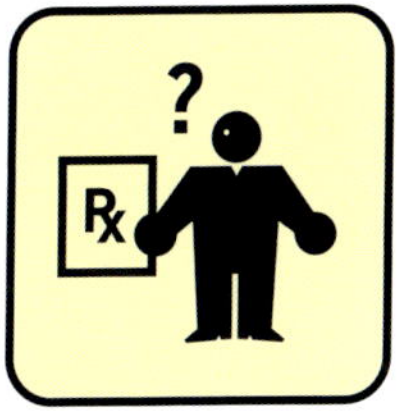
Rx

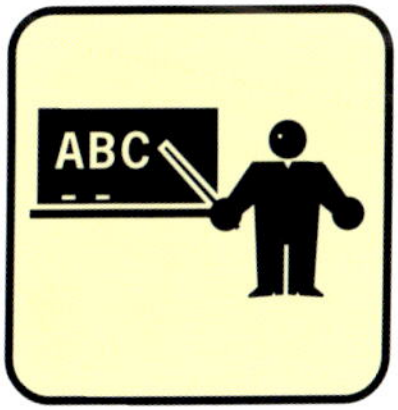
ABC

Chris Rooney   (USA)   www.looneyrooney.com

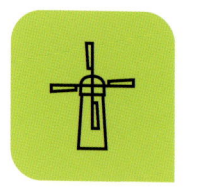

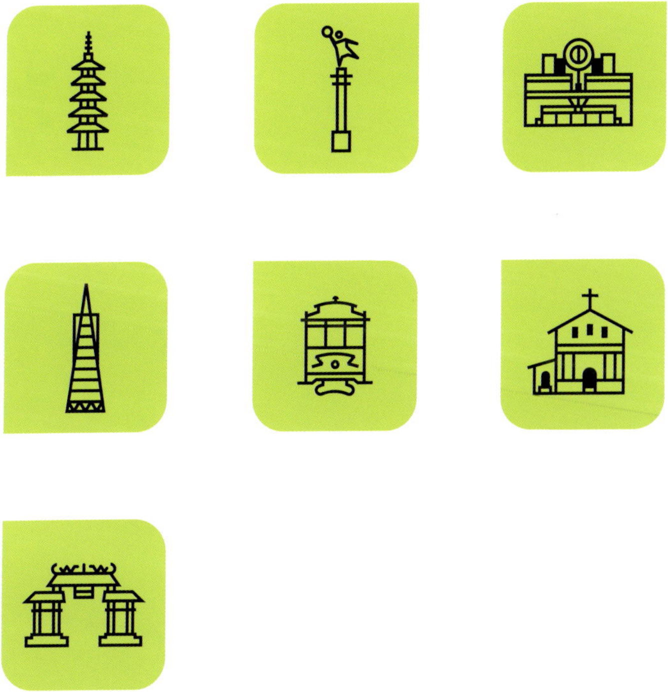

ROMANCE

CONFRONTATION

DIFFERENCES

MISCOMMUNICATION

GENDER ISSUES

POLITICS

BREAKING UP

DOMESTIC ABUSE

WORKPLACE

SELF-DEFENSE

S&M

POST-COITAL

Chris Rooney (USA) www.looneyrooney.com

COMMUNICATION

MEDIA PORTRAYALS

REPRODUCTION

EGO

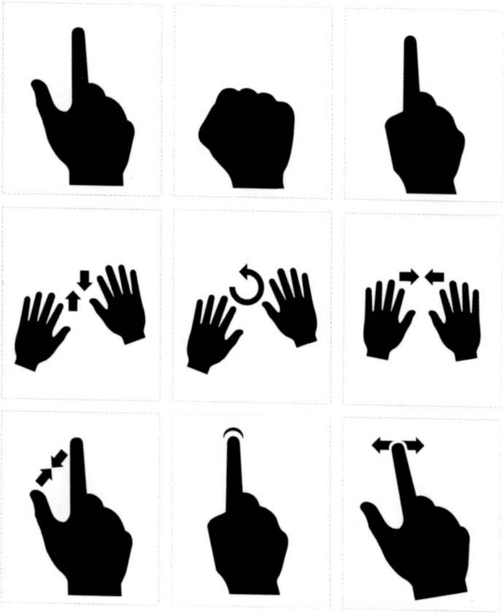

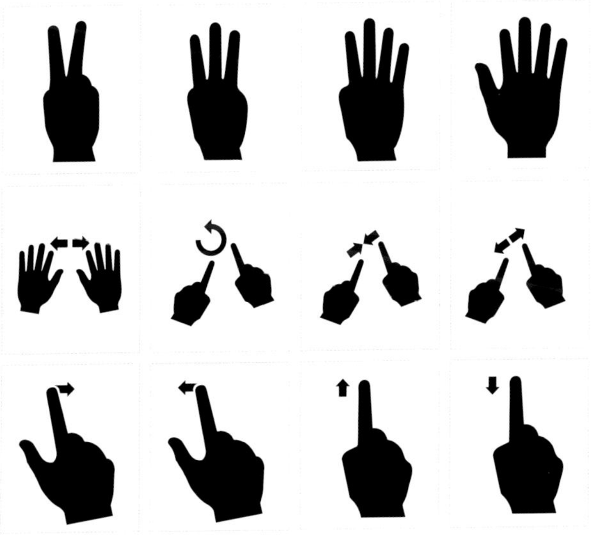

Ryan Lee [USA] www.rdlinteraction.com

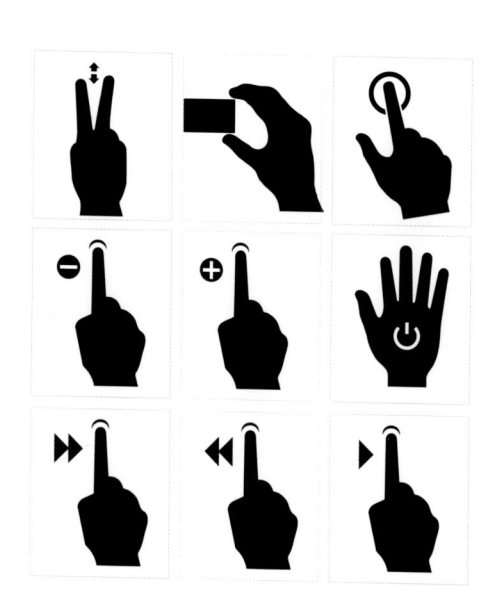

620

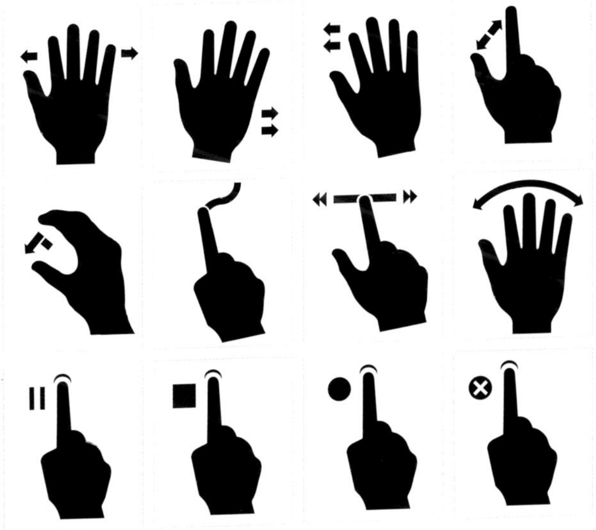

DANGER
Anti-climb paint

TO HOTEL PANORAMA

Lars Harmsen [GER] www.magmabranddesign.de

Louis Minnaar (SAF)

624

I ♥ RAP!

Bookslut.com

it rains a lot these days

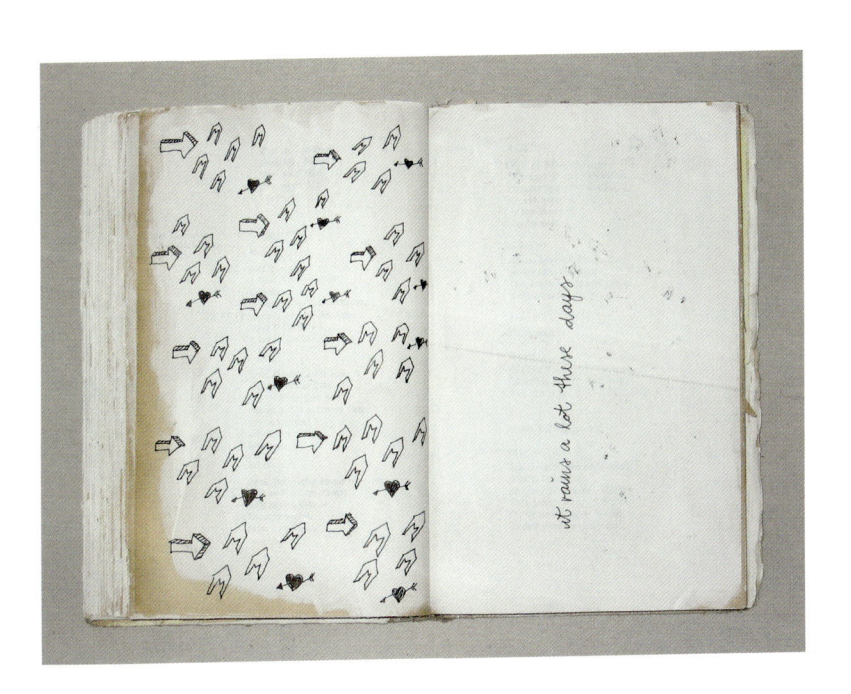

Sabrina Müller (GER) www.sabrinamueller.com

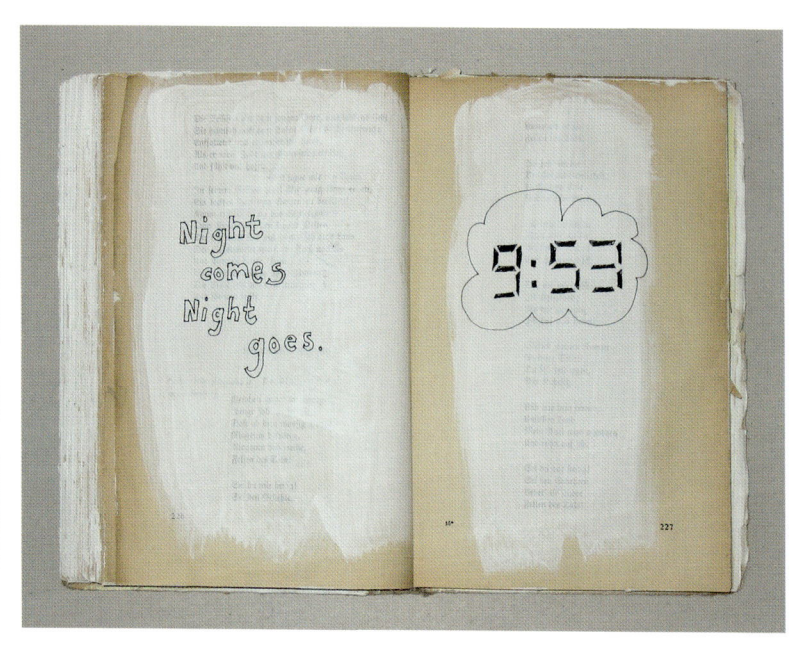

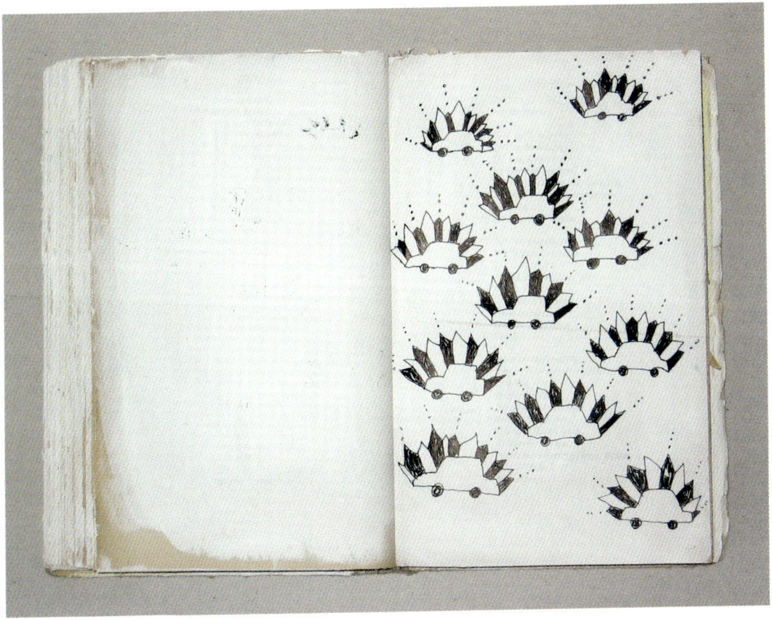

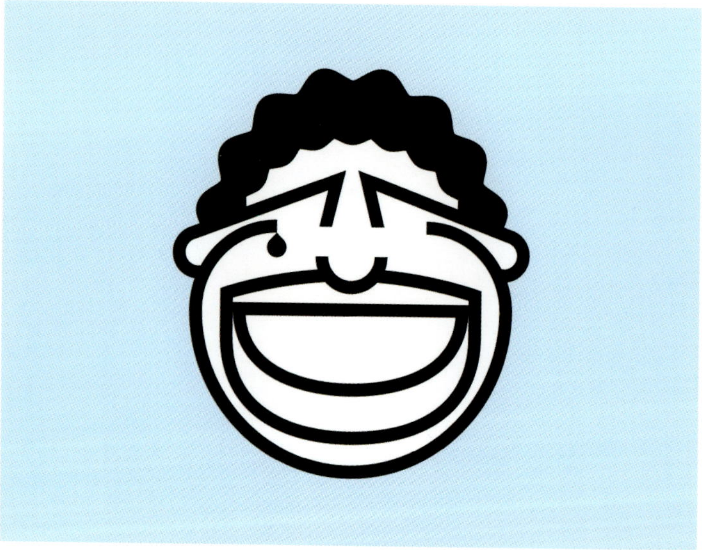

Hernan Berdichevsky & Gustavo Stecher (ARG) www.imagenhb.com

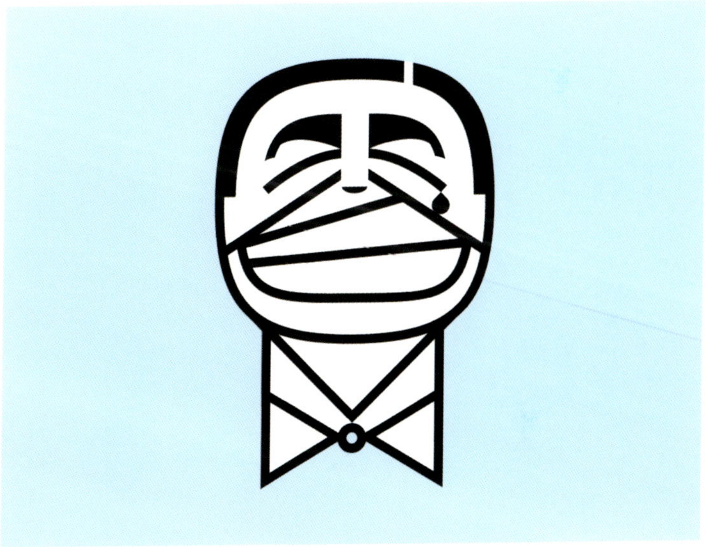

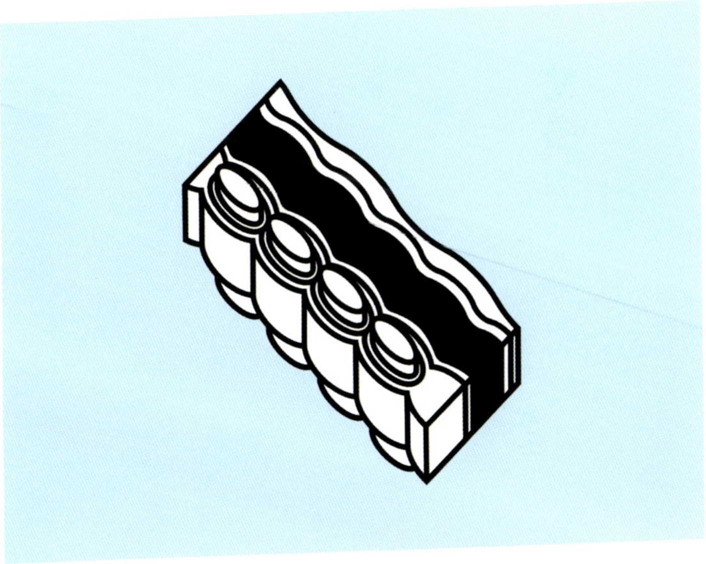

Hernan Berdichevsky & Gustavo Stecher [ARG] www.imagenhb.com

634

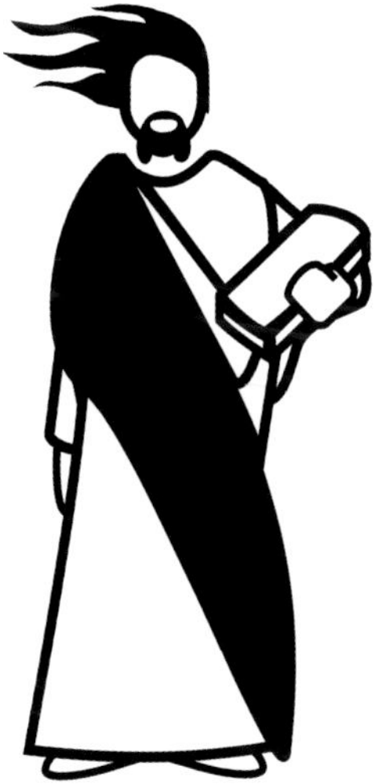

Linosso (GER) www.linosso.com

Moshik Nadav [ISR] www.behance.net/moshik

Moshik Nadav [ISR] www.behance.net/moshik

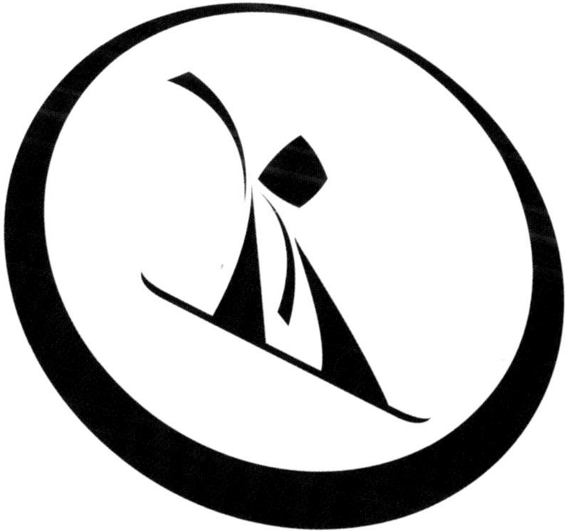

Moshik Nadav [ISR] www.behance.net/moshik

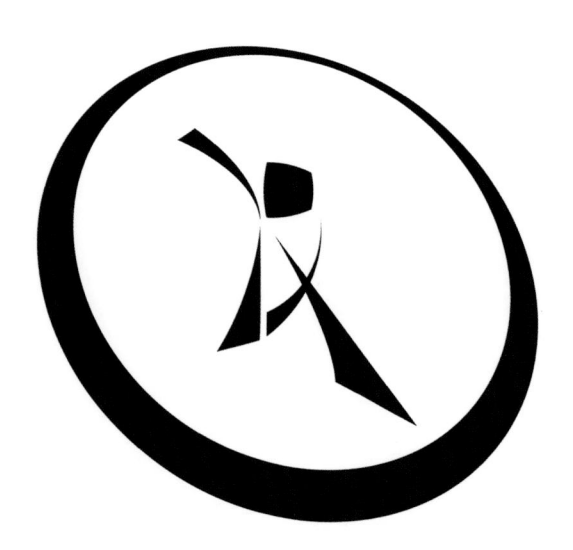

640

Moshik Nadav [ISR] www.behance.net/moshik

642

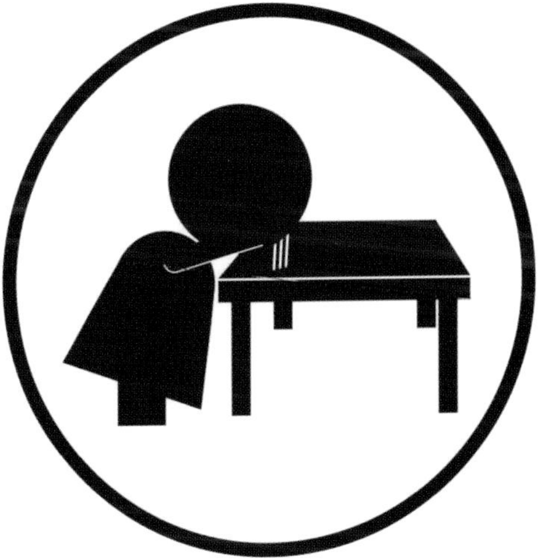

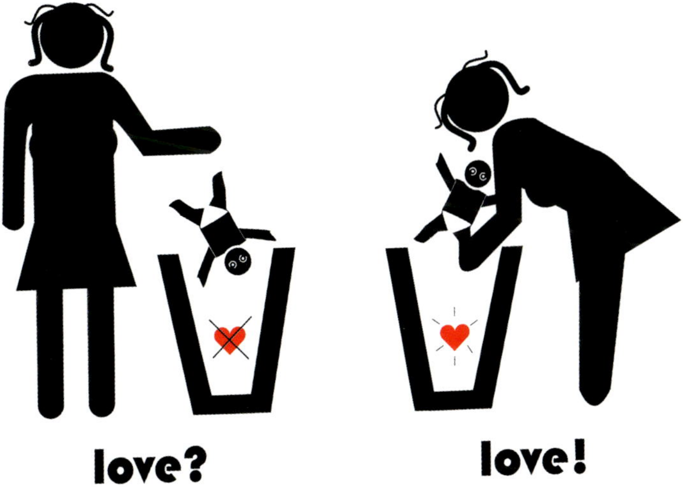

Giulio Vesprini (ITA) www.giuliovesprini.it

Zhebrakov Andrew & Khodjaev Stanislav (RUS)

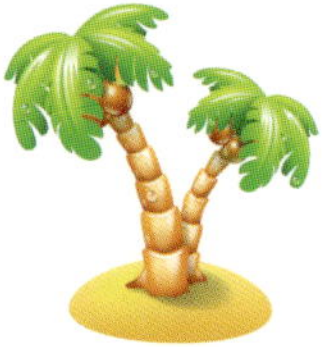

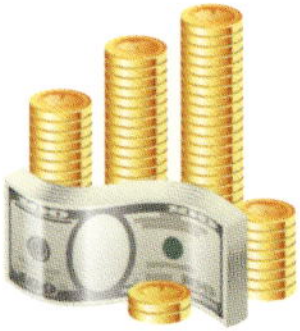

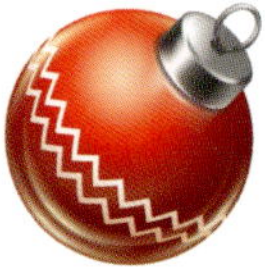

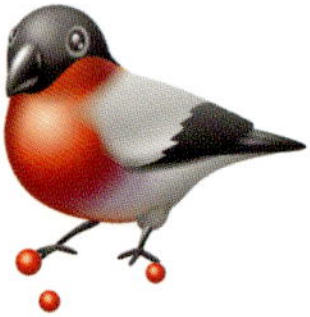

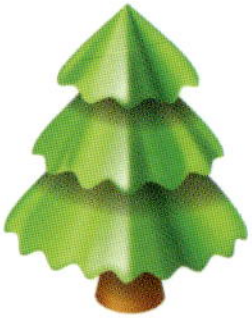

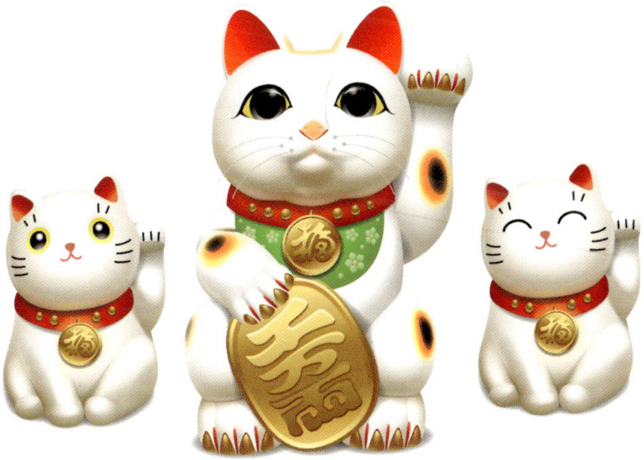

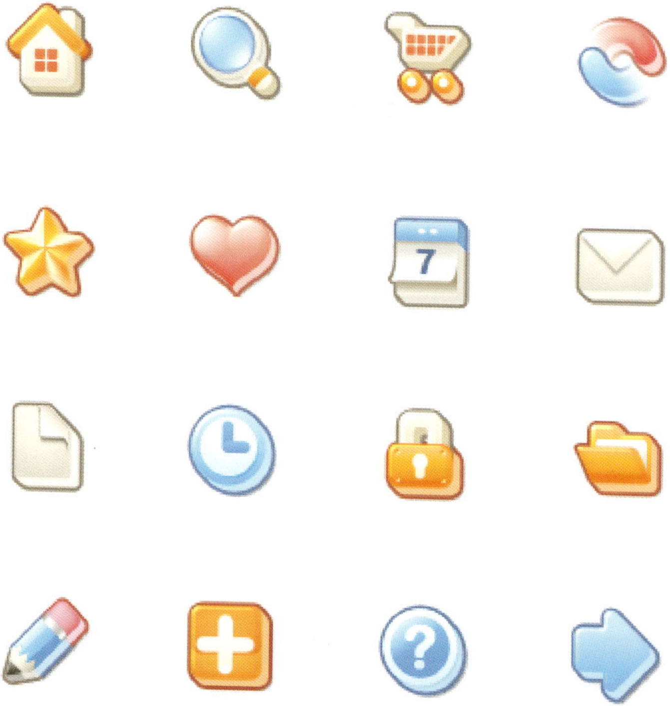

Zhebrakov Andrew & Khodjaev Stanislav [RUS]

january

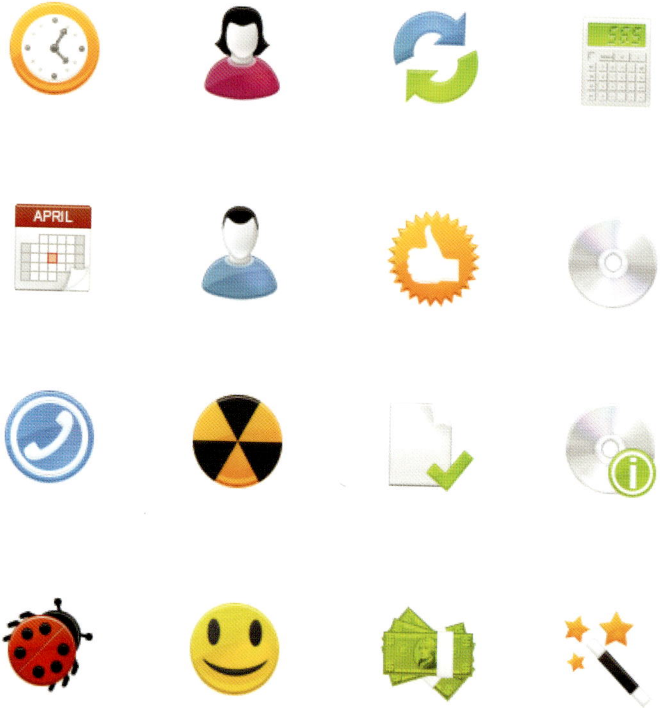

Zhebrakov Andrew & Khodjaev Stanislav [RUS]

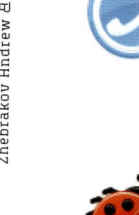

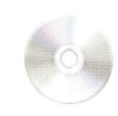

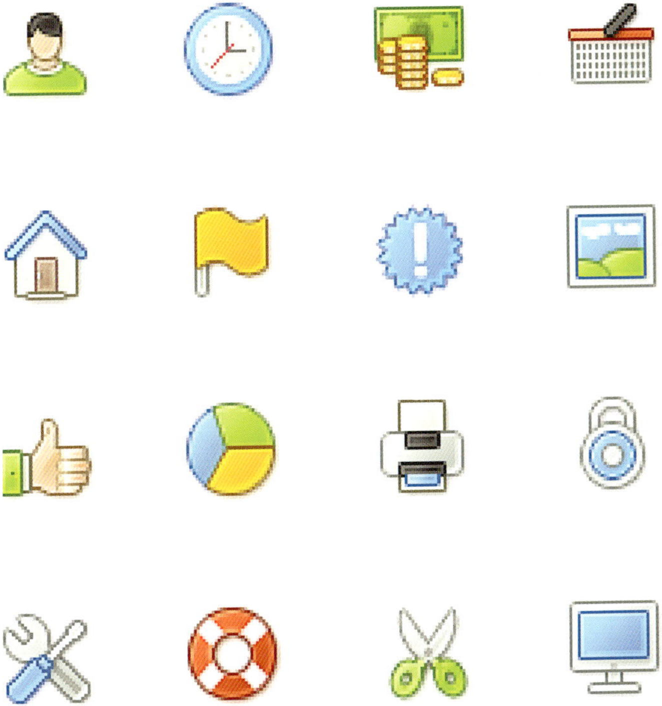

index

Surname, Prename	Loc.	Contact
Allport, Lara & Barett, Simon	(AUS)	lara@thenationalgrid.com.au www.thenationalgrid.com.au
Antonsen, Randi	(NOR)	antonsen.r@gmail.com www.randiantonsen.no
Aquini, Davide Giulio	(ITA)	info@ad-g.it www.ad-g.it
Arenz, Dominik	(GER)	contact@stereoswebfunk.de www.stereoswebfunk.de
Aspinall, Jamie Oliver	(SUI)	info@schnuppe.ch www.schnuppe.ch
Bade, Sebastian	(GER)	kontakt@grafischerpool.de www.grafischerpool.de
Baird, Richard	(GBR)	rich@richardbaird.co.uk www.richardbaird.co.uk
Bendandi, Wladimiro	(ITA)	info@d-plus.it www.d-plus.it
Berdichevsky, H. & Stecher, G.	(ARG)	herni@imagenhb.com www.imagenhb.com
Bertell, Erik & Piippo, Pekka	(FIN)	info@hahmo.fi www.hahmo.fi
Bittner, Beate	(GER)	b.bittner@glutrot.de www.glutrot.de
Bretzmann, Daniel	(GER)	input@eyegix.com www.eyegix.com
Bukhari, Masood	(USA)	masood@masoodbukhari.com www.masoodbukhari.com
Cabanzo, Luis Miguel	(ITA)	miguel@2ngry.com www.2ngry.com
Castillo, Marco Antonio	(MEX)	elmacizo@gmail.com www.behance.net/el_mrk

Pages

430-431

326-335

269　　442-443　　448

56-57　　236-243

14-19　　42-43

220-223

66　　276-286

362-365

180-184　　274-275　　630-634

308-313

235　　294-295

134-135　　172-173　　480-481

38-39　　52-53　　291-292　　296-301　　492-497　　518

568-573

20　　48-49

Surname, Prename	Loc.	Contact
Cehovin, E. & Devetak, T.	(SLO)	eduard.cehovin@siol.net www.cehovin.com
Correa C., Oscar H.	(COL)	oscarhcorrea@hotmail.com www.correadesigns.com
D'Addio, Gregory	(GBR)	g.daddio12@googlemail.com www.coroflot.com/greg_deAddio
Davie, Tom	(USA)	tom@studiotwentysix2.com www.studiotwentysix2.com
Designgruppe Koop	(GER)	a.koop@designgruppe-koop.de www.designgruppe-koop.de
Drouan, Marine	(GER)	info@mixher.fr www.portfolio.mixher.fr
Dümmel, Andreas	(GER)	neugier@pyruswerbeagentur.de www.pyruswerbeagentur.de
Eck, Andreas	(GER)	apfelgernhaber@me.com www.apfelgernhaber.de
Escobas	(MEX)	escobas@escobas.com.mx www.escobas.com.mx
Faerstain, Simon	(DEN)	simon@faerstain.dk www.faerstain.dk
Fenneman, Puk	(NED)	puk@coolpuk.com www.coolpuk.com
Fenzl, Jekaterina	(AUT)	katjara@ymail.com
Fetz, Michael	(GER)	m.fetz@fetzdesign.com www.michaelfetz.com
Figueras, Miriam	(ESP)	lasoga6@gmail.com www.cargocollective.com/mfigueras
Grundl, Jan	(GER)	jan.grundl@yahoo.de
Hadar, Yotam	(ISR)	yotam.hadar@gmail.com

Pages			
490			
174-179	244		
233			
214-215	360-361	409-411	
190-197			
186-189			
44-47	198	510-511	
231-232	434	440-441	447
106-109	254-259		
158-161			
8-13	118-121	454-457	
202-203			
336-337			
115			
462			
252-253			

Surname, Prename	Loc.	Contact
Harmsen, Lars	(GER)	harmsen@magmabranddesign.de www.magmabranddesign.de
Hartmann, Michael	(GER)	design@finalart.de www.finalart.de
Herzog	(GER)	popeia@buerodeluxe.com www.buerodeluxe.com
Himmes-Asbeck, Bettina	(GER)	Jay@be-him.com www.be-him.com
Hofacker, Sandra	(SUI)	info@apfel-z.de www.apfel-z.de
Holmes, Rachel	(GBR)	rachel_l_holmes@hotmail.co.uk www.behance.net/Rachel_holme
Holtzman, Eyal & Stel, Myrthe	(NED)	info@2kilo.nl www.2kilo.nl
Hosang, Randy	(CAN)	randyhosang@hotmail.com
Jensen, Bo Virkelyst	(DEN)	mail@addsoul.com www.addsoul.com
Kaljuvee, Kätlin	(EST)	katlinkaljuvee@gmail.com
Kama	(INA)	info@oxidizzy.com www.oxidizzy.com
Kettner, Florian	(GER)	info@rv20.com www.rv20.com

Pages					
58-60	287	394-395	478	482-485	623
34-37	534-545	551-553			
320-321					
354-355					
70-71	262-263	378-381	466-467	473	476-477
162-171					
136-141	574-575				
452-453					
51	69	72-75	114	185	200-201
387	460-461	472			
486-487					
21	40-41				
30-33	324	338-339			

Surname, Prename	Loc.	Contact
Klevenz, Alexandra	(GER)	info@freirausch.de www.freirausch.de
Klobes, Miriam	(GER)	info@dipl-designerin.de www.mk-kommunikationsdesign.de
Koh, Benjamin	(SIN)	juren85@yahoo.com www.pepper-cinnamon.net
Kühnel, Martin	(GER)	www.whatiswrongwithgrooving.com
Kuokka, Jenni	(FIN)	info@hahmo.fi www.hahmo.fi
Kurth, Mirco	(GER)	mail@no28.de www.no28.de
Lawal, Lanre	(NGR)	alphabetraffic@gmail.com
Ledwig, Christopher	(GER)	ledwig@f1rstdesign.com www.f1rstdesign.com
Lee, Eun Jin	(GBR)	hello@iameunjin.com
Lee, Ryan	(USA)	ryan@rdlinteraction.com www.rdlinteraction.com
Lemke, Harri	(GER)	kontakt@desingbuero-lemke.de www.designbuero-lemke.de
Lim, Jay	(MAS)	info@tsubakistudio.com www.tsubakistudio.net
Linosso	(GER)	s.wagner@linosso.com www.linosso.com
Lobina, Aurora	(ITA)	info@aurorise.com www.aurorise.com
Magoulas, Vasilis	(GRE)	info@vamadesign.com www.vamadesign.com
Mahn, Sandra	(GER)	mahn@zweinullsieben.com www.zweinullsieben.com

Pages

566-567	622		
116-117			
22-29	404-407	526-529	
554-555			
62-65	302-307		
288-289	548-550		
323			
128-129	204-213	224-225	366
523			
618-621			
113	122-127	199	558-563
388-391			
464	635		
499	519		
468-471			
67	248-251	498	

Surname, Prename	Loc.	Contact
Malmströmer, Anders	(SWE)	anders@malmstromer.se www.malmstromer.se
Marchionna, Sandra	(GER)	sandra.marchionna@freenet.de www.gut-ding.com
Markovic, Kristina	(GER)	info@kristinamarkovic.com www.kristinamarkovic.com
Melton, Marcus	(USA)	marcus@marcusmelton.com www.marcusmelton.com
Minnaar, Louis	(SAF)	louisminnaar@gmail.com
Moos, Linus von	(GER)	linus@ripsl.ch www.ripsl.ch
Morelli, Angela	(GBR)	an.morelli@mac.com www.angelamorelli.com
Morena, Anna	(GER)	mail@annamorena.de www.annamorena.de
Mühlbauer, Andrea	(GER)	andrea@purpleblackdesign.com www.purpleblackdesign.com
Müller, Claudia	(GER)	hello@studio-kniften.de www.studio-kniften.de
Müller, Sabrina	(GER)	hello@sabrinamueller.com www.sabrinamueller.com
Nadav, Moshik	(ISR)	moshik@moshik.net www.behance.net/moshik
Naewmalee, Nattanan	(GBR)	nutbass@yahoo.com www.nuatstudio.com
Nagorny, Andrey	(USA)	andrey@unit-y.com www.unit-y.com
Neri, Matteo	(ITA)	info@blackjackslab.com www.blackjackslab.com
Orjuela R., Maria Angélica	(COL)	mariemaor@gmail.com

Pages

346   356-357

264-267

500-501   524-525

260-261

624

515-517

578-583

491   502-509

449-451

530-533

626-629

636-644

76-95   408

564-565   576-578

270-271   290

152-153

Surname, Prename	Loc.	Contact
Ovalles, Alejandro	(VEN)	jaoc28@yahoo.com www.jaoc.net
Paccagnella, Fabrizio	(ITA)	info@spritzer.it www.spritzer.it
Passeck, Michael	(GER)	info@passeck-wernecke.de www.passeck-wernecke.de
Pavlovic, Alen	(CRO)	artra@kc.htnet.hr www.artra.hr
Pelzer, Klaus	(GER)	mail@b7UE.com www.b7UE.com
Prien, Marc	(GER)	info@empegra.de www.empegra.de
Radojevic, Milos	(SRB)	milos@geniuslogo.com www.geniuslogo.com
Rampazzo, Lucas	(BRA)	lucas_rampazzo@yahoo.com.br
Reiser, Felicitas	(GER)	feereiser@gmx.de
Reiser, Judith	(GER)	hello@judithreiser.com www.judithreiser.com

Pages

96-99   382-385   465   584-587

435-439

556-557

54-55   61   68   234

514

293-393

245-247

216-219   412-415

588-589

396-403

Surname, Prename	Loc.	Contact
Rodriguez Melo, Sergio	(COL)	www.flickr.com/photos/garbagcolombia
Rölle, Julio	(GER)	hello@44flavours.de www.44flavours.de
Rooney, Chris	(USA)	chris@looneyrooney.com www.looneyrooney.com
Rothenhagen, Christian	(GER)	moin@christianrothenhagen.com www.christianrothenhagen.com
Salas, Luis Felipe	(CHI)	fel_salas@hotmail.com
Schroeder, Kai	(GER)	ks-schroeder@gmx.de www.artvanced-design.de
Siedenburg, Ann Katrin	(GER)	post@katigraphie.de www.katigraphie.de
Stephan, Kerstin	(GER)	kerstinstephan@seefarben.de www.kerstinstephan.com
Suwannakrua, Teekatas	(THA)	teekatas@gmail.com www.raindropmemory.deviantart.com
Sysmäläinen, Julia	(GER)	j.sysmalainen@de.edenspiekermann.com
Timmesfeld, Feli	(GER)	timmesfeld@ergosign.de www.ergosign.de
Tom, Travis	(USA)	tntom70@aol.com
Vaz, Sandra	(ESP)	sandravaz81@hotmail.com www.sanvaz.com
Velásquez L., Diego	(COL)	vldiego26@gmail.com www.flickr.com/photos/diegovelin
Vesprini, Giulio	(ITA)	controlzeta.workdesign@gmail.com www.giuliovesprini.it
Wagner, F.e & Siedenburg, A. K.	(GER)	www.kokliko.de, www.katigraphie.de

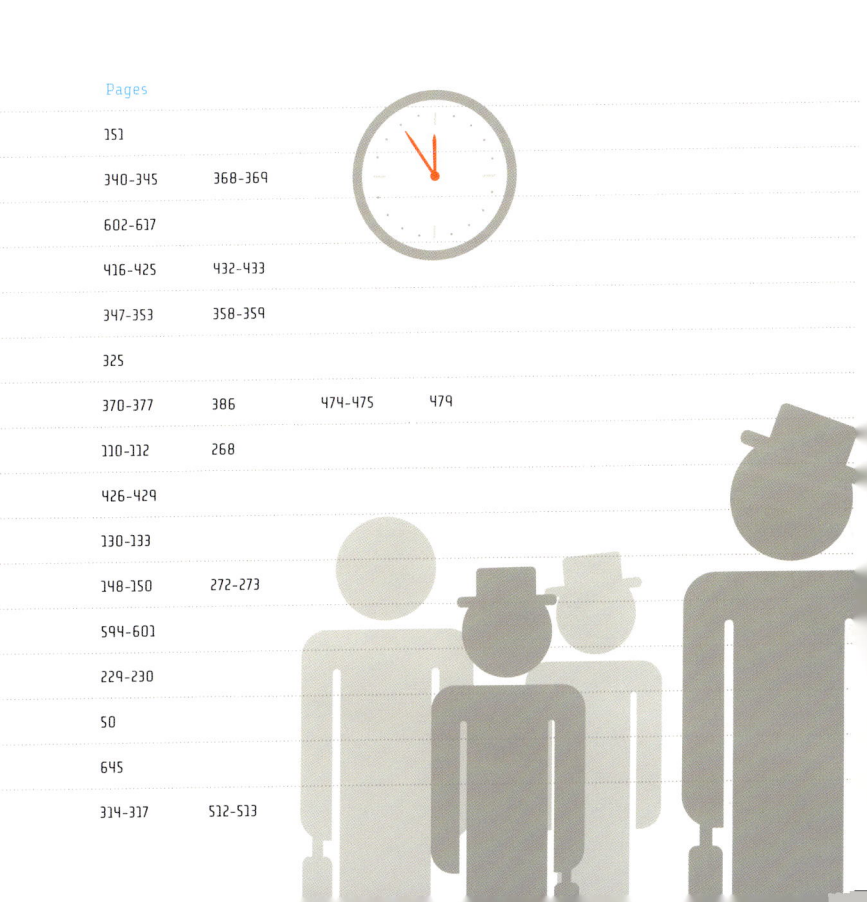

Pages			
151			
340-345	368-369		
602-617			
416-425	432-433		
347-353	358-359		
325			
370-377	386	474-475	479
110-112	268		
426-429			
130-133			
148-150	272-273		
594-601			
229-230			
50			
645			
314-317	512-513		

Surname, Prename	Loc.	Contact
Webb, James	(GBR)	james@webbandwebb.co.uk www.webbandwebb.co.uk
Weier, Andre	(GER)	info@nalindesign.com www.nalindesign.com
Weik, Marcel	(GER)	info@mwkd.de www.mwkd.de
Wiesenauer, Bernd	(GER)	info@uid.com www.uid.com
Wölfel, Peter	(GER)	peterwoelfel@online.de
Zelle, Steve	(CAN)	steve@idapostle.com www.idapostle.com
Zhebrakov, A. & Khodjaev, S.	(RUS)	info@icojoy.com

Pages				
590-593				
142-147	444-446			
154-157	318-319	367	463	625
458-459				
100-105	488-489	520-522	546-547	
226-228				
322	646-653			